Schooling for Change

The Falmer Press Teachers' Library

The Falmer Press Teachers' Library: 9

Schooling for Change:
Reinventing Education for Early Adolescents

Andy Hargreaves
Lorna Earl and
Jim Ryan

The Falmer Press

(A member of the Taylor & Francis Group)
London • Washington, D.C.

UK	Falmer Press, 1 Gunpowder Square, London, EC4A 3DE
USA	Falmer Press, Taylor & Francis Inc., 1900 Frost Road, Suite 101, Bristol, PA 19007

First published in 1996

A catalogue record for this book is available from the British Library

Library of Congress Cataloging-in-Publication Data are available on request

ISNB 0 7507 0489 6 cased
ISBN 0 7507 0490 x paper

Jacket design by Caroline Archer

Typeset in 10/12pt Garamond by
Graphicraft Typesetters Ltd., Hong Kong.

Printed in Great Britain by Biddles Ltd, Guildford and King's Lynn on paper which has a specified pH value on final paper manufacture of not less than 7.5 and is therefore 'acid free'.

Contents

Acknowledgments

This book has been in process for almost five years. Each of us has alternately labored over it and set it very far back on our desks and in our minds. Nevertheless, it has continued to surface as a book that needed to be written. Our conversations with real teachers and students, along with insistently encouraging colleagues, have compelled us to draw together and consolidate some of our ongoing work and present it in a way that is accessible to teachers working in the field.

Throughout this time we have been involved, with a number of our colleagues, in a program of work that has contributed to and also helped evaluate the progress of school reform efforts in what are known as the Transition Years of Schooling in our province of Ontario. A key part of our program was a report, *Rights of Passage* (Hargreaves and Earl, 1990) which two of us co-authored under a grant from the Ontario Ministry of Education in Canada. Our task was to review selected international research on schooling in the Transition Years (grades 7–9), paying particular attention to innovative programs and services in the area. We were asked to detail any implications for the development of Transition Years policies. To our pleasure and mild surprise, the report quickly came to be discussed and disseminated throughout Ontario schools and school systems. It fed actively into the policy development process for restructuring education in grades 7–9 in the province, and it began to be used and referred to in other jurisdictions across Canada, and beyond it too — for instance, in statewide reviews of the middle years of schooling in Australia (for example, Eyers, 1992). Because the report, as a Ministry document, is not readily available, we have extended and updated it for this book aimed at a wider audience. We are particularly grateful to the Ontario Ministry of Education for setting us on this course of investigating change during this particularly interesting time in the lives of young people.

Addressing a broad professional audience across a wide geographical spread is never easy in educational writing and research. The administrative details of different systems vary, as does the terminology used to describe them. However, from our international review, it is clear to us that the problems of change experienced by early adolescents and the problems encountered in trying to change our schools so that they meet these young people's needs more effectively are remarkably similar in may different countries. So, if the chosen spelling seems unfamiliar to you, or the details of our terminology are not always exactly the same as those used in your own system, please bear with us, for the messages matter for many systems, whatever words are used to describe their administrative specifics. Our spelling is North American. Our vocabulary is also often that of North American systems, though we transpose to other systems at points, and use more generic terms when we can. We talk about *students* of all school ages, rather than *pupils*; *elementary* schools, not primary schools; we describe schools as being run by *principals* but in some systems, these people would be known as headteachers; we use the term *school district* rather than school board or local education authority; we employ broad references to *teaching strategies* where some American readers might prefer *instructional strategies*; and we refer throughout to grades 7–9 as the focus of our work, when years 8–10 are the appropriate parallel in the British system which begins one year later than in North America.

While we have endeavoured to be wide-ranging in our reach, it is in the province of Ontario, Canada, that our own program of work has been located, in particular the report that is the basis of our work. We therefore offer a very special thanks to the many Ontario teachers and administrators who encouraged us, exhorted us to travel throughout the province to address groups of educators, challenged our evidence and our interpretations and stimulated us to continue our pursuit of deeper understanding of what schooling for young adolescents might be like. The search continues to be fruitful and to engage our time and imagination. No work of this magnitude is completed solely by the authors. We have been assisted along the way by the initial *Rights of Passage* research team, especially Margaret Oldfield. More recently our Research Officer, Shawn Moore, and Leo Santos, our indefatigable secretary, have spent many late nights deciphering our scrawl and reworking 'just one more draft'.

Finally, as is always the case, we have depended, leaned and prevailed upon our families, colleagues and friends as we have struggled to move this book from ideas and conversations to words on paper. Without them, it is doubtful that this book would ever have seen the light of day.

1 Triple Transitions

The Problem

In Western societies, early adolescence is typically a time when young people undergo a profound transition in their social, physical and intellectual development. It is a time of rapid change, immense uncertainty and acute self-reflection. The exhilaration and pain of growing up for many early adolescents resides in their having much less confidence in what they are moving towards than in what they have left behind.

Strangely, Western societies towards the end of the twentieth century also find themselves in the midst of changes and transitions of great turbulence and uncertainty. Economies are becoming more flexible and also more fragile. Technologies are becoming more complex. Organizations are dispensing with bureaucracy in exchange for flexibility and fluidity. Nations are worrying and sometimes warring about their identities as economies expand, borders become irrelevant and people turn in upon themselves. Gone are the old and obvious antagonisms between labor and capital; East and West. But with more pluralism, complexity and diversity, gone too are the old ideological certainties, the seemingly secure moral foundations on which learning was organized, people lived their lives, and duties and obligations were maintained.

Just when modern industrial societies seemed to be reaching maturity, when economies seemed capable of infinite expansion and welfare states of endlessly extending educational and social benefits to all, social, economic and political life have been plunged into unpredictability. It is as if societies themselves are being condemned to experience a kind of adolescence. Like adolescents, we all now live in exciting and terrifying times of transition and turmoil. The prefix *post* used to describe these times in terms of what Daniel Bell (1973) labelled *post-industrial* society, and C. Wright Mills (1959) first termed *post-modern* society, suggests much greater confidence about the passing of what went before, than about what lies in store ahead (A. Hargreaves, 1994).

Our future is very much an open book. It can be one of triumphant innovation; of diverse and self-fulfilling yet environmentally sustainable lifestyles; of people living and working together in communities of difference. Or it can be a future of division and despair where the successful are seduced into a technologically glitzy world of superficial consumerism and lifestyle choices, while the unsuccessful are condemned to unemployment, underemployment or

1

undemanding employment that offers them few real choices. The nature of our future depends, in part, on how we prepare the next generation who will live and make it.

Young adolescents are at a critical point in their development, as is the changing adult world they are entering. In large part, this explains why educators around the world seem to have identified the transition years of schooling as a focal point for educational reform. Reforming these transition years of schooling seems to promise a double indemnity — against serious harm coming to the future of our youth, as well as to the world they will inherit.

Secondary schools have not traditionally been particularly responsive either to the transitional needs of young adolescents or of wider social change. Secondary school systems evolved from small academies of subject specialization for selected elites, into extensions of the factory-like systems of mass education where students were processed in large batches, and segregated into age-graded cohorts or *classes*. These were taught ('instructed') through standardized and specialized curricula (courses of instruction). Instruction most commonly took the form of recitation or lecturing along with note-taking, question-and-answer and seatwork (Goodson, 1988; Cuban, 1984; Hamilton, 1989). These antecedent structures of schooling, defined for the age of large factories, heavy mechanical industry and specialized bureaucracies, have set the basic conditions for much of secondary schooling today. Whilst the surface and style of schooling may have changed, these deep structures of division, department and delivery have been reproduced from generation to generation.

'Real' secondary school teaching, the seemingly natural, normal and given way to organize teaching and curriculum, is therefore a highly specific socio-historical invention from a long-distant period (Metz, 1991). As we move into a more post-modern age, efforts at educational reform and restructuring have begun to address these fundamentally given, indeed almost 'sacred' norms of secondary schooling, as Sarason (1971) calls them. Departmental specialization has been questioned through proposals for core and integrated curricula (Drake, 1991). Intelligences are coming to be seen as multiple, not singular (Gardner, 1983). Flexible teaching approaches are being advocated that respond to a diversity of student learning styles (McCarthy, 1980). Assessment strategies are being sought that are more 'authentic' in evaluating what is actually learned by a range of methods, rather than just through pencil-and-paper exercises (Wiggins, 1992). Efforts are being made in many places to group students more heterogenously (Wheelock, 1992). Secondary schools are just beginning to confront major transitions in teaching, learning, curriculum, organization and assessment (Sizer, 1992).

So there are three transitions. In early adolescence, young people are changing. On the cusp of the century, societies are changing. And with accelerating programs of educational reform, secondary schools and junior high schools are also changing. In this book, we want to address this triple transition and analyze the challenges it poses for educators of early adolescents. We want to articulate what it means to educate early adolescents in the rapidly changing social, cultural and economic conditions that await and already surround us. We want to speak plainly about the challenge, and be practical, imaginative, yet properly circumspect about potential solutions. The scope of our task is great, so we cannot always be as detailed as we would like. But we hope to draw together some important threads, identify fruitful directions and stimulate focused debate.

The Book

Our purpose in this book is to consolidate the literature related to young adolescents and present it as a broad narrative summary that is easily read and accessible to teachers and administrators who want to understand the issues involved in educating early adolescents. For this reason, we do not itemize findings of individual projects in great detail, but cite studies and instances which bear on the points being made. Given the range of issues included in this work, our review is necessarily selective rather than exhaustive. It is designed to identify key themes within each of the areas of focus. Our review team concentrated its search on the United States, Great Britain, Canada, Australia and New Zealand. Material from other countries is also included in the review, to the extent that we could overcome accessibility problems and language difficulties.

The themes that we address in this book are very much based on our earlier report. They are:

- The key characteristics of elementary (or primary) schools and secondary schools and their impact on student learning and development. This is to build a sense of what students in early adolescence are transferring *to* and *from*; of what they are in transit *between*.
- The transition process itself, as it is understood and experienced by students, and as it is managed by teachers and administrators.
- The curriculum for early adolescents — especially issues surrounding the concept of a core curriculum, the criteria underpinning such a curriculum, and the particular forms that a core curriculum can take.
- Innovative strategies of assessment and evaluation which support and are integrated into the learning process itself during the transition years of schooling rather than ones which are merely undertaken as a kind of judgment, when the learning is over.

This book also expands our original report to include a more comprehensive look at issues of ability grouping, support for students, teaching and learning and the implications of all this literature for restructuring schools. As we discuss these issues we will also refer in places to findings we have gathered in subsequent phases of our work. One of these studies focused on the change process through which people anticipated and implemented newly developed

reforms for the Transition Years (grades 7–9). These reforms included a legislated mandate to detrack or destream grade 9 from a position where courses
were offered at three levels of difficulty to one where all grade 9 students
would be taught in mixed-ability groups. This study of *Secondary School Work
Cultures and Educational Change* (Hargreaves, Davis, Fullan, Stager, Wignall
and Macmillan, 1992), described how principals and teachers in eight varied
secondary schools were responding to these changes.

A third part of our program, *Years of Transition: Times for Change*
(Hargreaves, Leithwood, Gérin-Lajoie, Cousins and Thiessen, 1993), evaluated
issues in the Transition Years as they were exemplified in sixty-two Ministry
funded pilot projects, in order to explore directions for policy and implementation in Transition Years reforms. When we appraise some of the widely
advocated strategies for reforming education for early adolescents, we will draw
on some of the findings of this later study, in addition to the related literature, to
see what the concrete realities of restructuring in the transition years of schooling
look like in practice.

We do not want our review to assert over-confident claims about research
evidence. Nor do we want administrators to use it as a way of imposing new
policies on the teaching profession. Rather we urge you to use this material
along with your own and your colleagues' existing knowledge and experience
in a critical and reflective way. Science can all too easily be harnessed in the
service of greater administrative power! Research evidence is rarely sufficiently
solid, timeless or incontrovertible to justify this kind of direction. Nor do we
want to encourage over-zealous beliefs in and commitments to magic models
of restructured schools for early adolescents that some might advance as answers
to our problems. Although we have no cause to be complacent about current
arrangements for educating early adolescents, almost all purported solutions,
however promising, are themselves imperfect. Although most problems have
a solution; every solution brings more problems too! Productive change is a
process of continuous problem-solving and improvement; not an investment
in the false certainties of science, or the hyped-up promises of rapid reform.

Starting Assumptions

Our hope is that our book will help stimulate debate and evaluation, open
new horizons of perception and possibility, clarify directions for improvement and reform, and identify needs for further research. For this reason, our
tone is not always absolutely detached and dispassionate. We try to avoid the
blandness of superficial consensus by identifying what our recommendations
specifically do *not* mean, as well as what they do. Our style is therefore often
argumentative; and sometimes a little blunt. This is deliberate. We believe it
is time to stop tinkering around with the education of early adolescents, adding individual initiatives, making minor adjustments to outdated structures and

practices. It is time to commit to changes that put young people first and our accustomed habits, traditions and conventions of working as educators second. This does not mean becoming oblivious to teachers' own needs. But it does mean revisiting our priorities and putting students first among then.

This means that our review is not and cannot be absolutely neutral and impartial. While we endeavor to be rigorous about weighing the evidence, our analysis and summary is still guided by certain values and assumptions. In some literature reviews, these all too often remain undeclared and implicit. We want to place ours 'up front' — so that as a critical reader, you can engage not only with the evidence we present and see how far it validates our assumptions, but you can also engage in dialogue with the assumptions themselves, perhaps using them to revisit your own educational purposes and commitments. Three basic assumptions have guided our analysis. These are:

Assumption #1   Programs and services in the transition years should primarily be based on the characteristics and needs of early adolescents.

This means that those programs and services should *not* be determined by the inertia of historical tradition that has come to define our existing understandings of 'proper' curriculum subjects (Goodson, 1988; Tomkins, 1986) and of valid, workable methods of teaching (Cuban, 1984; Curtis, 1988; Westbury, 1973). It also means that programs and services for early adolescents should not be shaped primarily by the curriculum and credential requirements of what is to follow in the senior years, as is currently the case (Stillman and Maychell, 1984; Gorwood, 1986; Hargreaves, 1986). Rather, the different stages and sectors of the educational service should work together in a partnership of equals, building education as a continuous process which effectively meets the needs of young people at each stage of their development.

The main purpose of schooling for young adolescents, we assume, therefore, is *not* to prepare students for senior high school but to help make education a continuous process addressing the personal, social, physical, and intellectual needs of young people at each particular stage in their development.

Assumption #2   The different aspects of schooling (i.e., curriculum, pedagogy, guidance, assessment, and staff development) should be dealt with as an integrated whole, not as isolated subsystems.

It is little use encouraging teachers to be more flexible and learner-centered in their approaches to teaching, if they are left to work within traditional, judgmental, fact-centered systems of assessment and evaluation. There is little value in asking teachers to be more experimental and take risks in their teaching, when they work within closely defined, curriculum guidelines that put a high premium on coverage of content. There is also little point in encouraging *all* teachers to take more responsibility for the personal and social development of their students, unless the responsibilities of what is presently understood as 'guidance' are distributed more widely throughout the school (Levi and Ziegler, 1991; Hargreaves *et al*, 1988; Lang, 1985).

In other words, we assume with Sarason (1990) that programs and services for young adolescents are best approached as an integrated system if improvements are to be effective. In education, things go together. Everything affects everything else. Curriculum, assessment, pedagogy, guidance, staff development, and the like are best considered *together* in terms of the ways they can support the learning and development of early adolescents.

> *Assumption #3*   The development and implementation of any changes should be based upon, and take account of existing theories and understandings of educational change.

Simple and relatively superficial change, in terms of adopting new curriculum guidelines, installing computers, reducing class sizes or implementing detracking or destreaming, is comparatively easy to prescribe (although less easy to fund!). Complex and enduring change, in terms of new teaching strategies or greater attention to students' personal and social needs, is not (Miles and Huberman, 1984). In these matters, teachers do not change because they are told to, or even as a result of a few 'quick' shots of in-service training (Fullan and Hargreaves, 1991). Responsiveness to change, interest in change, and willingness to change, rather, are deeply rooted in teachers' own personal and professional development (Hunt, 1987) and in the extent to which their colleagues, principals, and schools can provide an environment or *culture* which supports and promotes change (Fullan and Hargreaves, 1991). In such schools, change is most effective not when it is seen as a problem to be fixed, an anomaly to be ironed out, or a fire to be extinguished. Particular changes are more likely to be implemented in schools where teachers are committed to norms of *continuous* improvement as part of their overall professional obligations (Little, 1984; Rosenholtz, 1989). We therefore assume that if it is to be effective, change in schooling for early adolescents, like any complex and lasting change, must address the deeper, more generic issues of staff development, school leadership and the culture of the school as a supportive community committed to continuous improvement. Without that, it is unlikely that deep change will extend much beyond paper into practice.

Shrewd readers and experienced educators will have discerned that our assumptions contain a conundrum. Our second assumption suggests that if some things are to be changed, then everything must change. Change must be wide-ranging. Our third assumption meanwhile, suggests that change must secure teachers' commitment and involvement, and be pursued as a continuous process. It seems we are suggesting that change must be quick and wide-ranging, and also specific and gradual. This is one of the most fundamental paradoxes of educational change and it is one that can perplex and infuriate educators. As we will point out at the end of our book, however, it is not necessarily a paradox of despair. Approached constructively, such paradoxes of change can be managed productively, leading to positive ways forward. Educational change, we will argue, can in fact be a paradox of hope through which we can create and go on creating a better education and better world for the young people who will make up the generations of the future.

Structure of the Book

Our book is organized into ten chapters. Chapter 2 looks at both the common and variable characteristics and needs of early adolescence. It examines the nature of the transition that young people are making in early adolescence — in themselves, in their social relationships and in their schools.

Chapter 3 describes the kinds of school organization and culture in elementary and secondary schools, respectively, that students are in transit between during this period of their lives. This chapter asks to what extent and in what ways the organization and culture of most existing elementary and secondary schools meet the characteristics and needs of early adolescents.

Chapter 4 focuses on the process of transition itself. It analyzes research on the experience of transition to secondary school; on the nature and duration of the anxieties among students that precede and accompany that experience; on the degree of continuity and discontinuity that is characteristic of school transition; and on the desirable and undesirable aspects of these continuities and discontinuities. The remainder of the chapter describes and evaluates programs and innovations that have been tried or suggested to manage and improve the experience of transition for young people.

Chapter 5 considers the needs of young adolescents for support and guidance at this critical time in their development. It evaluates specific systems of support. More widely, it contends that an integrated and comprehensive support system is necessary to give young people the information, security and confidence that they need to make wise decisions.

Chapter 6 concentrates on the curriculum for young adolescents. It analyzes the origins and effects of the current secondary school curriculum and looks at how well that curriculum meets the needs of students at this stage in their lives. It exposes the ways in which the subject-based curriculum serves many students poorly, but is realistic in addressing why that subject-based curriculum is difficult to reform or remove.

Chapter 7 assesses the case for a core curriculum and for common learning outcomes. Criteria for establishing different *kinds* of core curricula are also reviewed. The chapter also advocates greater curriculum integration, especially in secondary schools. Yet it does not do so uncritically. Our review exposes widespread confusion about what curriculum integration is, and dangerous zealotry among some proponents who want to eliminate boundaries between subjects and disciplines altogether. Our chapter therefore clarifies different meanings and purposes of curriculum integration, it examines what curriculum integration looks like in practice, and it identifies some of the persistent obstacles to introducing it and making it work in subject-based secondary schools.

Chapter 8 deals with assessment and evaluation. Assessment is the activity that is often claimed to determine almost everything else in school. It is 'the tail that wags the curriculum dog'. The different purposes of assessment are reviewed in this chapter, as are the kinds of strategies available for fulfilling them. Current widely used assessment strategies are reviewed and analyzed in terms of their capacity to support or inhibit meeting the needs of young adolescents. The chapter then describes and analyzes a range of innovative assessment strategies that are not isolated from the learning process, but integrated into it — strategies that are a central part of the learning process itself.

Chapter 9 addresses the issue of teaching and learning. Curriculum and teaching go hand in hand. None of the proposed directions in curriculum will have any impact on students unless changes occur in the way teachers teach. In this chapter, we examine changing conceptions of learning and their implications for teaching. Although there are particular teaching strategies which appear to have promise, we emphasize flexibility and thoughtfulness in the way teachers choose to teach in their classrooms.

Chapter 10 considers the book's findings within the context of processes of educational change and projects of school restructuring. It compares strategies of securing educational change through attending to issues of moral purpose, restructuring, reculturing, positive politics and organizational learning. This final chapter explores the paradox of hope that we spoke of earlier in our chapter where change must be wide and specific, cautious but quick if it is to be successful. It identifies how this paradox can be dealt with effectively as we build better schools for high quality learning among young adolescents today so that they can achieve a better livelihood of living and working tomorrow.

2   Adolescence and Adolescents

What is Adolescence?

If the prime purpose of education for young adolescents is to provide curriculum, teaching and other services based on their needs and characteristics, it is important to understand the nature of adolescence.

Adolescence itself, as it is understood and experienced in most Western industrial societies, is the transition from childhood to adulthood, beginning with puberty. It is a period of development more rapid than any other phase of life except infancy. Adolescent development is neither singular nor simple, and aspects of growth during adolescence are seldom in step with each other, neither within individuals nor among peers (TFEYA, 1989). Early adolescents (aged 10 to 14) are complex, diverse and unpredictable (Shultz, 1981; Thornburg, 1982). At this time in their lives, young people are no longer children, nor are they adults. For the first time, many remarkable things begin to occur in adolescents' lives. Adolescents discover that their bodies are changing dramatically; they begin to use more advanced mental abilities; and they become extremely conscious of their relationships with others (Palomares and Ball, 1980).

Development and Maturation

Adolescence is a time of enormous physical changes characterized by increases in body height and weight, the maturation of primary and secondary sex characteristics, and increased formal mental operations. As these changes occur, adolescents are very aware of them and must adjust psychologically to these changes within themselves and to the developmental variations that occur within their adolescent group. There is a strong concern among adolescents with how they match up to common behavioral and physical stereotypes (Thornburg, 1982). They also compare themselves to their peers, who may or not be maturing at the same rate (Babcock et al, 1972; Osborne, 1984; Simmons and Blyth, 1987). In addition, changes in school bring changes in the peer group, making social comparisons even more complex (Simmons and Blyth, 1987).

Just as with physical maturation, the rate of intellectual maturation varies among students, and even within individual students over time (TFEYA, 1989). Adolescents expand their conceptual range from concrete operational concerns with the here-and-now to hypothetical, future, and spatially remote aspects of abstract thought (Palomares and Ball, 1980). Conceptual changes occur as students assimilate knowledge about new phenomena and as elementary ideas are replaced by more predictive, abstract or robust notions (Linn and Songer, 1991). While children in this age range have high energy and sometimes short concentration spans, they are also increasingly able to focus attention for long periods on topics that interest them (Epstein, 1988).

We have seen that there are substantial variations within the stages of adolescence. There is also considerable evidence that children are entering puberty earlier than in previous generations. In the United States, for example, the average age for the onset of menstruation 150 years ago was 16. It is now 12.5. It is important to note, however, that even though girls and boys become biologically mature at an earlier age, many take longer to reach intellectual and emotional maturity (TFEYA, 1989).

Identities and Values

Because young adolescents find themselves in what feels like a rift between childhood and adulthood, affiliation and identity become major concerns (Palomares and Ball, 1980). Adolescents' value systems move from being defined mostly by their parents to being more strongly influenced by their peers. This issue is particularly salient in North America, for as one cross-cultural study of adolescent values tellingly shows, North American 15-year-olds are less likely to talk with their parents and more likely to refer to their peers about matters that concern them, than adolescents in virtually any other country (King, 1986). Accordingly, adolescence is characterized by a strong focus on and a high need for peer friendships, especially in North America. Adolescents become increasingly dependent on membership in their peer group. They develop more interest in and closer relationships with members of the opposite sex. They engage in a wide range of activities to help them establish a sense of self and personal identity. In their meta-analysis of research on students in middle schools, Manning and Allen (1987) report that such students, at this stage of their development, are developing their roles and values, exploring their identities, and identifying future aspirations. Young adolescents search for identity by establishing who they are, their place among their peers, and where they fit in the larger society.

Psycho-social Crisis

As adolescents grapple with, and make the psychological adjustment to all of the changes occurring in their lives, they inevitably face conflicts and inconsistencies among the various identities and values available to them. Negative resolutions of these conflicts can leave adolescents with a pervasive sense of alienation or estrangement: from parents, peers, and society in general. Calabrese (1987), in a review of research on adolescence, discusses the physiological and emotional problems of American adolescents as they relate to a sense of alienation (i.e., isolation, meaninglessness, normlessness, and powerlessness) and as they are evident in alcohol and drug abuse, suicide, behavioral problems, and sexual promiscuity. One of the main sources of alienation, according to Calabrese, is the use of adolescents for economic exploitation. They are often treated as a consumer market, a source of inexpensive labor, and as human capital. Materialism has a pervasive influence on adolescent values. Adolescents routinely adopt consumer fads and life styles to which they are exposed. Particular kinds of clothing or music, for example, provide them with a sense of identity and help them compensate for their sense of alienation (Ryan, 1995a).

There is also some evidence that adolescents feel a sense of powerlessness especially acutely, given the widely documented need they have for a sense of independence. As long ago as 1953, Noar (quoted in K. Tye, 1985) pointed out that:

> The establishment of an independent personality involves emancipation from parental control and securing equality of status in the adult world. It is this need that lies at the root of so much misunderstanding and conflict in the home and the school. If rebellion against grown-ups could be regarded as evidence of maturity, adults would look upon it with favor . . . Teachers who do not fully understand the need for independence are prone to bemoan the seeming loss of respect for their authority . . . Instead of encouraging growth in these directions, the school too often makes rules and regulations that deprive the pupils of independence of thought and action.

As Noar indicated, schools can exacerbate the adolescent's feeling of alienation. By providing anonymous structured environments which stress cognitive achievement rather than recognizing emotional and physical needs, middle and secondary schools often promote and reinforce the very sense of powerlessness and isolation to which adolescents are already inclined (Calabrese, 1987). In implicit but forceful ways, a bureaucratic and impersonal institution conveys a lack of caring — caring which so many students desire (Wexler, 1992).

Peer-Group Membership

Group affiliation is one of the central preoccupations of early adolescence. All other issues become secondary to the adolescent's search for belonging and acceptance among same- and opposite-sex age mates (Palomares and Ball, 1980; Shultz, 1981; Thornburg, 1982). Personal and social needs are particularly strong for early adolescents (Thornburg, 1982; Lounsbury, 1982). Students in this period of their lives need help in building their self-esteem and increasing their sense of belonging to a valued group (Shultz, 1981; Babcock *et al*, 1972; Kearns, 1990). They need a sense of social usefulness and guidance in making informed choices, especially about important life decisions (TFEYA, 1989; Cheng and Zeigler, 1986). Loyalty to the peer group and the importance of positive self-concept emerge repeatedly throughout the literature, as key social development characteristics of adolescents (Calabrese, 1987; Ianni, 1989; Kenney, 1987; Manning and Allen, 1987; Thornburg, 1982). Establishing social connections with peers strongly influences adolescents' sense of self-esteem and their development of social skills. The process of becoming a member of one or more peer groups presents a number of challenges to adolescents. Along with their strong need to be liked and included, adolescents must clarify in their own minds with whom they wish to identify, and evaluate the social implications of their own personalities (Palomares and Ball, 1980). By offering membership, the peer group provides an identity to adolescents, expanding their feelings of self-worth and protecting them from loneliness (*ibid*). Peer groups can supply adolescents with an important source of security, caring and dignity in a world and in schools that may often appear to them to be anonymous, complex, uncaring and debilitating (Ryan, 1995a).

The prevailing culture in North America and elsewhere has come to expect adolescents — even early adolescents — to begin to flirt and to experience some form of sexual interaction and dating. Increased sexual interest, influenced by hormonal and anatomical changes as well as cultural expectations, becomes a major concern of most adolescents. Almost all adolescents experience some form of sex-related activity, and developing meaningful personal standards of morality and behavior is another critical issue for students during these years (Palomares and Ball, 1980). Schools must recognize that the peer group is highly influential for young adolescents and that it can be, at one and the same time, both a major distraction and a powerful ally in the educational process.

Relationship to Society

Adolescent needs are not just personal or social in the sense of immediate relationships. They are also social in a much wider sense. There is mounting evidence from Britain and the United States that many young people in early and mid-adolescence think and worry a great deal about controversial issues like nuclear war and, more recently, the environment. In the 1980s, the shadow of nuclear threat caused misery and anxiety among a fair proportion of young people (Tizard, 1984). Issues like nuclear war and the environment may not be the foremost sources of worry among early adolescents, but they are certainly important ones. One of the central needs of early adolescents, therefore, is a capacity to understand and cope with the controversies and complexities of the world around them and develop considered attitudes towards them. This is also a time when young people begin to imagine and 'try on' the various

personae and roles that they might aspire to as adults and to explore the requirements of the world of work and adult responsibilities.

The characteristics of early adolescents we have described are attested to
in a wide-range of literature. If these characteristics are portrayed in language
that is sometimes a little too measured, perhaps even high flown; the words
of the Illinois Junior High School Principals' Association bring them down to
earth.

> Confused by self-doubt, plagued with forgetfulness, addicted to extreme
> fads, preoccupied with peer status, disturbed about physical develop-
> ment, aroused by physiological impulses, stimulated by mass media
> communication, comforted by daydreams, chafed by restrictions, loaded
> with purposeless energy, bored by routine, irked by social amenities,
> veneered by 'wise cracks', insulated from responsibility, labelled with
> delinquency, obsessed with personal autonomy, but destined to years
> of economic dependency, early adolescents undergo a critical and fre-
> quently stormy period in their lives. (Fram, Godwin and Cassidy, 1976:
> cited in Oppenheimer, 1990)

Though perhaps slanted a little negatively towards images of disturbance
and purposelessness, this characterization nonetheless brings to life the living,
breathing early adolescents that many of us teach, some of us will have had
as our own children and all of us have once been ourselves.

If schooling for early adolescents often leaves their problems and concerns unaddressed, it also often leads to suppression of their strengths. Adolescent energy can seem to us organizationally dangerous and imminently (indeed
literally) overpowering, so we organize learning individually, statically and
sedentarily so as to restrain it (Tye, B., 1985). Adolescents' obvious pleasure
in the sexual dimensions of life can create disquiet in those of us who feel
discomfort with our own. As a result, we often deny the existence, value and
necessity of adolescent desire or we surround and suffocate adolescent sexuality
with images of danger, disease and death (Fine, 1993). Adolescents' emerging
sense of irony, can, with raw perspicacity, sometimes make our bureaucratic
rules and regulations seem self-serving and foolish. So we turn clever irony
into smartness and impudence and thereby diminish and dismiss it.

Throughout this book, we will amplify how well or how badly schools
address these near-ubiquitous needs and characteristics of early adolescents in
Western societies. But we must not assume that early adolescents are all alike,
that there are no differences of need, concern or experience among them.

Variations Among Adolescents

Adolescence is a comparatively recent phenomenon (Bennett and LeCompte,
1990). It is also unique to Western and industrialized parts of the world. In other

societies and other times, the transition between childhood and dependency and adulthood and self-sufficiency has often been comparatively short. In traditional societies, for example, the period between childhood and adulthood frequently came to a close as the young person achieved physical maturity, economic self-sufficiency, and found a partner for marriage; events that often coincided with one another. This kind of transition was common in a number of aboriginal communities. Elders commonly prepared young people for adulthood at early ages by extending to them the right to make decisions about many things (Reddington, 1988). In contrast to many places in the Western world, these young people were permitted, to a large extent, to do what they wanted at the time and place of their choosing, including when they felt ready to engage in economic and family pursuits. As the Western world became more industrialized, however, adulthood came to be postponed for a much longer time, usually well after young men and women had reached physical maturity.

Bennett and LeCompte (1990) also contend that the particular form which schooling and economics have taken has had a substantial impact on the suspension of adulthood. The common practice in many industrialized countries is for students to spend longer and longer periods of time in educational institutions designed to prepare them to become economically self-sufficient in a world of work that many believe requires highly skilled and mature men and women. Unlike their ancestors, young people are thrown together in large groups, isolated from most adults, and denied many of the rights that adults enjoy. This has had a number of unintended effects. Among other things, schools now provide conditions which prompt young people to develop their own sub-cultures — often of an oppositional nature — which they often use to rescue a measure of dignity in a school (and world) where they are denied the right to make decisions for themselves (Hargreaves, 1982). The extent and nature of the distance between young people and the adult world and its perceived economic and social rights and opportunities, however, may vary between and among individuals and groups of adolescents. Gender, social class, race, ethnicity and place of birth are just a few of the variables around which such differences revolve, and which provide the basis for a range of different responses to schooling.

One of the most important and systematic sources of variation in the needs and characteristics of early adolescents is gender. In her study of female adolescents, Gilligan (1989) found that girls up to age 11 exhibit well-developed self-confidence and a healthy resistance to perceived injustice. However, after that point, they go through a crisis which erodes the self-confidence of their childhood. This crisis is in their response to adolescence and the structures and demands of the culture which sends girls the message that, as emerging women, they must 'keep quiet'. This trend has been confirmed in a number of other studies (for example, King, 1986; Bibby and Posterski, 1992). By age 15 or 16, Gilligan found, girls' independence has gone underground. They start not knowing what they had known before. Gilligan asks how parents, teachers and therapists who work with girls can prevent this crisis and decline in self-confidence during the early years of adolescence; thereby questioning and redefining what kind of women and men our society should be creating (Bibby and Posterski, 1992).

Gender is not the only source of variation among adolescents. Race, ethnicity and social class matter greatly also. Ianni (1989) and his associates observed and interviewed adolescents in ten US communities over a ten-year period. They found that the norms and behaviors of adolescents and their peer groups were primarily determined by the socioeconomic status and culture of their communities. Indirectly, as well as testifying to the diverse character of adolescence, this study also affirms the importance of parental influences and responsibilities for young people. The National Panel on High School and Adolescent Education (1976) noted that ethnicity and social class were both important variables in determining a student's learning experiences outside the school, expectations of success, and levels of self-esteem.

Another source of diversity is that of students' first language. In increasingly multicultural and globally mobile societies, more and more schools are being faced with issues of second-language learning that apply to more than one language community and more than one small minority of students. Second language learning often involves large, complex, multilingual communities (Corson, 1993). Because language is central to the identity and self-concept of developing adolescents, schools are increasingly being faced with challenges of catering to more and more second-language learning needs for more students, in more classes. Differences in language, however, are only a small example of the differences that may exist between the behavior of students of various non-European heritages and expected school conventions. In schools that some-times cater to students from over sixty different heritages, students bring cultural baggage to school with them that is often not recognized or understood by teachers and administrators. Differences in communication styles (Corson, 1992; Erickson, 1993; Erickson and Mohatt, 1982; Phillips, 1983; Ramirez, 1983; Ryan, 1992a), learning styles (Appleton, 1983; Phillips, 1983; Cazden and Leggett, 1973; Ryan, 1992b), conceptions of testing (Deyhle, 1983 and 1986), cognitive processing (Cole and Scribner, 1973; Das *et al*, 1979), self-concept (Clifton, 1975), family traditions and commitments (Divoky, 1988; Gibson, 1987; Olson, 1988), locus of control (Tyler and Holsinger, 1975), attitudes toward cooperation (Goldman and McDermott, 1987; Ryan, 1992c), aspirations (Gue, 1975 and 1977), authority (Reddington, 1988; Henrikson, 1973) and conceptions of space and time (Ryan, 1991) represent just a few of the dimensions around which differences occur. While such differences can be overcome by some students (Ogbu, 1992), they will nevertheless remain as complications for a number of adolescents as they strive to come to terms with their lives in challenging school environments.

The problems and challenges of adolescence are therefore filtered and reworked through young people's everyday experience of class, race, ethnicity, gender and language background. Being an early adolescent is a very different experience for the student of a white, wealthy family in an affluent suburb than for members of large African-communities in areas of severe urban poverty. It is different for young women than for young men. And it poses challenges for recent immigrants with inchoate grasps of the dominant domestic language of instruction; challenges that long-standing residents of the dominant culture can scarcely imagine. All students, regardless of race, ethnicity, social class, gender, or place of birth may take on any number of identities, and these may change from week to week and from situation to situation. And while these categories may influence how adolescents respond to schooling, it is difficult to predict how they intersect with one another or how they will be combined with the popular cultural resources at hand.

These variations pose serious and significant questions for the education of early adolescents. The faltering self-confidence of adolescent girls calls for strategies of gender equity that embrace active, confidence-boosting intervention, not strategies that treat boys and girls exactly the same, whatever their differences of need (Robertson, 1992). The disproportionate representation of working-class students (Weis, 1993), African-American students (Troyna, 1993) and Native or aboriginal students (Ryan, 1976) in lower tracks, indicates, as we shall see, not poor upbringing or family deprivation, but significant gaps between the knowledge and styles of learning and interaction that are valued and common in these students' homes and communities, and the forms of knowledge, styles of learning, and even basic structures of time and organization that characterize most of our schools. At the same time, some of the strategies that schools use to address issues of race only deflect or exaggerate the problems rather than solving them. These include channelling African-American students into competitive sports activities that reinforce racial stereotypes, offer few prospects of continuing sports careers beyond school, and depress and detract from the academic success needed to make gains and have choices in the real world of work (Solomon, 1992). They also include creating dubious course options, and relaxing standards simply to *graduate* students rather than *educate* them (Bates, 1987; Cusick, 1983). You do not get young people to jump higher by lowering the bar! If we want all young people to achieve better, we must therefore question the very structure of our school system itself, and its ability to respond to wide-ranging differences of language, race, ethnicity, culture and class in the student population.

Summary

Adolescence is not created exclusively by adolescents. It is in many respects an adaptation to and reflection of adult problems and concerns, and is partially created by adults distancing themselves from the problems of adolescence by claiming a lack of influence on their norms and values (Ianni, 1989). Lasch (1979) argues that in a society where self-possessed narcissism appears to be pervading wide areas of our culture, many adults seem all too keen to ape adolescent styles and values so as to symbolize their own everlasting youth and immortality, rather than asserting and leading with moral values of their own. Educating early adolescents well means accepting and engaging with early adolescents' concerns; not acquiescing blindly to them on the one hand, or rejecting them outright on the other.

Young adolescents, we have seen, have become impaled on the horns of a dilemma. These are the need for independence and the need for security. The needs of early adolescents are complex, crucial and challenging for anyone entrusted with the onerous responsibility of meeting them. This challenge is to meet their personal, social and developmental needs and establish the implications of their educational experiences for them as future adult citizens. This chapter has identified some of the key characteristics and needs of early adolescents, which are to:

- adjust to profound physical, intellectual, social, and emotional changes;
- develop a positive self-concept;
- experience and grow toward independence;
- develop a sense of identity and of personal and social values;
- experience social acceptance, affiliation and affection among peers of the same and the opposite sex;
- develop positive approaches to sexuality that embrace and celebrate caring, pleasure, emotion and desire in the context of loving, responsible relationships;
- increase awareness of, ability to cope with, and capacity to respond constructively to the social and political world around them;
- establish relationships with particular adults within which these processes of growth can take place.

In the remainder of this book, we will explore how well schools currently address these needs and how they might be able to do so more effectively in the future.

3   Cultures of Schooling

Transition as a 'Rite de Passage'

Adolescence in general, and the experience of transition to secondary school in particular, can usefully be viewed as a kind of 'rite de passage'. In their longitudinal case study of transition and adaptation to secondary school, Measor and Woods (1984) describe transition as precisely that. Transition to adulthood and to secondary school is one of the most important status passages that people experience in their lifetimes. Whether one is moving from childhood to adulthood in preliterate societies, from single status to being married, from marriage to divorce, or from elementary to secondary school, the movement marks a passage in status from being one kind of person with certain rights and expectations to another.

These status passages are important yet traumatic. With school transfer, they are sometimes particularly traumatic, argue Measor and Woods (*ibid*), because transfer to secondary school involves not *one* status passage, but *three*:

- the physical and cultural passage of adolescence itself that we call puberty;
- the informal passage within and between peer cultures and friendship groups where different kinds of relationships are experienced and expected;
- the formal passage between two different kinds of institutions, with different regulations, curriculum demands and teacher expectations.

The multiple-status passage of transition can be a particular source of anxiety because the messages and directions of the passage are not at all consistent with each other. Movement from elementary to secondary school and from child to adolescent represents an *increase* in status. Movement from the top of one institution to the bottom of another and from *older* child to *younger* adolescent represents *lowered* status. For the child, transition can be a good thing or a bad thing. Often it is both — and this can be confusing and worrying. Reflecting on their discovery of these multiple-status passages and their implications, Measor and Woods (*ibid*) comment that other literature on transition which 'concentrate(s) almost exclusively on the formal aspects such as the pupil's academic achievement, miss(es) a great deal and may come to the wrong conclusions'.

The next chapter looks closely at the process of transition to secondary school and the ways in which it is and can be managed. Here, we examine what it is students are in transit *between* — the culture of the elementary school and of the secondary school — and the continuities and discontinuities between these cultures.

Two Cultures of Schooling?

The differences between elementary and secondary schooling, and between elementary and secondary teaching, may in many ways be regarded as amounting to differences between two quite distinct cultures (Hargreaves, 1986). To move from one school to another is to change not just institutions but communities, each having its own assumptions about how students learn, how knowledge is organized, what form teaching should take, and so forth. Moving from elementary to secondary education commonly entails moving from a generalist pattern of curriculum and teaching where teachers have responsibility for more than one subject, and where, through themes and projects, they can explore the relationships among subjects, to a more specialist pattern where the curriculum and the teaching staff are divided up by subject specialization (Ginsburg *et al*, 1977). Elementary-to-secondary transfer entails students leaving behind a relationship with a single class teacher who knows them well, for less extensive relationships with a wide range of subject-specialist teachers (Meyenn and Tickle, 1980). In short, as Ahola-Sidaway (1988) has noted in her study of student transfer from elementary to high school in Canada, transfer entails movement from what, following Tonnies (1887), she calls the world of *Gemeinschaft* to the world of *Gesellschaft*, from a personal and supportive world of community to a more distant and impersonal world of association.

Among teachers, the main differences between elementary and secondary schools are usually felt to be ones of teaching style and strategy. There is evidence, however, that such differences are frequently exaggerated. An Inner London Education Authority survey of teachers in England found that many had very stereotyped views of the curriculum and teaching methods in the sector other than their own. Many of these views were not based on direct experience or visits (ILEA, 1988). Stillman and Maychell (1984) came to similar conclusions in their study of transfer from middle school (age 9–13) to secondary school in two English school districts. Secondary school teachers, they found, held on to 'a demeaning stereotype' of middle school teaching which:

> portrays a scene of noisy classrooms with children freely wandering around. What work is done is in small groups and based upon free-ranging topics. The formalities of school learning, the use of reference books, the ability to concentrate, the ability to take notes from the board and to process work is all supposedly absent.

Yet when Stillman and Maychell (*ibid*) compared the teaching strategies in the final year of middle school with the same age group in a parallel system of secondary schools in another school district, they found 'no indication of any real differences in classroom practice'. They attributed this misunderstanding to lack of experience that teachers have with any sector other than the one in which they are presently working.

The presumption that elementary or primary schools are awash with active learning and small group work is, in most respects, erroneous. Of course, a passing and somewhat superficial visit to almost any open-plan elementary school can give quite a contrary impression — of movement, diversity, students taking initiative and small group collaboration. It was just these sorts of passing impressions that misled noted American educational writer Charles Silberman (1970 and 1973), on returning from England in the 1960s, to report the occurrence of what he called a 'quiet revolution' in England's primary schools. Closer studies of primary-school teachers' classroom strategies unveiled a very different picture.

In a survey of 468 teachers in Northwest England, Bennett (1976) found that most used a mixture of styles. Only 9 per cent of the teachers met the criteria of progressiveness defined in terms of the influential and highly regarded *Plowden Report* on primary education (Central Advisory Council for Education, 1967). In a study of 100 primary schools conducted in the mid-1970s, Galton and his colleagues found a preponderance of didactic teaching and almost no evidence of discovery learning or cooperative groupwork (Galton *et al*, 1980; Simon, 1981). In common with other studies, this research team also found an unexpectedly high emphasis on basic skills among primary teachers (Bassey, 1978; Galton *et al*, 1980; Her Majesty's Inspectorate, 1978). And while they found many instances of students sitting together *in* groups, they came across very few examples of them working together *as* groups.

These results are consistent with findings elsewhere. Basic skills teaching in American urban elementary schools remains a salient feature of educational life. Goodlad (1984) notes, in fact, that in widespread calls and efforts to go 'back to basics', proponents overlook the fact that in many ways, we never really got away from them.

'Progressive' or 'innovative' practice in primary and elementary schools therefore seems to be less pervasive than commonly claimed. In many ways, recent years have also seen quite deliberate moves away from it in many districts. Another point is that even where 'progressive' or 'open-learning' practices do exist, they are not nearly so 'unstructured' as their critics commonly imagine. In Ireland, for instance, Sugrue's (1996) study of sixteen primary teachers identified by their administrators as positive exemplars of child-centred practice, finds that their classroom teaching is highly structured. These teachers spend a lot of time '*scaffolding*' learning for their students; creating clear frameworks which push students to the proximal limits of their development and understanding; extending those limits themselves still further. They also engage in *shepherding* their students; a metaphor that blends together the care, control and organization of large groups of young and often vulnerable children as they are steered through their learning and development. More recent forms of student-centered learning are, if anything, even more structured. Cooperative learning, for example, specifies strategies for making both individuals and groups accountable for their performance, and for creating positive kinds of inter-dependence among students (Johnson and Johnson, 1990).

Secondary school teaching strategies are as easily stereotyped as are those strategies teachers use with younger children. While Barbara Tye (1985), on the basis of her large-scale survey of American high school classrooms, con-cluded that 'all high school classrooms are discouragingly similar' with similar patterns of frontal presentation, closed questioning and deskwork, nonetheless, within and around this overall uniformity, there are some important variations.

Some of the most important variations are subject related — an issue we delve into in our chapters on curriculum. For instance, in England, Barnes and Shemilt's (1974) survey of secondary school teachers revealed that their pro-fessed orientations to teaching style and other matters, varied by subject along a continuum from a 'transmission' or relatively traditional, directive approach to an 'interpretation', process-based, student-centered one. At the transmission end of the continuum were mathematics, French and the so-called 'harder' sciences of physics and chemistry. Clustered at the 'interpretation' end were subjects such as English, with the social sciences of history and geography falling somewhere in between. Ball's (1980) case study of teachers' attitudes to mixed-ability teaching indicated that teachers in the French department stuck with predominantly didactic, teacher-centered approaches, but teachers in math-ematics and English did not. Differences in pedagogical approach have been recorded elsewhere between English and mathematics departments (Siskin, 1994; Stodolsky, 1988; McLaughlin and Talbert, 1993) and between academic and vocational subjects (Little, 1993). Our own study of how teachers in eight secondary schools responded to an upcoming mandate to detrack (or destream) grade 9, found that teachers in more practical and lower status subjects, such as technical education and family studies were among the most flexible in their strategies of teaching, especially with wide-ranging ability groups (Hargreaves *et al*, 1992).

In elementary and secondary schools alike, the pictures of pedagogy that accumulated research has revealed are complex. The differences in teaching style between elementary and secondary school are less dramatic than is often believed. So if pedagogy is not the key factor that distinguishes between the cultures of elementary and secondary schooling, what is? What are transferring students leaving and entering that is so different? A look at the cultures of elementary and secondary school respectively will give some clues.

The concept of school culture has been defined in many ways, and is still highly contested among writers on the subject. Corbett *et al* (1987) define culture as a shared set of norms, values and beliefs. In her analysis of the cultures of two different secondary schools and their impact on teachers' interpretations of tracking, Page (1987) argues that while the beliefs, values and assumptions are often tacit and regarded as self-evident by members of the culture, 'they nevertheless provide a powerful foundation for members' understanding of the way they and the organization operate' (p. 82). Wilson (1971) widens the definition of culture to include socially shared and transmitted knowledge of what is and what ought to be, symbolized in acts and artifacts. Such characterizations of culture are especially common in writings on corporate and more general organizational cultures (Deal and Kennedy, 1982; Ouchi, 1980; Schein, 1984; Wilkins and Ouchi, 1983) and in studies that apply these more general frameworks to education (Davis, 1989; Deal and Peterson, 1990). Their purpose is often directed to learning how to create strong organizational cultures that will lead to greater effectiveness.

In a critique of such work, Bates (1987) argues that by searching for the conditions and processes that lead to strong cultures, researchers place the interests of prescription above the need for understanding. Moreover, he contends, apparently common cultures (even strong ones) do not merely emerge from the group, or naturally represent their collective interests. The strong culture of an organization, rather, arises from managerial manipulation (also Jeffcutt, 1993). It supports and promotes dominant interests among those who have most to benefit from the organization, and either suppresses or seduces others with different interests, and alternative views to conform to the dominant pattern. Culture, then, does not just emerge naturally, but is actively created and contested against competing visions and values of what people in the organization should do. As Cooper (1987) tellingly puts it in the title of her analysis of workplace cultures in schools, 'Whose culture is it anyway?'.

Some writers prefer the term *ethos* to that of *culture* (Rutter *et al*, 1979; D. Hargreaves, 1995). The notion of a shared or common ethos is more pervasive but also more elusive than that of culture. The dictionary definition of ethos is that it is 'the characteristic spirit of a community or an age'. It is a kind of zeitgeist; diffusely felt more than specifically identifiable. Whilst spiritually appealing to some, the notion of ethos, however, tends to elude action and intervention. How do you create something as intangible as a 'spirit'? *Culture* can admit more readily that values, beliefs and the like can be created, negotiated, imposed or subverted. There can be majority cultures and minority ones; mainstream cultures and sub-cultures within them. *Ethos*, however, tends to encourage evasion of these issues, by appealing to a singular spirit that shines through us all.

One aspect of cultures to which Sarason (1971) has drawn attention is that cultural norms possess what he calls *sacred* and *profane* characteristics. Those norms that define professional purpose and are fundamental to teachers' belief systems (for example, commitment to subject specialty) are considered 'sacred' and generally not subject to change. 'Profane' norms by contrast, (for example, student discipline) are acknowledged as the particular way that things are done in the organization and are seen as more susceptible to change.

Andy Hargreaves (1992 and 1993) adds another dimension to the understanding of school culture. He points out that culture has both content and form.

The *content* of a culture is made up of what its members think, say and do. The *form* consists of patterns of relationships among members of the culture which may take the form of isolation, competing groups and factions, or broader attachment to a community, for instance.

We interpret culture here to mean the content of the shared sets of norms, values and beliefs of members of an organization *and* the form of the patterns of relationships among these members. Especially at the secondary school level, we will deal with both the content and form of school culture, as well as with its 'sacred' and 'profane' qualities. Cultures can be found in individual schools (Page, 1987), even among individual departments within schools (Johnson, 1990; McLaughlin and Talbert, 1993). They can also come to characterize whole forms of schooling, such as vocational schooling, private schooling or junior high schools. We want to explore the cultures of elementary and secondary schooling in particular.

Elementary School Culture

Elementary school cultures are built upon two central, interlocking principles — the first, widely acknowledged, the second less so. These are the principles of care and control.

A study in Quebec, Canada examined the key differences between elementary and secondary school cultures as they were experienced by a group of students in transition between the two cultures. Participant observation was used to gather data regarding seventy-six students in grade 6 (elementary school), and the sixty-eight who subsequently entered grade 7 in English Catholic high schools. Ahola-Sidaway (1988) concluded that elementary schools are like families, whereas secondary schools are based on formal contracts. Elementary students are part of the school neighborhood, have strong connections to the school community, are located in specific classrooms, occupy a designated desk, and have close ties to teachers, classmates, and their principal. Secondary students, on the other hand, go to school outside their community; occupy a large, complex building; have no home-based classroom, desk, or teacher; are controlled by bells, forms, and procedures; and have only a locker as their personal territory. Their connections are not based on relationships with teachers or classmates. Instead, peer cliques are formed around common interests.

Home, family, and community are the symbols of care that characterize the culture of elementary schools. The importance of care for elementary teachers and their students is also revealed in another study which found that student control in elementary schools is more humanistic than in secondary schools, where it is more custodial (Smedley and Willower, 1981). In a questionnaire study of the entry-level characteristics of 174 elementary and 178 secondary teachers, Book and Freeman (1986) found that elementary candidates had more experience working with school-aged children and more often expressed child-centred reasons for entering teaching as compared to their secondary counterparts who were more subject-centred in their approach.

In a study of fifty primary schools in London, England (one of the most systematic studies of school effectiveness ever completed), Mortimore and his colleagues (1988) identified positive school climate as one of twelve key factors associated with positive student outcomes. This 'positive' climate was a pleasant one with high emphasis on praise and rewards. Classroom management was firm but fair. Enjoyment, happiness and care were also core features of these positive climates. Mortimore *et al* (1988) stated that:

> Positive effects resulted where teachers obviously enjoyed teaching their classes, valued the fun factor, and communicated their enthusiasm to the children. The interest in the children as individuals and not just as learners, also fostered progress. Those who devoted more time to non-school chat or small talk increased pupil's progress and development. Outside the classroom, evidence of a positive climate included the organization of lunchtime and after-school clubs for pupils; involvement of pupils in the presentation of assemblies; teachers eating their lunches at the same tables as the children; organization of trips and visits; and the use of the local environment as a learning resource.

Happiness wasn't everything, of course. Focused, intellectually challenging work also mattered, along with a host of other factors. But the presence, persistence and pervasiveness of care in primary school was clearly associated with the effectiveness of these schools.

That care is central to the culture of elementary schools is partly a result of their size and structure. Johnson (1990) attests to one simple difference between elementary and secondary schools being that 'although elementary teachers may work with the same twenty students throughout the day, secondary school teachers are routinely assigned 125 students in five rotating classes' (p. 111).

The gender composition of elementary school teaching is another important determinant of its care-orientation. Elementary education is chiefly the work of women, and care and connectedness are central features of women's work and lives (Noddings, 1992; Gilligan, 1982). While several researchers have pointed out that male elementary teachers appear no less caring or attached to their students than their female counterparts (Nias, 1989; Coulter and McNay, 1993), the presence of women in large numbers in elementary schools may still be significant for shaping the caring qualities of that culture in gender-related ways (Acker, 1995).

In a Canadian study, Andy Hargreaves (1994) found care to be a central, positive and often overlooked principle for elementary teachers. It often underpinned their active preference for an individualistic approach to their work and for spending most of their time working in their classroom with their own students. So strong was this *ethic of care* (Gilligan, 1982) for these elementary teachers that a number of them expressed serious reservations as to whether they really wanted additional preparation time because this would take them away from their classes and from the children for whom they cared. This sentiment is exemplified in the following quotes from Hargreaves' (1994) study:

> I wonder if I had much more time away, if I would feel I was losing something with the kids. And yet I could certainly use the time.
>   There is an amount you can increase it to and then you are missing the kids. This is what I said to (the principal) the other day. It's fine having all these spares, but when do you ever get the kids?

Hargreaves argues that while the commitment to classroom care of these teachers was admirable, it did not stand alone. Care was bound up with two other arguably less desirable conditions — ownership and control. Teachers in portable classrooms confessed to becoming overly possessive about their classes — 'you get very mothering . . . because they're your family and you have this little house'. This caused some difficulties in liaison with special education resource teachers where disputes could arise about who had 'ownership' of the students. Teachers in this study also spoke of the satisfaction of having their own class, of being in control. As one of Johnson's 'good' teachers confessed with regard to having student teachers in her class:

> I love student teachers, because they're young, energetic, fresh, un-biased . . . but my classes lose when I'm not with them. That is not saying that I'm anything special (but) I know what I'm doing; I know where I'm going. It's difficult to put that on paper and have somebody come in and work with the class the same way that I work, and cover the same areas, the same material, in the same ways. I'm very jealous about that. I don't like to give it up. (Johnson, 1990, pp. 279–80)

This complicated interplay of care, control and ownership in the commitment of elementary teachers may have important implications for students and their movement towards independence as they approach adolescence. The nature of teachers' commitment may explain why many studies of primary and elementary education have found images of student independence and initiative to be somewhat illusory, with teachers allowing more discretion over *when* things are studied rather than over *what* or *how* things are studied (Pollard, 1985; Berlak and Berlak, 1981; Hargreaves, 1977).

In discussions about transition to secondary school, it is common for secondary schools to be cast in the role of uncaring villains. Certainly, the evidence we have reviewed points to higher commitments to care among elementary teachers than among their secondary counterparts. But this may not be unconditionally good news. For many elementary teachers, the packaging of care with ownership and control may make it difficult for students to develop the independence, autonomy and security to grow beyond those who care for them most. It may make transfer to secondary school less like a series of increasingly bold and exploratory steps away from home and more like a terrifying leap from the nest. One of the best things that elementary teachers might do for their children is, like good parents, to give them the strength and security to grow away from them. This may mean unhinging care a little from its other associations with ownership and control and with the accompanying sentiments that these are '*my* children' in '*my* class'.

Some developments in elementary and primary education are helpfully moving in this direction already. At a time when knowledge is becoming more complicated and differentiated and can no longer be coped with by a single generalist teacher, calls for greater subject-specialist expertise in elementary teaching form an important part of the international agenda to improve the quality of teaching in elementary schools (Hargreaves, 1989; Department of Education and Science, 1983; Campbell, 1985). This is giving elementary students a wider range of contacts with more specialist teachers especially in subjects like music and art, but also leading to more coordination and consultation between teachers in and out of the classroom. For example, many school systems now operate with specialist teachers working cooperatively and collaboratively with classroom teachers to provide appropriate and flexible curricula for specific children and groups of children in regular classes. In some places, classroom teachers also work closely with teacher-librarians to offer programs to expose children to the much wider source of skills and knowledge provided by the school library. These shared activities have begun to break down the exclusive sense of ownership that many elementary teachers have held with their classes. If the principle of care can be preserved within these changes, and teachers can work as partners to meet these needs for care, then, in the upper elementary years especially, students may have a sounder basis of developing independence to prepare for secondary school. The responsibility for narrowing the gap between the two cultures of schooling belongs to both secondary and elementary teachers.

Secondary School Culture

When students move to secondary school or to junior high or middle schools, what kind of culture are they entering, and how different is that from the culture they have left? Apart from the obvious factors of sheer size and complexity, research and other writing on secondary schools in particular points to three dominant and interrelated factors of their culture: *academic orientation, student polarization* and *fragmented individualism*.

Academic Orientation

Due to its complex nature, understanding high school culture is no small task. Pink (1988) describes the complicated character of high school culture when he portrays the secondary school as a complex organization generating its own norms and operational ethos. He states that conflicting programs not only divide the school but also cast a dubious shadow on the possibilities for goal consensus. Pink notes that high school culture is characterized by departmentalization and isolation (also Johnson, 1990; Siskin and Little, 1995). This complexity makes it difficult to bring about change at the secondary level (Rossman *et al*, 1985). A major stumbling block in the path of secondary school change is teachers' academic orientation (Boyd and Crowson, 1982). This is closely intertwined with teachers' orientation towards subject matter and content and has profound implications for teachers' approaches to pedagogy, their attitudes to change and their responsiveness to curriculum integration. We will deal with this issue in detail in our later discussion of curriculum. Here, we want to note two particular consequences for the wider culture of the secondary school in terms of students' norms and values, and their social relationships in school. These consequences are ones of polarization of students through ability grouping and of isolation and alienation among students through neglect of their personal and social-development needs.

Student Polarization

The predominantly academic orientation of secondary schools puts a premium on a rather narrow definition of what counts as achievement and success. As we will see later, there are many other kinds of achievement, in addition to academic ones, on which secondary schools place considerably less value. Embracing a narrow view of achievement as *academic* achievement creates large rates of failure by *definition* (ILEA, 1984; Hargreaves, 1989). Secondary schools in most countries still place highest value on the academically bright (Lawton *et al*, 1988).

The predominance and preeminence of academic achievement persists in spite of increasing evidence that the future needs of society stretch well beyond narrow academic content (Snyder and Edwards, in press) and in the face of growing recognition that intelligence is much more complex and multidimensional than was once believed. In the United States, in the past decade alone, at least seven eminent national commissions have published gloomy reports outlining the failure of secondary schools to meet the needs of all of their students (Brown, 1984). Goodlad (1984), in an eight-year study of the state of the public education system in the United States, described it as being 'nearing collapse'. Schools become increasingly stratified as they are called upon to train students in accordance with their mental abilities and specific skills (Cremin, 1961). The majority are trained to fill the requirements of a hungry marketplace while a few attend universities and colleges (Greene, 1985). Adler (1982) bemoaned the existence of what continues to be a class society in schools and the manner in which students are placed into tracks or streams that exude inequality. This sentiment is echoed by Goodlad and Oakes

(1988) who point out the sorry record of schools in promoting the achievement of Black, Hispanic and poor children. They go on to say that the attainment of those students whom schools educate least well will become increasingly important and that existing tracking policies actually restrict students' access to knowledge.

If, as we shall argue later, the proper purpose of education for young adolescents is to provide a broad and balanced education for all students and to stimulate and recognize a wide range of achievements, then a uniform policy of ability grouping or tracking is inconsistent with such goals. To say that different forms of achievement are equally worthwhile, then to group students according to only one or two dimensions of achievement, is inconsistent. The existence of separate, insulated tracks is an example of such inconsistency in the context of a commitment to broad educational goals.

Allocation of students to streams or tracks is supposed to be based fairly on merit and ability. In practice, it is a complex and subjective process as counsellors and teachers use test scores along with behavioral and attitudinal criteria to assign students to streams (Cicourel and Kitsuse, 1963; Oakes, 1992; Troman, 1989). This may be one reason why poor and ethnic minority students are disproportionately represented in lower streams (Hout and Garnier, 1979). All told, student assignment factors are difficult to sort out and their 'fairness' is questionable (Oakes, 1992).

A common argument in favor of streaming or tracking is that students feel more positively about themselves and achieve better when they are with other students they perceive as similar to them. Research evidence does not support this claim. Placing students in average and low tracks appears to lower their self-esteem, not raise it (Esposito, 1973). High-track students are more enthusiastic and low-track students more alienated (Oakes, Gamoran and Page, 1991). High-track students convey greater self-confidence, not only about their academic competence, but generally (Oakes, 1985). One response to these findings might be that the lowered self-esteem of low-stream students may be due not to their stream placement, but to factors located in the students, themselves. However, some of the research indicating lower aspirations among low-stream students has found this result even when home background factors have been held constant (Alexander, Cook and McDill, 1978).

Students in lower streams receive poorer instruction from less qualified teachers (Murphy and Hallinger 1989; Oakes, 1992). Ability grouping assignments result in differences in pace. The resulting differences in coverage mean that the low-track students fall further behind. These differences tend to stabilize track placements because the prerequisites for moving tracks have been missed (Oakes, 1992). Although there are strong pedagogical arguments that ability clusters should promote mobility between groups, research indicates that once students are channeled into a track, such mobility is conspicuous by its absence (Murphy and Hallinger, 1989). Lawton *et al* (1988) found greater emphasis being placed on discipline and control in lower stream programs as compared to high stream programs where quality of teaching was accentuated.

There is also typically less emphasis in low-track classes on curriculum goals like interest in the subject, basic concepts and principles, and problem solving, even though these goals are increasingly seen as essential for all students (Oakes, 1992). In general, students in lower tracks form sub-cultures that are not as valued. The good student is one who has acquired good academic and social skills, as well as having a positive and cooperative disposition (Lawton *et al*, 1988). Students who do not meet these criteria are prone to drop out of the school picture. In general, lower track students spend less time learning, are taught lower level skills and are exposed to a narrower range of learning materials (Trimble and Sinclair, 1987; Murphy and Hallinger, 1989; Oakes, 1985). In short, they receive less opportunity to learn (Oakes, 1992).

Experiences such as these help create what David Hargreaves (1982) calls a 'loss of dignity' that is unintentionally inflicted by the secondary school system on its students. Not surprisingly, students in lower streams feel less connected to their school than their higher stream counterparts (Goodlad, 1984; Oakes, 1985; Murphy and Hallinger, 1989). In many cases, lower stream students may go further and protest their loss of dignity by forming counter-cultures of opposition — inverting the school's values and making these inverted values their own — to provide a source of status and identity for their low stream group (Willis, 1977). In a study of secondary school boys, David Hargreaves (1967) found these inverted values embraced fighting, swearing, untidy dress, sexual promiscuity, and general anti-school attitudes. Pressure to conform to the norms of the stream peer culture are strong. In high schools, if students do not belong, they risk being perceived as 'losers' (Lawton *et al*, 1988).

It is common to imagine that the attitudes, behavior and work habits found in low tracks are a reflection not of tracking but of the social back-grounds, the home and the community environments from which low-track students come. One of the most interesting challenges to this view is Lacey's (1970) classic study of an English grammar school. What is interesting about Lacey's study is that it focused on students selected for grammar school (the top 10–20 per cent of the ability range) who on entering it, all saw themselves as having been 'best pupils' within their previous primary schools. The students were streamed soon after entry at age 11 and, at first, this produced a wide range of responses of individual anxiety among many lower stream students, as they tried to accommodate to the new classification that streaming had placed upon them. After a year or so, these individual responses began to cohere into a shared, protective culture, (a kind of 'support group') with strong anti-school elements, which rejected academic values, gave high status to misbehavior, and so on. Lacey's explanation was that, once a school *differentiates* students into separate groups by some valued criterion, this leads to *polarization* between the groups, with the more successful groups embracing the official values of the school, and the less successful ones inverting them. Streaming is therefore a system of *differentiation* that creates student *polarization* and leads, in lower streams, to a higher incidence of truancy, delinquency and dropout. The contribution of streaming to student polarization has been replicated in other studies (Hargreaves, 1967; Ball, 1980). Indeed, Hammersley (1985), claims that the research on differentiation and polarization, is one of the most powerful examples of cumulative research knowledge in education.

Tracking or streaming is a product of the overwhelming academic orientation that characterizes the culture of secondary schools. This culture values academic achievement above all else and ranks students in relation to it. Students who are out of tune with this very particular value system respond to the differentiation by polarizing themselves in relation to the school's values and the successful students who identify with them. Counter-cultures form, gangs are created and the school becomes divided into very different student subgroups, often at odds with each other. There is not one secondary school culture here but many, and the school's capacity to have students learn and work together as a single community is undermined. In the past few years, policy makers and national opinion leaders in many countries, motivated by concerns for school effectiveness and equity have responded to these conditions with recommendations for abolishing tracking (TFYEA, 1989; Radwanski, 1987).

These policy declarations offer the possibility of alleviating the polarization among student groups that characterizes many streamed secondary schools, and of building secondary schools as more cohesive communities among staff and students alike. Unfortunately, politically prescribed elimination of tracking does not ensure that these problems will be resolved. It merely supplies the opportunity. We will explore some of the organizational and pedagogical challenges of teaching mixed ability classes later. More generally, on the basis of existing research we want to warn readers of the dangers of replacing one problematic secondary school culture (a tracked and polarized one) with another that may be equally problematic (a fragmented, individualized one).

Fragmented Individualism

Although much educational research is critical of many of the consequences of tracking, it has to be acknowledged that, in terms of academic achievement, research findings on the respective merits of tracked and untracked systems have been inconclusive (Reid *et al*, 1981; Brophy and Good, 1974; Findley and Bryan, 1975; Kulik and Kulik, 1982 and 1987).

On reflection, this is not surprising, as an important study by Ball (1980) points out. While it is common for schools and teachers to agree on the principle of mixed-ability *grouping*, agreement is less common about mixed-ability *teaching*; about how classes should be taught. This explains two important findings in comparisons between mixed-ability and streamed classes. First, in a comparison of streamed and unstreamed primary school classes, student achievement was more closely related to the teacher's attitude towards streaming than it was to the existence or non-existence of streaming itself. Teachers in unstreamed classes often continued to teach them as if they were still streamed (Barker-Lunn, 1970). Second, as Ball (1980) found, having avoided discussion of how the new mixed-ability classes should be taught, teachers continued to use the same teaching methods commonly used for their subjects.

These findings serve as a reminder that the central issue in destreaming or untracking is not so much how students are grouped, but how they are taught. Heterogeneous grouping creates a possibility. It does not, of itself, solve any problems. Ball's research alerts us to a danger that may occur with untracking if appropriate teaching methods and the conditions needed for them are not directly addressed by the school as a whole community. If teaching methods are left to individual teacher discretion, or even to the discretion of departments, many teachers may resolve what they see as a 'problem' of heterogeneous grouping by using systems of worksheets through which students proceed at their own rate, according to their own abilities. This may resolve some problems of classroom management, but it may also lead to students becoming isolated, separated from their teachers, and segregated from their peers, as they work in their own little space with their own private sheets.

If anything, the increasing availability of computer-assisted learning can exacerbate these trends towards individualization; isolating students in front of individual monitors as they progress through the self-paced learning of basic skills exercises (Goodson and Mangan, 1994; Stoll, 1995). Individualization is, of course, not a necessary consequence of computer-based instruction. Kutnick and Marshall's (1993) study of experimental and control groups engaged in computer-based learning shows that students do not collaborate spontaneously or effectively in group-sizes greater than two. They need to be taught the skills of cooperation separately if group collaboration of any sort, on computers or off them, is to be effective.

In these ways, secondary schools may suffer from a *culture of individualism*. Hargreaves (1982) describes how secondary schools are deeply imbued with such a culture of individualism. They are places where teachers own the classrooms and students move around the school like frantic passengers in an overcrowded airport. He calls this phenomenon the loss of corporate territory. The lack of a sense of home or collective responsibility leads to a weak sense of institutional pride (also Rutter *et al*, 1979). Hargreaves (1982) describes secondary schooling as a 'curiously fragmented experience' for students; of school bells sounding every forty minutes or so to signal a changing of the guard. Isolation is still the norm for secondary school students' experience (Firestone and Rosenblum, 1987). And the world in which they are isolated can be a large, complex and intimidating one. This is particularly disturbing for young adolescent students whose needs for care, security and group attachment, we have seen, are exceptionally strong at this stage of their development.

Self-image is important in the personal development of the adolescent. Adolescence is a time for establishing and testing perceptions of self as worthwhile individuals (Carter, 1984; Seltzer, 1982). Interaction of teachers and peers with the adolescent individual are essential elements in the formation of self-perception. Yet, Karp (1988) observed that student dropouts in Ontario, Canada generally suffered a lack of self-esteem and were frustrated in a school system they felt cared little about them. More caring teachers and interesting courses were designated as two key ingredients that would have kept them in school (also Wehlege and Rutter, 1986; Fine, 1986).

The culture of individualism is a source of concern for students' experience of school, their satisfaction with it and their willingness to stay on. It is also a concern in the longer run, in terms of the kinds of adults these isolated, individualistic students will become. Will they make up a future 'me generation' — individualistic, materialistic, hedonistic and self-seeking? A major study by the University of California reported that first-year university students are more materialistic and less altruistic than they used to be (Association of Universities and Colleges of Canada, 1982). While the literature suggests that the American high school graduation certificate is no longer perceived as a guarantee of material success, the full- and part-time job is seen as a way of realizing materialistic goals. Etzioni (1982) claims that materialistic pursuit is related to the 'ego-centred mentality' that is 'rooted in American individualism'. The current culture of secondary schooling may in many respects reinforce the individualism of the wider culture, unintentionally instilling its students with the very values which will lure them early to the workplace, rather than ones that will secure their attachment to the school and the community of learning that it represents.

The 'me generation' applies to teachers, students, and parents alike. The quest for self-fulfillment has, in many respects, been subsumed in a sea of individualism and isolation. Teachers become isolated from their students and the public through the guise of professional expertise and specialization (Hargreaves and Goodson, 1996). Many secondary school students experience inequality in a meritocratically inclined system that is seen to favor academically bright students. They experience this alone in the culture of individualism, or within the refuge of a student counterculture. What they experience little of is care, concern or community (Sergiovanni, 1994). With their dignity damaged and their attachment severed, it is little wonder that such students opt for the more immediate attractions of the labor force.

Secondary school culture has thus become as much of an enigma as adolescent society itself. It is complex, unpredictable and skewed toward a very particular set of academic values. It is not as if secondary teachers do not really care for their students, but the existing structures and sacred cultures of secondary schooling, that are deeply embedded in a traditional academic orientation, make it difficult for them to develop or show that caring. Most secondary teachers see too many students, too infrequently and too briefly (Johnson, 1990; Sizer, 1992). This is a system developed less for care of the student than coverage of the subject.

Ultimately, solutions to these fundamental problems, these failures to meet the personal, social and developmental needs of adolescence are to be found in curriculum and teaching; in what secondary schools teach and how they teach it. In addition, there are other measures that secondary schools can adopt

Figure 1

Planning	Presence/Absence of Continuity	
	Continuity	*Discontinuity*
Planned	Planned Continuity	Planned Discontinuity
Unplanned	Unplanned Continuity	Unplanned Discontinuity

to provide more care, more adult support, and a greater sense of belonging and responsibility for their students. We will discuss these measures in later chapters.

Transition And Continuity

It is clear that transferring from elementary to secondary school, and to and from junior high or middle school involves making a transition between different cultures of schooling. In this transfer, there are continuities and discontinuities, some of them planned, some of them unplanned (Derricott, 1985). Four aspects of transition are therefore theoretically possible in the transition between the two cultures (summarized in figure 1).

Unplanned discontinuity is perhaps the main focal point for research and writing on student transition. The differences between elementary and secondary school are described here as being too sharp. The size of the leap made at transfer may be too great, perhaps explaining why short-term student anxiety commonly follows transfer (Nisbet and Entwistle, 1966; Youngman and Lunzer, 1977; Galton and Delamont, 1980). Much of the criticism regarding transfer and transition has been leveled at secondary schools. Their curriculum, culture and orientation have been criticized for being overly directed towards the academic needs of their older, university-bound students, creating a curriculum which is too fragmented and insufficiently interesting and motivating for younger and less able students (Hargreaves, 1982; Goodlad, 1984). The size and bureaucratic complexity of secondary schools have been held responsible for leaving students with no sense of home or place, no attachment to their school as a community (Hargreaves, 1982; Radwanski, 1987). The limited contact and absence of discussion about either curriculum or teaching issues between the teachers in elementary and secondary schools make it unlikely that continuity will occur with any regularity.

Criticism for excessive degrees of unplanned discontinuity has not been placed entirely at the doors of secondary schools, though. Many of the recent moves towards elementary students being taught by a wider range of subject-specialist teachers have exposed some problematic, long-standing assumptions about elementary teaching. We have seen that the care which elementary teachers admirably show for their students sometimes gets a little too tied up with how such teachers also value their ownership and control of 'their own' classes, 'their own' kids. Care of one's own class can sometimes become too precious and perhaps get in the way of students' needs for developing independence. There are clearly issues for elementary schools to address here, too — particularly with regard to teachers working together more closely as colleagues and learning to share some of the care for their students that they might otherwise have wished to keep to themselves.

Unplanned discontinuity may not be the only source of problems for transition. *Unplanned continuity* also poses difficulties. Continuity may not be wanted in some things. Elementary schooling is not always as geared to active-learning or child-centred education as it is imagined to be, and teaching strategies heavily focused on the separate teaching of basic skills and drills may be more prevalent than is often thought (Goodlad, 1984). In this respect, elementary schools or junior high schools, it has been found, can sometimes be almost more like secondary schools than secondary schools themselves (Tye, 1985; Delamont and Galton, 1980), more royal than the king!

One final problem that administrators need to watch is where the process of transition and continuity is *overplanned*. Measor and Woods (1984) argue that the student culture is a powerful reference point for adolescents. Its myths and messages cannot be eradicated, nor perhaps should they be. The messages of the student culture, can, however, be supplemented by improved official information, by more informal contact between the sectors, and by planned involvement of students in various aspects of the transition process as well. These are the subjects of our next chapter, where we review and discuss research on the transition process itself.

4   The Transition Process

Problems of Transition

The last chapter showed that transition to secondary school is an important status passage in a young person's life. It offers the promise of elevated status, more independence, more interesting experiences and opportunities. It also poses problems of lost security, threatening encounters and unknown expectations. The passage of transition is one of mixed messages and contradictory possibilities. Only one thing is certain about the passage of transition to secondary school. It cannot be avoided. Well prepared or not, all students must undertake it.

Research concerned with the transition from elementary or primary school to secondary school varies in terms of the part of the transition period that is studied. Most studies seem to accept the transition period as extending from the last year of elementary or primary school (the pre-transition period), through the first month or weeks of secondary school (the immediate transition period), and extending to the latter part of the first year of secondary school (the post-transition period). Major studies, such as those by Power and Cotterell (1981), Evans (1983), and Measor and Woods (1984), follow students from their last elementary school year to the end of their first secondary school year. Because some school districts have instituted middle or junior high schools, students sometimes undergo multiple transitions during their early adolescence. A few studies are concerned only with the expectations of students in the last year of elementary school or with the perceptions of students on starting high school. Such studies miss important information about changes during the first year of secondary school.

There are at least three areas in which transition to secondary school can result in potential problems:

- student anxiety about transfer and the extent to which that anxiety persists;
- adjustment to secondary school and the short- and long-term implications of transition for achievement, motivation and commitment to school;
- continuity or discontinuity in the curriculum and the implications of gaps or repetition in the curriculum for student learning.

Anxiety

Student anxiety is the most obvious and commonly cited area of concern in the transition to secondary school. There is some evidence that many students, in their final year of elementary school, do indeed feel anxious or apprehensive about some aspects of high school. A questionnaire study by Garton (1987), suggested that this anxiety reflected concern about relations with older students, harder work, bigger buildings, and different sorts of teachers. Mertin, Haebich, and Lokan (1989), found a preponderance of negative features in students' drawings of what they thought high school would be like. These related to vulnerability, aggression involving older students, and negative views of academic work. The major concerns of the transferring grade 8 students in a study in Ontario, Canada, were finding their way around the new school, their ability to handle longer exams, uncertainty about the consequences of incomplete homework or missed classes, anticipated confusion with class rotation, and gaining entry to extracurricular programs. Once in grade 9 in secondary school, the students still expressed concern about their ability to handle longer exams and uncertainty over consequences of incomplete homework and gaining entry to extracurricular programs (though a smaller proportion raised this concern than had in grade 8). The grade 9 students also expressed concern about their ability to understand teachers (which was more prevalent among high and middle track students) (Bulson, 1984). Reviewing the literature on transition, Cheng and Ziegler (1986) report that many students are worried about their progress in school, their readiness and their knowledge of important school policies.

Studies in England confirm that student anxiety commonly focuses on a mixture of concerns about the unfamiliarity and difficulty of work; the size of the school and the chances of getting lost in it; homework and bullying (Neal, 1975; Norfolk Middle-school Headteachers, 1983). In their longitudinal case study of student transition to secondary school, Measor and Woods (1984), found just such anxieties about relationships with older students, the size of the school, the difficulty of the work, the strictness of the discipline, and the impersonal nature of the teachers. Their intensive case-study approach also identified an important dimension of transfer-anxiety that other studies, based on interviews and questionnaires, have tended to miss. They call this dimension 'pupil myths'. Measor and Woods (1984) found that students create stylized and exaggerated stories and warnings, regaled in graphic detail, of the dissection of live rats, unspeakable organisms being preserved in formaldehyde, all new students having their heads flushed down the toilet on their birthday, and so on. Most of these stories, told over and over again in the same way by many different students, are factually false. Yet no amount of rational persuasion or assurance by teachers during induction programs and the like will convince students that they are without foundation (Freund, 1985). Their occurrence and persistence in many different countries around the world testifies to their resilience.

These stories persist, say Measor and Woods, because they serve power-ful symbolic functions which touch on students' emotions and reach down to their unconscious. Effectively, they warn students about the upcoming inver-sions in their status (heads down the toilet), about the areas of the school that are controlled by older students and that are to be avoided or treated with cau-tion (the washrooms), and about the generally 'tougher' environment and expectations that secondary school will present (live dissections). What is revealing about the mythical status of these stories, say Measor and Woods, is that, by the end of that first year in secondary school, the transferring students become tellers of the very tales to which they were once subjected. Clearly, the story is more important than the storyteller and provides a way of conveying, through the student culture, signs and warnings about the change to come, the status passage ahead.

Teachers often treat these myths as part of the problem — as an unneces-sary source of anxiety for students that should be rationalized and explained away. Measor and Woods suggest that the myths might, in fact, be part of the solution in that they provide a way of passing on warnings through the culture that is increasingly important to early-adolescent students — that of their peers.

Secondary school is not always an unremittingly frightening prospect for students. It is a time of mixed and conflicting emotions. In many respects, stu-dents also look forward to secondary school, particularly to taking new sub-jects. On the basis of interviews with students and parents, Trebilco, Atkinson and Atkinson (1977) suggested that the transition to secondary school was viewed with positive anticipation. Similar findings of a lack of anxiety among primary students were reported by Ford (1985). These are important insights and findings. As we will see when we look at how secondary schools might be reorganized to smooth the process of transition, eliminating *all* vestiges of discontinuity between elementary or junior high school and high school may be a mistake; depriving students of their felt entitlement to a clear status pas-sage that is substantial and significant.

In part, the differing results regarding transfer anxiety reflect the fact that transition is a process that evokes generally mixed feelings among students. But there are also sources of variation between schools and between types of students in the degree of anxiety that is generated. At the school level, Garton (1987) found that students' attitudes and expectations reflected the degree of contact with the high school and the existence of an induction program involving visits to the secondary school (also Breen, 1983). Galton and Willcocks (1983) found that, in elementary schools which exaggerated (unintentionally) the tra-ditional nature of the secondary school to which students would be transferring (by using warnings like 'you won't get away with work like this there'), students' anxiety was *higher* before transfer than it was for students from other feeder schools, but *lower* afterwards, once the high school teachers were found to be less threatening than had been imagined. In a sense, these 'teacher myths' about high school may function like the 'pupil myths' described by Measor and Woods. This is not to advocate the use of 'teacher myths' in the transition process; simply to point out that, once we acknowledge their existence, 'pupil myths' do not seem quite so immature by comparison. Both serve to transmit important warnings in a context of high emotion and low information.

The amount of experienced anxiety about transfer also differs between types of student. In Australia, Breen (1983) and Richards (1980) both found that information provided by elementary teachers can usually predict quite well those students who may have trouble moving to secondary school. Anxieties are usually greater for boys than for girls (Garton, 1987; Mertin, Haebich and Lokan, 1989). Boys are more likely than girls to be involved in school problem behavior, both as perpetrator and as victim (Simmons and Blyth, 1987). Anxieties vary between different student 'types', but these patterns of variation are quite complex in character, showing no clear distinction by ability, for instance (Youngman and Lunzer, 1977). As we shall see shortly, the most important between-student differences in attitude to transfer are not ones of short-term anxiety, but of longer-term adjustment.

Anxiety about secondary transfer is indeed short-term. Power and Cotterell (1981) followed students from early in their last elementary school year through to the end of their first secondary school year. There were anxieties at first but these did not persist for long. Overall, students found high school to be better than they expected: more interesting and less difficult, and classrooms were less structured and less involving than what they had experienced at elementary school. Other studies have also suggested that anxieties about the social and organizational aspects of secondary school disappear after a short time (Breen, 1983; Knight, 1984; Mertin *et al*, 1989; Trebilco, Atkinson and Atkinson, 1977).

Galton and Willcocks (1983) studied students undergoing transfer from six schools and administered a questionnaire dealing with children's anxiety twice during the transfer year. In the main, the pattern of anxiety about change was one of high anxiety just before transfer, followed by a decline in November and again the following June (also Nisbet and Entwistle, 1969; Youngman and Lunzer, 1977). However, when students were transferring from schools with a more characteristically 'primary' atmosphere, anxiety levels were the same after one year in secondary school as they had been on entry. The differences here had perhaps been understressed and the importance of the change played down.

Whatever the source of anxieties and however traumatic they can be at the time, they are nevertheless short-lived. It is important to remember that there are also positive aspects to transfer, such as the great expectations that students have of their new school, sometimes heightened by well-orchestrated induction programs. But at the heart of their promise may be the greatest danger of all — of expectations being unfulfilled and disenchantment setting in. These dangers alert us to the longer-term implications of transfer.

Adaptation

Perhaps the most important implication of Galton and Willcocks' (1983) thorough study of student transfer is not what it reveals about short-term student anxiety, but what it shows concerning longer term adjustment to secondary school.

- Although almost all children in the sample made good progress in tests of basic skills in the last two years of elementary school, only 63 per cent made gains on the same tests one year after transfer, and these were smaller than in previous years.
- Almost a third did worse on their tests at the end of the first year at secondary school than they did in their last year of elementary school.
- Students experienced a decline in achievement in their first year of secondary school, lost motivation and enjoyed school less.
- In the whole-class teaching environment of the secondary school, many students became 'easy riders', doing just enough to avoid the teacher's attention.

These disturbing declines in student progress were also reported as evidence to an influential committee reviewing the quality of secondary education for the Inner London Education Authority in England (ILEA, 1984). In Australia, Power and Cotterell (1981) also found a decline in student satisfaction over the first year of secondary school (also Breen, 1983; Evans, 1983; Richards, 1980). This longer term decline in satisfaction with school is generally regarded as a more important and intractable problem than the anxiety associated with the first contact in the new school.

Some groups are more at risk than others in the longer term process of adjustment to secondary school (for example, Karp, 1988; King *et al*, 1988; Radwanski, 1987; Wehlage and Rutter, 1986). They include:

- students from backgrounds of lower socioeconomic status (SES) (Nisbet and Entwistle, 1966; Spelman, 1979; Wehlage and Rutter, 1986). This link raises questions not merely about supposed deficiencies in lower SES students that need to be identified and remediated, but also about norms and orientations of secondary schooling being based on the goals and purposes of the middle-class, that nonetheless form the dominant culture (Fine, 1986);
- students (and these are often also students from lower SES backgrounds) who have to endure long bus journeys to their new schools, especially in remote communities (Gorwood, 1986; Ryan, 1976) — leading to problems of fatigue, reduced time for homework, and restricted opportunity to identify with and commit to the broader dimensions of their school beyond scheduled classes;
- students from a range of ethnoracial groups (LeCompte and Dworkin, 1991). A study of dropouts in Boston middle schools found that practices of attendance, suspension, and retention (requiring students to repeat grades) increased student disengagement from school and encouraged at-risk students to drop out. Black and Hispanic students

had higher rates of absenteeism, retention, and suspension than the general school population (also Wheelock, 1986; Wehlage and Rutter, 1986);

- lower achieving boys. King *et al* (1988) found that the majority of school-leavers in their study in Canada were boys and that they were far behind their peers in accumulating the necessary credits for graduation. A study of grade 9 students found boys more frequently at risk than girls. Many had not been identified as at risk in grade 8 and only 23 per cent received guidance services in grade 9 (Stennett and Isaacs, 1979). In Galton and Willcocks' (1983) study, the rates of achievement of boys and girls were virtually the same before transfer, but one year later, 45 per cent of the boys had fallen below their elementary school score, while only 15 per cent of girls had done so;

- students with academic problems (Karp, 1988; Ainley, 1991); for whom there is often less support in large impersonal secondary schools and for whom being placed in low tracks or streams may create particular difficulties;

- less athletic boys (ILEA 1988), who are prone not only to the obvious threats of bullying, but who are also at risk of being marginalized if the co-curricular life of the school is unduly dominated by athletic priorities;

- girls who are at risk of relinquishing the strength of confidence and self-concept they once had in elementary school (Gilligan, 1989; Robertson, 1992; Simmons and Blyth, 1987). Simmons and Blyth (1987) found that girls during transition scored less favorably than boys in self-image. Girls continued to place a higher value on same-sex popularity than did boys. Girls' greater tendency to place a high value on body image and same-sex popularity also made them more vulnerable in the transition to a new school as the peer group by which they judged themselves was disrupted.

The Inner London Education Authority (1984) report argues for more effort spent identifying students with difficulties prior to transfer (particularly with regard to reading level) and greater concentration of resources on at-risk students prior to transfer. In this regard, it suggests that the final year of primary school may be more crucial than previously recognized (ILEA, 1988). King *et al* (1988) suggest that schools should concentrate on such things as reversing previous patterns of academic failure, building student confidence, improving guidance services, providing alternative programs, establishing firm attendance policies, reducing course failure rates, and creating a positive school atmosphere that encourages students to feel a sense of belonging to the school.

Particular measures of this kind are exceptionally important, but enormous efforts on the part of national, state and school district initiatives have not proven to be very successful at reducing the long-term dropout rate. Perhaps, as Wideen and Pye (1989) suggest, this is because such measures focus too much on the specific characteristics and risk-factors associated with drop-outs, and not enough on the policies, practices, cultures and structures of schooling that are linked to student disaffection in general, and dropping out as one manifestation of such disaffection. This poses questions not just about the needs of particular students but about the overall structure of secondary education today, and how appropriately and effectively it is meeting the needs of its young clients. Some of the issues requiring attention reach right down to fundamental, 'sacred' aspects of secondary schools — to issues of curriculum, for instance.

Curriculum Continuity

Power and Cotterell (1981) found that the biggest declines in student satisfaction in the first year of secondary school concerned 'usefulness-relevance' and 'clarity-difficulty' of school work. Moreover, they reported differences in the way attitudes to particular subjects changed. Where there was continuity in the curriculum there was little change (for example, science); where the curriculum and teaching changed to become more expansive, there was an improvement (for example, English); and where there was inconsistency, there was a deterioration (for example, mathematics, social science). The extent of discontinuity varies between different regions and districts. In general, however, there are disjunctions in many subject areas (Cunningham, 1986; Kefford, 1981; Knight, 1984; Pike, 1983; Powell, 1982).

Many writers argue that the curriculum should be an uninterrupted, ordered sequence in the educational experience of young people (for example, Gorwood, 1986; Derricott and Richards, 1980). Some teachers, however, are opposed to relying too heavily on what students have done before, lest they be handicapped by prematurely applied labels. Students, these teachers feel, should be allowed to begin secondary school with a 'fresh start', a 'clean sheet' (ILEA, 1984).

Stillman and Maychell (1984) point out that this 'clean sheet' philosophy is not a tenable one, at least in curriculum terms. While there might be a case for change in curriculum being sharp rather than smooth, this, they say, should be planned, in full knowledge of what has gone before, rather than left to chance and circumstance. The decision either to start afresh or to go over the groundwork, they note, arises not from careful planning but from lack of communication. Unplanned repetition of content in some cases and substantial gaps in learning in others, are the unfortunate consequences of elementary and secondary schools not joining together to plan curriculum across the transfer divide.

Gorwood (1986) found that the unwillingness of teachers to consult on curriculum continuity is more a product of reticence than apathy. Whatever the reasons, the overall outcome is poor or inconsistent attention to curriculum continuity across the elementary-secondary divide. Where this matter *is* given attention, it tends to be in certain subjects only (mainly the high-status academic areas such as mathematics, English, French, and science) but not, for instance, in art, humanities, music, or health education (Stillman and Maychell, 1984). Moreover, in their observation of meetings set up to establish curriculum continuity in particular subject areas, Stillman and Maychell noted a tendency to rush prematurely into specific decisions about content, rather than discussing the 'deep structure' of the subject and the essential skills, concepts, attitudes and knowledge that elementary and secondary teachers should attend to at different stages. This was supported by an investigation of pilot projects in an Ontario school district (Manning, Freeman and Earl, 1991).

Another way to address the problem of curriculum continuity is not to leave its resolution to the voluntary efforts of teachers or administrators, but to impose a common curriculum or curriculum framework by legislative decree, so that progress from one stage or year to the next is the same for all schools and teachers. Do teachers still need to take some responsibility for curriculum continuity from one stage to the next, or can written frameworks do all this for them? We will address these issues in chapter 6.

Summary

Short-term problems of student anxiety, longer term problems of declining achievement and motivation, and persistent problems of curriculum continuity are key issues in the transition process. Schools and school systems are by no means oblivious to these difficulties and many have made positive efforts to improve and adjust their practice in order to respond more effectively to transition issues. The remainder of the chapter reviews some of the specific measures that have already been taken, and others that have been proposed in this important area of school reform.

Responses to Transition

Reforms designed to improve the experience and consequences of transition appear to fall into five broad areas. These fall short of reorganizing the basic structures of secondary schooling which are the subject of later chapters. The more specific areas of reform are:

- choice of secondary school;
- planning, communication and joint work between secondary school and elementary school teachers;
- record-keeping systems and practices;
- induction programs and procedures;
- institutional reorganization, especially in the form of middle schools.

School Choice

Some of the issues involved in transition from elementary to secondary school are complicated by questions involving the choice of school. In Gorwood's (1986) study of transition in one school district in England, the average number of feeder schools from which secondary schools drew their students was eighteen, with a range of between seven and twenty-eight. In the large Metropolitan area that made up the Inner London Education Authority in England, students in one secondary school could come from as many as thirty or forty primary schools (ILEA, 1984). In Ontario, Canada there is an average of about five feeder elementary schools for every secondary school but, in many urban areas, students may attend any secondary school of their choice. In rural areas, they may have to travel long distances to the only accessible secondary school. That students can transfer between Catholic school and public school systems, as well as into and out of specialized programs like French immersion only adds to the complexities. Growing tendencies towards administrative decentralization, site-based management, greater parental choice of school, and market models of schooling in general pose even further challenges to liaison and continuity.

For those principals and teachers seriously committed to building constructive liaison between elementary schools and the secondary school into which they feed, this complexity can be quite dispiriting. Yet it does not affect all areas alike. Outside metropolitan areas, the choices are much reduced, particularly in small towns and rural communities, and the theoretical possibilities for liaison (notwithstanding problems of distance) are much improved. Even where choices are more dispersed and the number of schools involved in having their students move to any one secondary school is high, possibilities for focused liaison still exist. In practice, most of a secondary school's students come from only a small number of feeder elementary schools, with just a few students coming from elsewhere. Focusing liaison and continuity efforts on what is seen to be a coherent *family* of feeder schools helps meet the needs of most transferring students. Moreover, once active liaison is set in motion, the process becomes self-fulfilling, as the elementary schools build up an image and identity of being a particular secondary school's 'natural' feeders (Freund, 1985).

Choice and continuity do not sit well with each other although some might claim that a written, mandated curriculum imposed on all schools circumvents this problem (we will return to this issue later). More generally, however, we want to suggest that the obstacles presented by the co-existence of choice and continuity are not insurmountable and coherent liaison procedures can be established in a way that will address the needs of *most* of a school's entering students. In smaller towns and rural areas, as schools are geographically clustered into more natural 'pyramids', arranging this liaison should be more straightforward, although distance and time present their own unique difficulties even there (Walsh, 1995).

Planning, Communication and Joint Work

One way to remedy the unplanned repetitions and discontinuities of transfer is to increase the amount of direct teacher contact between the two school levels (ILEA, 1988). These contacts can take four broad forms:

- exchange of information, especially in the form of student records (which we shall discuss separately);
- meetings between teachers at the two levels;
- shared experience and joint work between teachers in the two sectors;
- teacher education and training at pre-service and in-service levels which familiarizes teachers with the issues that concern both elementary *and* secondary educators.

Meetings are one way of achieving understanding and continuity between elementary and secondary systems. From their participant observation of curriculum and liaison meetings, Stillman and Maychell (1984) found that the following factors contributed to greater effectiveness in these meetings:

- involvement of staff from the school district, to lend the meetings authority and direction;
- presence of the participating headteachers (principals). Without visible involvement of the school leaders, teachers often do not feel sufficiently empowered to make important decisions themselves;
- a balance of primary (elementary) and secondary school staff so that no one group dominates the decision-making process;
- involvement of subject teachers and not merely 'guidance' or 'admin-istrative' staff, in discussions that will and should inevitably affect their own teaching;
- a rotating 'circus' of venues to meet, moving from one participat-ing school to another. This is not merely a shrewd act of diplomacy. It also increases familiarity and understanding among the participants of each other's schools;
- privacy, to generate open discussion. Gathering in the corner of a hectic staffroom does not create the best atmosphere;
- time, especially scheduled time in the school day. This is more likely to secure commitment, to make the job manageable, and to signal the seriousness of the task;
- if curriculum matters are on the agenda, devoting some time to dis-cuss general principles of the curriculum areas in question. Giving some (focused) time to discussion of shared goals and objectives before moving to safer practicalities and specifics;
- good meeting management, including appointing a skilled chairperson

(perhaps a school district coordinator would do), having a focused agenda, and circulating some materials, including professional reading, beforehand;

- patience, because meetings between teachers from the two sectors often begin cautiously. As we saw in the last chapter, elementary and secondary teachers often have somewhat stereotyped views of each others' practices and fence cautiously around each other in the early stages (ILEA, 1984). Trust and openness take time to build. The first planning meetings will not always be entirely successful. Early superficiality should be anticipated and will need to be tolerated.

One final and extremely important condition that is usually necessary for successful liaison meetings is that of establishing norms of collegiality and collaboration. Little (1984 and 1989) argues that significant changes and improvements of any kind in education are only likely to happen where what she calls 'norms of collegiality' prevail in a school; where teachers plan together, help and support each other, exchange materials and resources, and work together with children. Unfortunately, most schools are still dominated by norms of privacy, autonomy and non-interference among teachers (Lortie, 1975; Johnson, 1990; A. Hargreaves, 1994). These 'norms of privacy' have profound implications for teachers' working relationships concerning issues of transition. Firstly, they restrict the depth and openness of communication and discussion between secondary teachers and elementary teachers, because secondary schools do not want to appear to be 'dictating' to their elementary counterparts. (Gorwood, 1986; Stillman and Maychell, 1984). Secondly, teachers *within* secondary schools seldom communicate across departments, have little understanding of what their colleagues do, and find it hard to act in any united and consistent way when developing policy that affects their school (Johnson, 1990; Hargreaves and Macmillan, 1995). To a lesser extent, Stillman and Maychell (1984) found that this also applies to their elementary school colleagues. This aspect of liaison and teacher collaboration is exceptionally important but little understood. For teachers to communicate and collaborate effectively *across* schools, they must also communicate and collaborate effectively *within* them. Developing effective transition and liaison meetings is, in this sense, more than merely a matter of agendas and procedures. It reaches right down to the culture of each school that is involved in transition, and the working relationships that make up those cultures (Hargreaves, 1992).

Elementary and secondary teachers working together can have a powerful effect on the transition. It is not just *talk*, but *work* that binds teachers together in the development and pursuit of common understanding and common goals (Measor and Woods, 1984; Wood and Power, 1984). Teachers learn more from experience than persuasion (Fullan, 1982). Activities are more educational than arguments (Lieberman, 1986).

Innovations that help develop shared experience between elementary and secondary teachers include:

- school visits by involved teachers;
- shared induction programs;
- visits of teachers and students to their partner school(s);
- secondary teachers having teaching responsibility in one or more of the feeder elementary schools, either on a concentrated basis shortly before transfer, or as a regular assignment;
- joint appointment of certain teachers between elementary and secondary school who can serve as 'link' teachers;
- joint staff development;
- exchanges of staff between 'related' elementary and secondary schools on a longer term basis of a semester, or a year;
- jointly planned and taught projects and experiences for students (for example, science fairs or residential experiences).

Measures like these help to break down stereotypes and develop openness and trust across the elementary-secondary divide (Gorwood, 1986; ILEA, 1984; Stillman and Maychell, 1984; Freund, 1985; Cheng and Ziegler, 1986).

Teacher training can also help foster the breadth of understanding and experience that would improve liaison and continuity between elementary and secondary education. The fact that most teachers are currently certified to work in only elementary or secondary schools magnifies the division between the two cultures of schooling. Certification to work at both levels might alleviate some of the problems (though it might require a longer teacher-education process). Another route to encouraging teachers to gain experience (and not just additional qualifications) at both levels would be to require such experience as a prerequisite to principalship.

Training teachers in the specific skills and qualities required for working with early adolescents is another possible strategy, one that is advocated particularly strongly by supporters of separately established middle schools. For instance, a survey of members of the National Middle School Association described the most effective middle or junior high school teacher as a person who genuinely likes and respects people, who is committed to working with young people in transition from childhood to adolescence, to listening and talking to them, and to assisting in their development of positive self-concepts (Steer, 1980).

The Task Force on Education of Young Adolescents in the United States recommended that middle-level teachers learn to work as members of a team, that they be given the opportunity to understand pre-adolescent and adolescent development through courses and direct experience in middle-grade schools, and that they receive instruction in the principles of guidance to enable them to serve as advisors. The task force advocated certification in middle-grades teaching in order to give legitimate status to middle-grades teachers. Certification at this level, they said, will also encourage universities to offer specialized courses in middle-grades pedagogy (TFEYA, 1989).

Whichever strategy is adopted — certification and training specifically geared to the middle years, or encouraging broader experience and under-standing among teachers as a whole — a review of the certification process seems appropriate as one way to establish collaboration among teachers for con-tinuity in the experience of students.

In summary, an increase in meetings and joint curriculum planning be-tween elementary and secondary school levels may help create a stronger bridge between the two cultures of schooling. However, elementary and secondary teachers may ultimately need to 'walk a mile in each other's moccasins', to spend time working in and with each other's schools, if they are to gain a sufficiently deep understanding of that culture which is not their own.

Record Keeping

Another way for teachers to liaise about student progress is by exchanging information. Student records are one of the key items of information teachers pass on to one another. Cheng and Ziegler (1986) argue that records of students leaving elementary school should be made available to secondary teachers to show them what incoming students already know. They should be sent, along with samples of students' work, in time for secondary teachers to plan the first semester. Progress reports should in turn be sent by the secondary school to feeder elementary schools. The exchange process, they say, should run in both directions.

The Committee reporting on the quality of secondary education in the Inner London Education Authority (ILEA, 1984) found that use of student records was most successful when:

- records are passed on no later than half-way through the summer term so there is ample time for secondary teachers to consult them and program accordingly;
- records are passed beyond administrative staff to subject teachers themselves, the ones who actually teach the students. This should happen in every instance of transfer;
- some of the more sensitive information is not widely distributed to all and sundry, but sent only to the relevant guidance or administrative staff;
- formal records are augmented by larger profiles and portfolios of chil-dren's work to give a sense of the children's strengths and weaknesses.

The most important issue for student records is *when* and *how* secondary teachers use them. No matter how elaborate and systematic a student record may be, it is of no value whatsoever if no one uses it. Stillman and Maychell (1984) found that many schools do not use their student records. They believe in the 'fresh start' philosophy. If they consult them at all, they do not do so until

Christmas. This, observes the Inner London Education Authority Committee (1984), can have a backwash effect on elementary teachers themselves. If they perceive that their secondary colleagues make little use of the records they send, then they may see little point in filling them out conscientiously. Generally, the Committee found that:

> the schools between which information about pupils is transmitted most successfully are those in which records are passed on and distributed as appropriate, but which also make personal contact about any children for whom recorded details need elaboration. (ILEA, 1984)

Records are not a bureaucratic substitute for communication, but an important part of the wider process of understanding and liaison between elementary and secondary schools. Secondary teachers are more likely to take student records actively into account in their planning when:

- they trust their elementary counterparts. This trust, we have seen, is built not on bureaucratic procedure, but on shared experience and joint work that bridges the cultural divide (Stillman and Maychell, 1984);
- secondary teachers know their own criteria are being actively taken into account by elementary teachers when the records are being written. For this reason, the Inner London Education Authority Committee (1984) recommended that Department Heads of English and Mathematics communicate information about the attainment and progress of the previous year's incoming students *back* to the feeder elementary schools by Spring, so that these factors can actively be taken into account in writing the new round of reports (ILEA, 1984; also Cheng and Ziegler, 1986);
- the reporting system is integrated with the assessment system as a continuous record of student progress, to lend greater weight to the information being passed along (Hargreaves *et al*, 1988; Broadfoot *et al*, 1988). Ways of achieving this will be described in chapter 8;
- information is shared through personal contact and discussion (ILEA, 1984).

Student records need to be well-written. But, ultimately, they are only as good as their readers. Considerable effort is often expended on the design of student records. Countless hours of elementary teachers' time are devoted each year to compiling them. If the records have no readers or are read only in emergencies, all this precious energy is wasted. If as much effort could be channeled into ensuring conscientious use and interpretation of student records as is channeled into their compilation, students would benefit immeasurably from the improved programming that would almost inevitably result.

Induction Programs and Procedures

Transition, as we have seen, is both a short-term and a long term phenomenon. In the short term, the effort to assist students focuses on inter-school transfer and, more specifically, on orienting students to their new environment. As students move from elementary to secondary school they and their parents need to explore their choices, have opportunities to experience secondary school facilities, meet with secondary school staff and consider their strengths and weaknesses in relation to the course options and selections. One of the aims of orientation programs is to decrease students' feelings of apprehension and alienation (Ascher, 1987). When we think of students entering high school, we usually consider how well we prepare them for course choices (Levi and Zeigler, 1991). Transition activities, however, need to prepare students more generally for their first year at a new school, with all the attention to social and personal issues which that implies.

The Inner London Education Authority report recommends involving elementary teachers more in planning pre-transfer visits, preparing students and then accompanying them to the new school. It suggests longer visits, incorporating more active experiences, and visiting the secondary school when it is working normally (ILEA, 1988). Bulson (1984) suggests that entering students be given exposure to high school curricula through visits to secondary schools. To alleviate their concerns, students also need clear information on homework and attendance policies and training in exam writing skills. Some prior experience with class rotation and exam writing may help accustom students to secondary school practices.

Other types of orientation programs have proven helpful. A March-to-November program for parents, students about to transfer, and their elementary teachers, designed by an Indiana middle school, resulted in significant improvements in parent-school relationships (Deller, 1980). Cheng and Ziegler (1986) found that summer head-start programs and summer camps for incoming students received positive evaluations in empirical studies.

Parents should be seen as potentially valuable sources of information about their children's progress and adjustment in transition (ILEA, 1988). Individual parent-counselor conferences before transfer have received positive evaluations, as have peer-group orientation programs and clear, fair, well-communicated policies on student behavior, homework, discipline, and academic standards (Cheng and Ziegler, 1986). The same authors advocate that transition be a concern of the whole school — teachers, administrators, nurses, students, and their peers — not just guidance staff (*ibid*).

Recognizing how important the informal peer-group culture is for transferring students, Measor and Woods (1984) suggest that schools allow and encourage students to become more actively involved in managing the transition process, not just during induction. Secondary students can, for instance, author an 'alternative guide' to help their transferring counterparts orientate themselves to secondary school.

Personal and social development programs, led by home-base teachers during the first days of secondary school, can also actively involve students in the induction process (for example, by sending them with maps, in groups, to find their way around the school) (Hamblin, 1978; Baldwin and Wells, 1981). Such programs can be a useful adjunct to the basic administrative work and general 'chats' that otherwise normally make up the first days of secondary school (Galton and Willcocks, 1983).

Ho (1992) describes a transition program that focuses on inter-school communication (through key personnel), student orientation (through an educational planning unit; individual interviews with a counselor; a grade 9 orientation program that addressed study skills and social and academic issues; and an open house at the secondary school) and parent orientation (through an information night, teacher interviews and an open house at the secondary school).

The most common activities in induction programs are having students visit the secondary school for an orientation day, descriptions of the secondary school program at parent/student orientation nights, and visits to the element-ary school by the secondary school counselors or administrators. These can be offered in a myriad of ways and can be supplemented with such things as student handbooks, taught classes and programs that address transition issues, elementary students attending regular classes in the secondary school, exchanges of letters between students in the elementary and secondary schools, or senior grade buddies for entering students. All of these activities are designed to give young adolescents and their parents the chance to make wise decisions based on accurate and comprehensive information about themselves and the school programs in their community.

Although it is guidance counselors who are often responsible for coor-dinating transition programs, they need not carry the total weight of planning and organizing these activities. Administrators, secretaries, teachers, librarians, parents, community members and students themselves are all potential con-tributors to an increased understanding of and smooth adaptation to the new environment.

Induction days sometimes form a dramatic, even glitzy part of a second-ary school's overall induction program. These special days with their flashes and bangs in the science display, impressive gymnastics performances in physi-cal education and the like, can create a real sense of eagerness and anticipa-tion among the transferring students about the excitement ahead. In a sense, such induction days can be seen as 'warming up' the students for the pass-age, making it attractive and desirable (Freund, 1985). Insofar as they allevi-ate anxiety and create positive attitudes to transfer, induction days have real advantages. But they also carry dangers. The chief danger is disenchantment. In an interview case study of student transfer to a senior high school for older students, Thomas (1984) found that the anticipation and excitement generated about the prospects of more independent learning quickly turned to disillu-sionment when worksheets and dictation were found to prevail; when the school could not deliver on its promises. This points to the importance of there not being too great a discrepancy between what students experience on their 'induction day' and what they are likely to experience in the remainder of their secondary school career.

Institutional Reorganizations

One commonly proposed solution to the problem of meeting the special needs of the Transition Years is to create an institution specially for that critical period of development for young people — one which would protect them, insulate them and smooth the transition between childhood and adolescence. Such an institution, it has been proposed, is the middle school.

Research and other literature on middle schools is hard to evaluate. Much of the favorable literature is associated with organizations that have adopted a position of broad advocacy in relation to middle schools, such as the National Middle School Association in the United States and the Saskatchewan Middle School Association in Canada (George and Oldaker, 1985; National Middle School Association, 1982). Other literature is less consistently favorable in its findings. For example, a study by Tye, K. (1985) of patterns of curriculum and teaching in junior high and middle schools found very little difference between the two institutions.

Several researchers (Hawkins *et al*, 1983; Earl, 1987; Pugh, 1988; Eccles and Lord, 1991) have reviewed the literature on age or grade grouping in an attempt to illuminate its effects on student achievement, parent and student satisfaction, curriculum program costs, student attitudes and self-concept. The results have suggested that teachers' classroom practices, not mechanical arrangements such as grade span, are likely to provide the best explanations of student learning and development (Epstein and Peterson, 1991).

Researchers of the English middle school have found its claim to offer students a smooth transition more rhetoric than reality. Using varying research methodologies with different samples and settings, all these authors found that, in the middle of the middle, at exactly the point where the division between primary (elementary) and secondary education had formerly been, there was not a smooth transition at all, but an abrupt break. The frequency of homogeneous-ability grouping increased sharply as did the incidence of subject-specialist teaching and the number of teachers with whom students had contact (Hargreaves, 1986; Hargreaves and Tickle, 1980; Taylor and Garson, 1982; Meyenn and Tickle, 1980). Hargreaves' study (1986) attributes this break to the fact that middle schools emerged less for reasons of educational idealism than administrative convenience (they were cheap!); that the schools had few teachers who had been specifically trained for the middle years; and that most middle school teachers had been recruited from former elementary or secondary schools and were assigned to the years of the middle school that corresponded most closely with their prior experience. Tye, K. (1985) and others (for example, Alexander *et al*, 1978) similarly contend that middle schools emerged in the United States largely for reasons of administrative convenience as well.

Some evaluations of middle schooling are more positive. A national survey of principals and seventh grade teachers in the United States, found that seventh graders in grade 6/7/8 middle schools, in comparison with the same grade group in grade 7/8/9 junior high schools, were somewhat more exposed to organizational structures and teaching practices that are in theory more appropriate for high-order learning and social development (Braddock *et al*, 1988). After middle schools were implemented in 1980 in St. Louis, student attendance improved, students scored higher on achievement tests, and there were fewer discipline referrals and student suspensions (Wiles *et al*, 1982). However, since the evaluation was done only two years following implementation, the longer term impact of middle schools is unknown.

Simmons and Blyth's (1987) research points to some long-lasting disadvantages of the junior high school transition in a large city, especially for girls, and suggests some advantages of K-8 or middle school systems. They argue that middle schools make the transition easier because it occurs before puberty and involves a move to a building which is usually smaller than a junior high school. Earlier transition has the advantage of coinciding less with other adolescent changes, reducing the cumulation of change, and involves a less dramatic increase in the numbers of peers and older students.

Perhaps a trade-off is involved in the choice between middle schools and junior high schools. McPartland's (1987) comparison of the effects of self-contained classroom teaching and departmentalization found that self-contained classroom teaching benefited student-teacher relations at a cost to high-quality subject teaching, while departmentalization improved the quality of subject teaching at a cost to student-teacher relations.

The research evidence on middle school systems, then, appears to be not sufficiently positive or negative to warrant their wholesale implementation, or indeed their unscrambling, as a response to the problem of transition. Middle schools offer possibilities, not guarantees. Where they fall short of their ideals, this may be due not to inappropriate goals, but to problems in meeting them because of shortages of specially trained staff, external pressure for accountability, real or perceived expectations of the schools that are to receive middle school students, and so on (Hargreaves, 1986). What is important for students at this stage is not the walls within which they work, nor even the name given to the building that those walls make, but the quality of teaching, learning, and personal care that occur within them. In this respect, changes within the early years of secondary school may be just as effective for student progress and adjustment as changes to the whole infrastructure of schooling.

Summary

Transfer is something to be eased. It is also something to be developed and improved. We have discussed practical ways of doing both these things; some of them very specific, others more broad and ambitious. Even in the case of very specific changes, though, we have found that deeper principles beneath them have generally needed to be addressed. Effective meetings between teachers from the two sectors depend not only on the practicalities of paper procedures, but also on the degrees of trust and knowledge that teachers have of one another's practice — not merely across the elementary-secondary divide, but within their own particular milieu as well. This means that an important prerequisite for effective communication across the elementary-secondary divide, may be highly developed forms of collegiality among teachers on each side of it — quite a tall order!

Administrators looking for quick procedural solutions to the problems of transfer and transition are likely to be disappointed. Before very long, their change efforts will need to address the deep principles underlying the specific innovations that they are trying to implement. Administrators who thought they were faced with just a few changes in procedure, have often later found themselves with the challenge of changing their whole school. If substantial and significant improvements to the education of early adolescents are to be secured, the underlying principles, deep structures and ingrained cultures of secondary schooling in particular, will ultimately need to be confronted.

5   Care and Support

The Need for Support

Young adolescents, we have shown, experience several 'rites of passage'. They go through puberty; they move from a family orientation to identification with a peer group; they transfer from one school to another and they begin to make personal and educational decisions that will have a long-lasting impact on their lives. This microcosmic world of self-exploration for young adolescents is embedded in the broader macrocosm of a world culture in transition, with national and world economies, social and ethnic makeup and global political structures changing at a dizzying pace. Young adolescents are a mirror image of their society, reflecting all of its problems (for example, learning difficulties, abuse, poverty, racism). They also experience a genuine concern about what the future will have to offer and about their place in it. As they face what is, for them, their first major 'identity crisis', young people need clear information, direction and extensive yet low-key support so they can develop a positive self concept, adjust to profound personal changes and acquire the coping skills, independence and critical judgment required to take their place in the larger community.

Providing support for young adolescents is a daunting task. Every school has enormous variability in the needs and requirements of its students according to age, maturity, achievement, family circumstances, interests, ambitions, ethnicity, gender and a whole host of other factors. Schools must serve not only their 'at-risk' students but the larger group of 'mainstream' students who need support as well. Indeed, we will see that one of the fallacies of secondary schooling and junior high schooling is that these schools can somehow remain indifferent or inhospitable places for the majority of their students who appear to be getting by, while mounting special, bolted-on programs for 'at-risk' students who don't appear to fit. Supporting and caring well for students who are at risk means having schools organized and structured to support and care well for all students. One of the most compelling reasons for school restructuring is to create schools that are more welcoming, inclusive and caring communities for all their students — mainstream and at-risk alike — and not just ones that cruise along in the slipstream of their high academic achievers (Stoll and Fink, 1996).

In chapter 2 we explained why the personal and social needs of young adolescents are so important. We pointed to the twin horns of the adolescent dilemma — the need for independence and the need for care — and showed how most secondary schools and junior high schools appear to neglect and sometimes even undermine the realization of these needs. Grades 7 and 8 of junior high school, we noted, are where discipline, control and regimentation appear to be greater than at any other point in the system. Many secondary schools, meanwhile, are like overcrowded airports, with the school bell signaling changes of flight every fifty to seventy minutes as students scramble to their lockers to exchange equipment for the next class (Hargreaves, 1982).

High school students, especially those who are not college-bound, tend to see their teachers as having no interest in them (Wehlage and Rutter, 1986). Students who have dropped out are perceived less favorably by their former teachers than by parents, peers or employers (Karp, 1988; Gedge, 1991). When these students are asked if there is one thing that would have kept them in school, they most often point to more caring teachers, to there being one adult who knows them well and cares for them (Karp, 1988). Potential dropouts or not, most students regardless of heritage, gender, or social class want teachers to care about them (Ryan, 1994).

Decades ago, Emile Durkheim (1956) argued that with the decline of the church's responsibility for the care and socialization of children, state education must now hold the prime responsibility for moral education of the young. Morally, he argued, education was important for creating a set of common values and sentiments in the young, beyond the pursuit of private interest that would occur if this task were left entirely to the family. Since Durkheim wrote, families themselves have changed. The customary concept of family consisting of two parents in their first marriage with their own dependent children applies less and less (Elkind, 1993).

Many young adolescents today are living postmodern lives in fractured families, culturally diverse communities and fast-paced worlds of visual imagery. Yet in the school day, these postmodern lives are trapped in modernistic institutions with bureaucratic schedules, compartmentalized knowledge and little care. Etzioni (1993) believes that if the moral infrastructure of our communities is to be restored, schools will have to step in where other institutions have failed. For this to happen, secondary schools will need to be very different places than they are now.

Sergiovanni (1994) argues that schools must play a much more vital and central role in community building, in providing care, developing relationships, creating common purpose and fostering a sense of attachment among people to something greater than themselves. Following Tonnies (1887), he proposes that schools should build community in three senses:

- *community of kinship* as a unity of being as among family, neighbors or colleagues — where a strong 'we' feeling is created in the social group;

- *community of place* as in 'my class', 'my neighborhood' or 'my school' — where there is common membership and a sense of belonging;
- *community of mind* where people bond together through shared goals, values and conceptions of being (p. 6).

How to become communities *of* students, communities *for* students and how to make connections to communities *beyond* the immediate body of students, poses some of the greatest challenges to the structure and organization of secondary schools, and to the ways they can and should provide support for their students.

Reforms that Neglect

The failure of large numbers of secondary schools and junior high schools to support and care for young adolescents effectively is one of the most striking themes in the literature on the sources of dropout and on the nature of secondary school life more generally (Wideen and Pye, 1989). Yet, the personal and social needs of early adolescents are paramount for their well-being now, and for their chances of academic success, social responsibility and personal fulfillment in the future. Much of the rhetoric of educational reform, however, seems at best oblivious and at worst actively hostile to these needs; showing a distinct lack of sympathy for anything that is not tightly disciplined, strictly academic and narrowly focused on the immediate task of learning.

In the United States, for example, the '*Goals 2000: Educate America Act*' identifies eight national goals for education. Two of these refer to teacher education and professional development, and one to parental participation. The other five refer to outcomes of academic learning and productivity. The necessity of a disciplined school environment is also listed, but what is envisaged is an environment free from danger and harm, not one that positively contributes to students' well-being and development. Tough compliance with discipline appears; the supportive interests of care do not.

Some of the numerous education reforms at state level are fortunately not so singular in their academic emphasis, nor so strident in their exclusion of the seemingly soft 'under-belly' of care. For instance, two of the six learning goals and their specific outcomes for the State of Kentucky explicitly emphasize self-sufficiency and responsible group membership. Similarly, the ten essential learning outcomes that students in the Canadian province of Ontario should achieve by the end of grade 9, include the outcomes that students should:

- 'solve problems and make responsible decisions using critical and creative thinking';
- 'apply the skills needed to work and get along with other people' (these include working collaboratively, being sensitive to cultural differences, and being able to resolve conflicts cooperatively);

- 'participate as responsible citizens in the life of the local, national and global communities';
- 'make wise and safe choices for healthy living' (Ontario Ministry of Education and Training, 1995, pp. 27–9).

In England and Wales, by contrast, the National Curriculum has defined a compulsory, detailed nationwide curriculum in subject-based terms that has largely excised care from the curriculum. The 'foundational' subjects of this curriculum, closely linked to learning outcomes at specified 'key stages' of children's education, are overwhelmingly the higher status subjects of the conventional secondary school curriculum. Aesthetic, practical, and personal and social subjects have been squeezed to the margins by this curriculum (Hargreaves, 1989; Goodson, 1994). Laden with content, weighed down with assessment demands and constantly pressed for time by the compulsory foundation subjects, the teachers of the National Curriculum have reported being able to devote little time or energy to other areas (Helsby and McCulloch, 1996).

For a while, in the late 1970s and early 80s, it seemed as if the Cinderella subjects of English secondary schooling had finally been able to go to the ball with their higher status sisters. In an emergent, grassroots movement, responsive to surrounding social changes and the needs and interests of adolescents, more and more British secondary schools began mounting required programs in social and personal education for all students. These were not just programs in personal coping and survival skills for the least able, for those the system has already failed, as had previously been the case. The programs extended to political education and to discussion of peace, race, the environment and a wide range of other social issues for all students.

Much of the impetus towards a National Curriculum and its force-fed diet of academic subjects, came from Right Wing think-tank and pressure groups, who advised the British Conservative government that personal and social 'non-subjects' focusing on 'burning issues' were not proper subject matter for school teaching at all (Scruton *et al*, 1985; Scruton, 1985; Cox and Scruton, 1984). These 'non-subjects', it was argued, embraced issues of social and political complexity, well beyond the maturity and judgement of most under-16s; many teachers were not sufficiently skilled to deal with them in an impartial way; and they would 'squeeze' other 'more important' subjects out of the school curriculum.

Critics responded by arguing that young people need to develop the reasoning skills, affective concern and powers of independent and critical judgement to deal with and think through these issues on which humanity is divided and which already preoccupy many young people anyway (Hargreaves *et al*, 1988; Stradling *et al*, 1984). Whatever the arguments, it is clear that the English and Welsh National Curriculum successfully halted the personal and social education movement in its stride, shuffling it to the periphery of teachers' and schools' priorities.

Best (1994), for example, provides case study evidence that the caring roles of secondary school teachers suffered because of the National Curriculum. Preparation for the National Curriculum distracted teachers from their home-room roles and led subject teachers to give even greater priority to their subjects. The intensity of assessment and examination demands meant that personal and social education and care in general 'goes to the wall' for many teachers. Liaison between elementary and secondary schools was shelved as each sector concentrated on its own National Curriculum requirements. Moreover, the National Curriculum and academic competition between schools in league tables of performance affected teachers' career prospects such that the caring or pastoral side of the teachers' work was no longer viewed as an important criterion for promotion (also Watkins, 1994).

Commitments to care may also be placed at risk by current efforts to redefine professional standards for teachers. These tend to model the classical professions by defining teachers' expertise mainly in terms of specialized knowledge and technical skill (Hargreaves and Goodson, 1996). Such professional standards tend to stress subject mastery, technical know-how (what is termed 'pedagogical content knowledge') of how to teach one's subject, and rational reflection. Care, commitment and emotional engagement are largely absent from emerging definitions of professional standards for teaching in the United States and from the criteria for being categorized as an 'advanced skills teacher' in Australia (Ingvarsson, Chadbourne and Culton, 1994).

The Case for Care

Much school reform seems to say that care doesn't matter. The emotional labor of caring is rarely recognized as central to teachers' professionalism either. Yet, as writers like Noddings (1992) argue, not only is care a vital prerequisite for student learning; it is an essential form of learning itself:

> If the school has one main goal, it should be to promote the growth of students as healthy, competent, moral people . . . Intellectual development is important, but it cannot be the first priority in schools. (p. 10)

Students, she says, care little for what it is they have to learn (a problem of curriculum). They also complain that teachers 'don't care' about them (a problem of support). The issue for schools, her work suggests, is not to dance to the rhythm of the school effectiveness movement, in pursuit of the goal that 'all children can learn', but to ask what it is that children *should* learn. Care, in both the formal curriculum and in the human relationships through which it is studied, is one of the most important things that students should learn, says Noddings.

There are several ways in which schools and educators should widen their horizons beyond the academics, and envision a clear place for care in young people's learning, Noddings argues. Some of these key domains, or centers of care, as she calls them, are:

- *care for the self* — for one's physical being (not just by self indulgent 'working out' but also through physical service to others), for one's spiritual life, work and recreation;
- *care for intimate others* — for partners and lovers as young people prepare for long term intimacy; for friends and neighbors; and not least, for children (the less mature) by having structured opportunities to work with and support younger children in the school setting;
- *care for associates and acquaintances* — for colleagues and communities in reciprocal relationships of help and support: a vital preparation for positive (and productive) workplace behavior and for service to the community;
- *care for non-human animals* — for pets in particular and the wider living world in general;
- *care for plants and the physical environment* — for tending one's own garden, for appreciating the local and global balance of nature, and for sustaining the wider environment;
- *care for the human made world of objects and instruments* — for the craft maintenance of material possessions (rather than throwaway materialism), and for the aesthetic and architectural environment in the country and in the city;
- *care for ideas* — for the passions of the intellect and the creativity of mind: not in the sense of processing blandly presented facts, but in terms of the insight and imagination that knowledge and reflection can bring.

It is not that academics are unimportant and care is everything. Indeed schools in inner cities and schools for the poor which try to provide caring safe-havens for their students but do not stretch them intellectually, do them little service in the long term (Hargreaves, 1995). But in most cases the relationship between care and academics is sadly askew in the other direction. Many young people will not learn the academics if they do not care for what they learn. They will lose attachment to their learning, if they feel isolated, lost and uncared for in their schools. And without learning the skills, responsibilities and rewards of caring for and cooperating with others, all the intellectual advancement in the world will not make them better people or more moral citizens (as many highly intelligent totalitarian leaders have demonstrated). Care matters. We cannot afford to neglect it.

Traditions of Care and Support

Despite their shortcomings in supporting students, secondary schools and junior high schools are not entirely bereft of care, or devoid of structures for providing it. Indeed, in the United States and the United Kingdom respectively, two very specific traditions of support have become firmly institutionalized within schools.

In the United States, the care functions of high school education have traditionally been allocated to specialized guidance and counseling personnel. These personnel advise students on course selections and career decision-making. They counsel individual students on personal problems that may be interfering with their learning, and deal with students who have behavioral problems too serious to be coped with in the classroom. Where students' problems are especially severe in terms of extreme poverty, abuse in the home, family dysfunctions, pregnancy, alcohol, drugs or crime, guidance and counseling personnel liaise with social service and juvenile justice agencies outside the school and with other teachers responsible for teaching the young people concerned within it. Where liaison arrangements have been established with 'feeder' schools (elementary and junior high), much of the responsibility for this often falls to guidance and counseling staff. Such staff often work with individual students, sometimes with small groups referred to them for special programs of work, and with classes to whom they teach course modules on careers etc. Guidance and counseling are regarded as specialized work requiring professional qualifications beyond those necessary for regular classroom teaching.

Guidance and counseling are the domains where high schools demonstrably care for their students in the United States. They provide students with trained staff qualified to deal with non-academic problems and they ensure that by allocating resources and attention to this area, the school and its teachers cannot neglect their duties of care and support. However, over time, it has become clear that a separate and specialized guidance and counseling system has brought as many problems as benefits.

- The professionalization of guidance and counseling, often with its own clinical language, sometimes tends to overemphasize 'deeper' problems of a psychodynamic nature, behind the seemingly 'simpler' ones that students present (Cicourel and Kitsuse, 1963).
- The professionalization of guidance counseling tends to disempower ordinary teachers from assuming greater responsibility for dealing with students' problems.
- The institutionalization of guidance and counseling as a separate and specialized function can encourage classroom teachers to feel that care, support and relationships are not their responsibility, because they are being accommodated elsewhere.
- The large number of individual contacts that guidance and counseling staff have with students can overload the staff with casework, and

reduce the general quality of care they give to most students because they concentrate on more intensive 'problem' cases among a few. All young adolescents benefit from opportunities to discuss personal issues with a receptive and supportive adult. In reality, there is usually a relatively small number of 'at risk' students whose circumstances demand this service most frequently. Guidance counselors must wrestle continually with the dilemma of meeting the ongoing needs of the many with the urgent, crisis-driven demands of the few (abuse, bereavement, bullying, etc.).

- Guidance and counseling staff can consume scarce time with individuals that might well often be better spent on in-class support roles with larger groups. They can spend too much time trying to 'put out fires' instead of helping create a climate that prevents fires from igniting in the first place.

'Good guidance' is a collaborative, total school activity that provides systemic support for students (Levi and Zeigler, 1991; New York State School Boards Association, 1987). Such a total school support program often includes secretaries and custodians (in Britain, aptly called caretakers), as well as teachers who are actively engaged with the student body in creating a 'sense of home' in the school. This does not eliminate the role of the guidance counselor. Rather the guidance program can be an integral part of the school, receiving strong administrative support, that is a shared responsibility of guidance counselors, administrators, regular and special education teachers, students and parents, all working together (Levi and Zeigler, 1991; Cheng and Zeigler, 1986). Early adolescents need help to remedy their weaknesses and develop their strengths without being stigmatized, labeled or separated from their peers through isolated, individual programs of treatment (MacIver and Epstein, 1991). The role of guidance and counseling staff is beginning to be transformed in many secondary and junior high schools but needs to be pushed considerably further.

Current directions in guidance point towards counselors spending less time with a small number of students with personal problems and shifting their emphasis from reactive to proactive programming (Bailey *et al*, 1989). In this kind of model, all teachers are counselors. Teachers who are specifically trained as counselors may help many more students by working in a preventive mode with small groups, who have similar problems around specific issues (for example, drug abuse, family stress, pregnancy) (Bailey *et al*, 1989; Aubrey, 1985; Capuzzi, 1988; Cole, 1988; Tennyson *et al*, 1989). A total school support program, with all teachers (and often the whole staff, including secretaries and custodians) actively engaged with the student body goes a long way towards creating a sense of home and community that allows young people to come to grips with the troubles and challenges that face them in their lives.

The emerging yet still needed changes of direction in guidance and counseling can be summarized as follows:

from working with individual students	⟶	*to* working with small groups and whole classes of students
from reacting to problems	⟶	*to* prevention of problems
from working outside classrooms	⟶	*to* working within classrooms
from providing separate specialist help to students aside from their teachers	⟶	*to* providing specialist advice to classroom teachers, who can then work better with the students
from individual casework	⟶	*to* group coursework

Reconceptualizing the guidance counselor's role is not only important for improving the quality of guidance in particular. It is also essential if secondary schools as organizations and the deployment of staff within them are to be restructured in ways that provide more meaningful and effective education for early adolescents. Such restructuring presupposes breaking down the strict separation between classroom teachers and guidance counselors so that staff resources can be deployed more flexibly to meet students' needs.

In the United States, the guidance system was invented to support the academic system. In the United Kingdom, this function fell to a system called *pastoral care*. Until the 1960s and 1970s, secondary schools in the United Kingdom were divided into grammar schools for high ability students and secondary modern schools for the rest. These schools were often relatively small, specializing in academic and vocational options respectively. With the advent of all-ability comprehensive schools in many areas the end of grammar and secondary modern schools saw the end of many smaller secondary schools too. Unless the secondary sector was divided up in some way by using middle schools or junior high schools, comprehensive schools became large, difficult-to-administer and impersonal organizations. Within these burgeoning bureaucracies, it was feared, students' individual welfare needs would be overlooked and the lines of staff responsibility for welfare and discipline would become unclear and break down (Reynolds and Sullivan, 1987).

At the same time, secondary school reorganization posed major problems for the careers and status of secondary modern school teachers. Likely to be outstripped by their better qualified grammar school counterparts in their competition for what, in the United Kingdom, are highly desired and lucrative Head of Department subject posts, these teachers required new posts of responsibility to match the status and salaries they had accumulated through their secondary modern experience (Burgess, 1987; Hargreaves, 1980).

These problems of discipline and student welfare in large schools, and of secondary modern teachers' career interests, ironically led comprehensive schools to adopt and modify a system that first gained popularity in the elite private sector: the *house system* of pastoral care (Lang, 1983). The students of such schools were divided into several 'houses', each with a name, comprising members from every age-group in the school, and led by a senior teacher who was 'Head of House'. The house system was a vertical grouping which coordinated administration, handled discipline, sorted out student problems and provided a base for in-school sports competition. Increasingly, such vertical house systems were replaced by lateral year systems, led by a Head of Year and often involving time at the beginning of one or more days per week when students would meet with their age-peers in their home-room, with their home-room teacher. These home-rooms in any one year, made up the year group as a whole. Whether based on house systems or year systems, pastoral care became a widespread feature of secondary school organization in Britain.

The 'conventional wisdom' of pastoral care in comprehensive schools was that it was predominantly concerned with the care, welfare and personal needs of students (for example, Marland, 1974; Blackburn, 1975) — either because such welfare is important in itself or because it can help the smooth running of the academic system. In practice, studies of pastoral care revealed preoccupations with administration, paperwork, student referral procedures, discipline and punishment (Burgess, 1983). The authors of one study of teachers' perceptions of pastoral care concluded:

> There is little evidence . . . that the institutionalization of pastoral care roles necessarily leads directly to a greater concern for pupil welfare. Indeed, teachers seem more likely to perceive such roles in terms of their resolution of problems of teachers' control and administration. (Best, Ribbins, Jarvis and Oddy, 1980, p. 268)

The need for much of that control, they argue, has arisen from the expectation that the main purpose of the pastoral system is to provide 'back-up' for the academic system in school (pp. 257–8). Yet, it is often this academic system and its inadequacies that is the problem for students. The curriculum and tasks that students have been set create many of the problems with which the pastoral system has to cope. The result, is what Williams (1980) calls *pastoralization* where

> the (pastoral care) tutor uses the relationship of mutual trust . . . to deflect legitimate grievance away from the inadequate types of learning experience offered within the school. (pp. 172–3)

The problems of a separate pastoral system therefore, are that:

- help and support get crowded out by administration and paperwork;
- care is sacrificed to control in a system set up to administer punishment and discipline;
- the existence of a bureaucratic system of disciplinary referrals encourages classroom teachers to take less responsibility for their own discipline problems at the point where they occur (Reynolds and Sullivan, 1987; Galloway, 1985);
- the pastoral system may support and protect the academic system and secure students' compliance with it, when the academic system itself may be at fault;

- the pastoral system may solve career problems for 'non-academic' teachers, more than welfare problems for students.

The guidance counselor and the pastoral care tutor each personify the problems of taking the care function out of the classroom, and building a separate system around it. Young people's minds are not strictly divided into affective and cognitive components, nor should the organization of schools be. Good learning takes place within a context of ordered, constructive and caring relationships. Where these classroom relationships are wanting, no separate system of care and support, however elaborate, will substitute for them. Care belongs primarily in the classroom, and the purpose of school organization should not be to create surrogate caring relationships elsewhere, but to develop systems that make constructive classroom relationships possible for students and teachers alike.

Guidance counseling remains solidly institutionalized in North American high schools — although efforts have begun in places to restructure secondary education so that teachers of younger adolescents can work in smaller mini-schools or sub-schools where care is not a specialized function, but integrated into the everyday life of the classroom as part of every teacher's responsibility. In Britain, separate specialized structures of pastoral care have been discredited for some years. A number of promising alternatives have emerged in their place. These include courses of personal, social and moral education taught by trained specialists (although these tend to be directed towards older adolescents) (David, 1983); extended home-room systems that sometimes include a taught program of personal and social skills, and which involve most teachers in the school taking some responsibility for student welfare (Baldwin and Wells, 1981); and systems of self-assessment and reporting that encourage students and teachers to engage in dialogue together about learning and progress (Munby, 1989; Hargreaves *et al*, 1988). The scope of these developments has, however, been limited by the subsequent introduction of National Curriculum testing which neither allocates statutory time for children's personal and social education, nor assesses that education as a valued part of their learning.

There is a place for specialized counseling of young adolescents, but its influence needs to be more modest. At the same time, other systems of support that involve more teachers taking responsibility for the care of their students need to be strengthened. These are of two broad types: specific measures for offering advice and creating a 'sense of home' for students, and more fundamental reorganizations of student grouping, curriculum delivery and other areas that make the experience of schooling more caring and personal in general.

Specific Solutions

One way to make students feel part of their school as a community is to create a clear 'sense of home'; a time and place where people care about students' personal and social development. Mentor systems are one way to achieve this (McPartland *et al*, 1987).

Mentors

Many sources in the literature recommend that teachers be matched with individual students to provide advice on academic and personal needs. The aim is to help students by providing each of them with the support of a caring adult who knows them well (TFEYA, 1989; Bloomer, 1986; Lake, 1988a).

When we studied pilot project schools making innovations in grades 7, 8 and 9, one of our cases involved the establishment of a mentor system. Here students said it was possible to talk about things with their mentor that might be more difficult to discuss with their parents; they enjoyed the 'change of pace' in the school day; and they liked the idea of mentoring as a service to which they could turn, if needed. In another case, the mentoring arrangement also included extended opportunities for learning (remediation and enrichment) and practice in time management as students negotiated and planned their personal and learning needs with their mentors (Hale, 1990). Mentor relationships seemed to work best when the mentor already had another connection with the student through a course or an extracurricular activity. Students often reported that mentor relationships felt artificial and they therefore made little use of them. Mentoring was also time consuming, especially in schools already undertaking several other innovations (Hargreaves *et al*, 1993). Artificiality may point to the need for more sensitive matching. Time constraints might suggest the need for less frequent use. But these problems are in many ways to be expected if mentor relationships are bolted-on to existing school structures (where students have fragmented and uneven contact with teachers), and to teachers' present commitments. The problems suggest a need to change the school structure; not to add something to it.

Teacher-Advisors

The Task Force on Education of Young Adolescents (1989) describes how a teacher-advisor program might work. The Task Force advocates having teacher-advisors as part of a team-teaching structure (i.e., different from the existing secondary school norm). Advisors would receive in-service training in adolescent development and principles of guidance. Teacher-advisors would not do formal counseling (which would remain the domain of mental health professionals) but would act as mentors and advocates for students. Guidance counselors would assist advisors in their roles. Teacher-advisors would be the primary contact between the school and parents. In that role, they would collate grades and comments from other teaching-team members, enter them on students' report cards and discuss them with parents. When behavior problems arose, the principal would consult the advisor assigned to the student in question before taking any action (TFEYA, 1989). Lounsbury and Clark (1991) suggest that providing students with opportunities to discuss topics of importance to them in a group advisory period helps retain students in school. This extends sound principles of guidance into wider classroom relationships. The success of such measures presumes changed structures of teaching and learning.

The Crittenden Middle School in Armonk, New York, for example, has instituted a program to bring a small group of students together with a teacher-advisor to work through a scripted discussion guide on issues relevant to the students' experience. In addition, O'Rourke (1990) describes a variety of methods and resources (for example, drama, role-playing, journal writing) for counselors and teachers to use collaboratively with young adolescents to help them express themselves and explore troublesome issues.

Home-rooms

Strengthening the role of the home-room teacher can do much to provide an atmosphere of care and a sense of home for students in secondary school (McPartland *et al*, 1987; Kefford, 1981). The role of the home-room teacher is often not designed to foster students' personal and social development. Administration, form filling, announcements and messages, along with loosely structured general 'chats' have often consumed much of home-room time (Blackburn, 1975). The personal and social development needs of young adolescents have not traditionally been a home-room teacher's priority. Strengthening the home-room teacher's role is not just a matter of providing more time. Unless objectives of what the role should achieve are developed, finding something to fill up the time in home-room period can become a problem (Baldwin and Wells, 1981; Button, 1981; Hargreaves *et al*, 1988).

A home-room 'curriculum' focused on the personal and social development needs of the young adolescent in a supportive-group context, is one way to use homeroom time constructively. In the United States, Simmons and Blyth (1987) argue that one way to build self-esteem is to help students achieve peer-regard and to give them social support. In Britain, a whole range of sophisticated 'tutorial' programs for home-room use have been commercially developed. Such programs dedicate a considerable amount of active, cooperative group work in home-room time to the development of generic skills and attitudes like listening skills, leadership, and trust; through to specific school-based matters like bullying or the management of homework; and to other social issues, such as gender and race stereotyping (Button, 1981; Hamblin, 1978; Baldwin and Wells, 1981). Critical evaluations of these programs have been broadly positive (Bolam and Medlock, 1985). However, subject teachers can feel anxious and threatened when required to teach unfamiliar subject matter (for example, about bullying), in ways that might diverge from their usual classroom style. For these reasons, it is unwise to institute such home-room programs without substantial commitments to professional development for the teachers concerned (*ibid*).

Extracurricular Activities

Extracurricular activities provide opportunities for the school and for teachers to demonstrate caring. The often informal atmosphere that characterizes these settings provides both students and teachers with opportunities to interact without constant reference to the usual hierarchy that generally sets the stage for student-teacher relationships. Also the fact that both teacher and student may be engaged in tasks that share a common purpose (for example, producing a school newspaper) tend to bring them together in ways that classroom activities often do not.

Students may have particular ideas about just how they expect caring to manifest itself in the school. In one multiethnic school setting, for example, students believed that teachers could display caring in two ways (Ryan, 1994). The first was the effort they put into their teaching. Students felt that those teachers who put time and effort into their lessons did so, in part, because they cared about their students. They also believed that teachers who took the time to get to know them personally really cared about them. For teachers the best time to establish these caring relationships was before and after the bell rang. In the hallways, at lunch time in the cafeteria, in the few moments in the classroom before the formal lesson begins and after it ends, teachers have opportunities to interact with students more informally. These moments, however, are fleeting and in many of these instances teachers often feel under obligations to supervise students and ensure that they conform to certain standards of behavior. The best opportunities to get to know students, teachers maintain, occur around extracurricular activities. Although teachers may still have some supervisory duties, the fact that they and their students are often mutually engaged in common pursuits pushes this usually differential relationship to the background. Both teacher and student also have much more time to interact with and get to know one another in these situations.

Community Connections

The Task Force on Education of Young Adolescents advocates adolescent involvement in community service inside and outside school as another way of building self-esteem (TFEYA, 1989). Such service is a way of helping adolescents move toward independence, broadening their learning experience outside of school. The community in general is seen by many writers not merely as a resource for learning, but also as a source of attachment, connectedness and motivation in the lives of students (Marx and Grieve, 1988). Lawton *et al* (1988) stress the importance of strong links between the community and the school in ensuring effective schools. Hargreaves (1982) argues that the emergence of the community school may be the vehicle to seal the gap between home and school, especially where the community school classroom contains people of various ages and interests, helping to break down the careful age-grading currently existing in most secondary schools.

Cheng and Ziegler (1986) encourage administrators to make themselves accessible to students and their parents and to create opportunities for informal socializing among staff, students and parents. Licata (1987) suggests three very specific ways of doing this — lunch with the principal for each student, a week-long camp to build school social ties, and a physical education Olympics.

Epstein (1988) introduces the concept of 'schools in the center', through which schools can promote interaction with the community by:

- encouraging mutual-help relationships between students and senior citizens;
- providing information to parents on adolescent development, school programs and goals, how to help children succeed in school, parenting approaches, community resources for families, and by inviting parents to bring their skills to the school;
- forming partnerships with local employers to allow students to explore career options.

This raises the more general question of how to forge relationships between schools, their parents and their communities as a whole, in order to create a supportive context for relationships between students and their communities. Relationships with the community are exceptionally important, but they are often dealt with superficially. Hargreaves (forthcoming), describes four models of school-community relationships.

- *Market-based relationships of parental choice* treat parents as clients and consumers who can send their children to the school of their choice (Kenway *et al*, 1993). Schools and parents are connected by individual contractual relationships. These tend to fracture more collective relationships between schools and communities (Blackmore, forthcoming; Wells, 1993). Moreover, parents who do influence the school's direction tend to be small fractions but highly organized factions of the wider community — white, articulate, well-organized and middle class and not at all representative of wider interests and constituencies (Delhi, 1995; Wells, 1993).
- *Managerial relationships* presume that schools are rational organizations within a decentralized system. 'Goals and priorities are set centrally for local interpretation and implementation. Decision-making is viewed as a logical, problem-solving process' (Logan, Sacks and Dempster, 1994, p. 10). In its establishment of parent councils, school councils and school development planning, the managerial approach

is better at creating committees than building communities. It grants untoward influence to atypical parents, diverts teachers' and principals' energies to procedural accountability more than to personal responsiveness, and has as yet shown few or no demonstrable benefits for teaching and learning practices or student outcomes (Taylor and Teddlie, 1992; Weis, 1993). In these respects, parent councils and similar managerial measures are at best just 'the tip of a more complex and powerful iceberg' of school-community relations (Fullan, 1996).

- *Personal relationships* between teachers and parents, by contrast, concentrate on the most important interest that parents have in school; the achievement and wellbeing of their own children. Few parents wait anxiously for the new school development plan to arrive in the mail. But they are extremely keen to see reports about their own individual children. What matters here is the quality of information passed between school and home, and how meetings are conducted with parents at times like parents' nights. Hargreaves (forthcoming) describes a successful example of grade 8 children running parents' night themselves, showing portfolios of work and conducting interviews with parents in their own language, while the teachers circulate around the parent-child meetings to advise, extend, support and comment where necessary.

- *Cultural relationships* embrace principles of openness and collaboration with groups of parents and others in the community. Schools gain more support from communities when they involve them in the uncertainties of change, rather than informing the community later once professionals have decided for themselves (Ainley, 1993). Multiple, informal relationships with community members work better than occasional bureaucratic meetings. Advocating a turn towards more feminist principles of working with parents and the community, Henry (1994) suggests that 'authentic causal contact or informal relations between parents and educators may be more important than formalized events' (p. 18).

Drawing these threads together, Epstein (1995) proposes that we attend to and bring together several different kinds of school-community programs and patterns of involvement that promote greater:

- parenting skills, leading to improvements in the home environment;
- two-way communication between home and school;
- organized parent support through use of volunteers and parents as teacher aides;
- learning at home through specific interventions of home tutoring;
- decision-making involving parents, including developing parent leaders;
- coordination with community services, including ways of integrating school and community services on the school site.

Peer Support

It is no surprise that peer counseling or peer support programs are becoming an integral part of schools' efforts to care for young adolescents. At this stage in their development, adolescents place a high value on peer relationships and go to their peers for help (Palomares and Ball, 1980; Cheng and Ziegler, 1986; Manning, 1992). In an evaluation of a peer-counseling program, Gutmann (1985) found that peer counselors were successful in increasing favorable attitudes to school work and in helping students deal with problems such as loneliness, sexuality, dating, family, friendships and work.

Peers can serve as major players or facilitators in transition programs for students entering the school. They can act as a welcoming or reception committee; they can lead assemblies; they can be trained as assistants to the counselors and conduct initial interviews with incoming students; they can teach study skills; they can serve as peer tutors; and they can provide a personal link to the inside life of the school. Many schools that receive immigrant students assign a 'buddy' to help the student become familiar with the school and also the language. In the process, the peer counselors also learn about themselves and develop skills that extend beyond the regular program. The payoff for the school and both groups of students can be significant (Bowan, 1986).

Career Education

Young adolescents in our schools today are likely to have an average of five different careers in their lifetime. Most of the jobs that they will enter do not even exist yet. There are no longer jobs where the unskilled or uneducated can lead satisfying working lives. The social and economic health and wealth of nations is dependent on the future productivity of these young people. Little wonder that career education and guidance are seen as critical elements in the education of early adolescents. Young adolescents need to clarify their own sense of self and translate their understanding into occupational terms; they need to acquire an understanding of occupations that allows for this translation and they need to try on various vocational self-concepts to explore how well they fit. As early adolescents mature, they acquire vocational maturity as well — a more differentiated view of the world of work and a capacity to understand and work with various career-related processes and concepts. Relevant and accessible information is essential if they are to make wise educational decisions that will avoid premature closure on future career options.

Self-assessment and career exploration are part of an iterative process that requires careful attention to career choices and the skills associated with them as an integral part of the curriculum in the middle years. The movement of career education curriculum is away from add-on or stand-alone programs toward integrating subject matter with career information, as well as developing social and organizational skills for job readiness (Levi and Ziegler, 1991). This shift has a number of implications in terms of:

- experiential education programs — moving to earlier, broader based opportunities for examining many options;
- attention to young women — encouraging girls to think broadly and non-stereotypically;
- attention to diverse cultural backgrounds — rural, poor, multicultural, native or indigenous peoples;
- guidance counselors and teachers being trained in job trends within a changing labor market — all teachers being current experts in careers related to their field;
- the infusion of career information into every subject of the curriculum;
- recognition that the majority of students do not attend university.

The literature provides a number of examples of innovative career education curricula which engage students in active involvement with the world outside school. Cooperative-education programs, job shadowing and workplace visits are becoming an important part of schooling. Yet they are too often confined to vocational students on the assumption that 'academic' students need to concentrate on their regular courses to qualify for university. School-work connections are important for all young adolescents as a vehicle for developing appropriate skills and attitudes and becoming familiar with career alternatives (Greenberg and Hunter, 1982; Gould, 1981).

Academic Support

The diversity that is evident among young adolescents inevitably means that some students will learn more slowly than others. Schools and teachers must organize and provide instructional support to ensure the success of all students, including those who are at risk of academic failure and those who need periodic assistance. Academic support can be provided through special education support, pull-out programs, in-class tutoring, extra periods of instruction, summer school, community placements, community tutors and many other approaches. Virtually every discussion of academic support, however, focuses on how to improve and extend instruction or opportunities for students to practise their skills. The Task Force on the Education of Young Adolescents (1989) recommended that all middle schools address the needs of these students proactively through specialized instruction, extra coaching and additional time to learn.

The kinds of mentor/advisor programs described earlier often perform an academic function as well as a personal one. Teachers who act in this capacity or who serve as home-room teachers can provide assistance with academic problems and coach their students. One interesting program designated a period each day for four days a week for mentor-monitoring. In this program, students timetabled their own activity for this period and had it approved by their mentor teacher. Students who were progressing well could opt to attend elective sessions being offered by teachers in the school or work on independent projects, while those who were having difficulty scheduled additional help from the appropriate teachers (Hale, 1990). This scheduled time for individualized activity not only provided routine opportunities for academic support but also reinforced student self-evaluation and encouraged personal time management.

Once again, though, specific pull-out assistance works best when the classroom and curriculum are already organized to provide high levels of in-class support as well. This is true for special education support in general where *restorative* models designed to pull children out of class, fix them up and put them back, have increasingly been replaced by *integrative* models that provide support in the context of the learning the child is already doing in his/her class (Wilson, 1983). Such *integrative* models, whether they be of counseling or special education support, pose challenges for changing our existing structures of schooling and the way we group students by age, divide the curriculum by subjects, and assign teachers individually to classes.

School Restructuring

The issue of school reorganization or school restructuring and how to achieve it is so important, that we devote all of our final chapter to it. But some of the implications of school restructuring for providing better student support need to be anticipated here. Two restructuring options for educating early adolescents are recommended strongly in the literature.

- reducing school size to create a more intimate, supportive environment;
- creating mini-communities within larger schools, for the same reason.

Reducing School Size

A study of school transfer in New York City found that some of the problems of transfer stemmed from the immense size of the school system and its rigid, bureaucratic structure (Cohen and Shapiro, 1979). Similarly, Simmons and Blyth (1987) found that large school size has a direct, small, negative impact on self-esteem of both male and female junior high school students in grade 7. Movement from a small intimate school to a less intimate, larger, and more heterogeneous environment creates difficulty for children (Walsh, 1995). McPartland *et al* (1987) reported that small schools with staff organized by self-contained classes or by functioning interdisciplinary teams had more desirable teacher-student relationships than did large, departmentalized schools (supported by Davis, 1988; Pinkey, 1981; Johnson, 1990). Fowler's (1992) review of the literature on school size found that large secondary schools with a graduating class above 750 appear to have deleterious effects on student attitudes, achievement and voluntary participation. However, it should be noted that these personal and social gains do come at some cost to curricular choice — the range of programs being much more restricted in small high schools (Barker, 1985).

Creating Mini-Schools

Even where they can often be shown to be desirable, small schools are often prohibitively expensive to construct and may pose problems of establishing sufficient diversity in the program. The same supportive effects that a small school offers can be created by other means. To reduce the discontinuity between the self-contained elementary school and the departmentalized mode of high school, many sources in the literature recommend the creation of 'schools within schools' (Lake, 1988a). In addition to creating a less impersonal climate, this arrangement allows peer friendship groups to be maintained, reducing another aspect of discontinuity in school transfer (ILEA, 1988).

The U.S. Task Force on Education of Young Adolescents (1989) suggests that schools be divided into clusters of 200 to 300 students each, comprising a cross-section of the school population (i.e., ethnic and socioeconomic background; levels of physical, emotional and intellectual maturity). Students remain in the same group as long as they are enrolled in the school, thus creating a stable cluster of peers and teachers. Each 'house', as the Task Force calls them, is supervised by a 'house leader'. The school, in turn, is managed by a building administrator (the former principal) assisted by a building committee comprised of teachers, administrators, support staff, parents, students, and community representatives (TFEYA, 1989). 'Houses' can be organized on an annual basis or continue throughout a student's tenure in the school (Simmons and Blyth, 1987). Even if students take most of their classes within their 'house', they might still leave it for specialized subjects, such as music, languages, science, health, and physical education (Burke, 1987). The Task Force on Education of Young Adolescents (1989) suggests a minimum of five teachers for every 125 students (one for every twenty-five students). Teachers would share responsibility for the same group of students, building interpersonal bonds among the students, between teachers and students, and indeed among teachers themselves.

Other sources in the literature suggest different arrangements. In the first years of secondary school, students can be assigned to the same class grouping and have the same teachers for a number of periods (Simmons and Blyth, 1987; Cheng and Ziegler, 1986). In this system, the school structure in later years can still approximate a more traditional secondary arrangement, with subject-oriented departments and individual student timetables.

There is evidence that 'schools within schools' programs produce significant achievement growth, improve attendance and behavior, and generate student, staff and parent satisfaction (Burke, 1987; McGanney *et al*, 1989; Moon, 1983). The increased teacher-student interaction has been shown to improve student motivation (Cheng and Ziegler, 1986). Evans (1983) investigated the effectiveness of transition subschools and concluded that they helped new students integrate into the larger school.

One of Theodore Sizer's nine common principles for members of *The Coalition of Essential Schools*, to be used as a basis for restructuring to meet their local needs and situations, is the principle of personalization.

> Teaching and learning should be personalized to the maximum extent feasible. To that end, a goal of no more than eighty students per teacher should be vigorously pursued. (Sizer, 1992)

Hewitt (1994) outlines three different models for restructuring a large secondary school of 1500–1800 students to create schools-within-schools using cross disciplinary teams and more flexible timetabling.

Upper School grades 11, 12	House A grades 9–12	House B grades 9–12	Grade 12	Family students	F	F	F
			Grade 11	Family	F	F	F
Lower School grades 9, 10	House C grades 9–12	House D grades 9–12	Grade 10	Family	F	F	F
			Grade 9	Family	F	F	F
Each 'school' has a separate head	Each 'house' is led by an assistant or vice-principal, or department head		Each family group of 100 students is led by a team of teachers				

In a collection of richly described cases of restructured schools brought together by Lieberman (1995), there are vivid portrayals of what these abstract models can look like in the everyday life of schools. Whitford and Gaus (1995), for example, describe an elementary school that changed from 'traditional top-down management; an orderly, strict environment; respectable test scores; and an experienced staff', with teachers working in self-contained classrooms, following detailed curriculum guidelines and drill-and-practice worksheets, to the following arrangement:

> Now the school is organized around three primary and two intermediate multi-age, heterogeneous teams of eighty-eight to 120 students and four to five teachers. On the primary teams are children whose ages would traditionally place them in grades K-3; the intermediate teams are composed of those students once grouped as fourth and fifth graders. Children generally remain on a primary team for four

years and on an intermediate team for two years. One result of this non-graded way of organizing children is that yearly retention or 'failing a grade' has been eliminated. Instead, children are given longer spans of time to develop and to demonstrate the abilities needed to progress from the primary to the intermediate program and from intermediate to middle school.

Within the teams, teachers use flexible grouping; that is, they group students in a variety of ways in addition to by demonstrated ability. By not relying exclusively on ability grouping, students have opportunities to work, play and learn with and from many different youngsters.

The adults in the building are interacting in new ways as well. Teachers on the same team have a common planning time daily. They also send representatives to the school's participatory management committee.

Although this example is drawn from elementary and intermediate age-ranges, the principles of restructuring so that small teams of staff work together with cohorts of students in more cross-disciplinary ways, are very similar to those that have been advocated for secondary schools. These basic principles are that:

- Students know each other better. They experience community. They work better as a team.
- Students know teachers better. They build trust with them more quickly and feel more comfortable in class.
- Teachers know students better. They can care for them more adequately, plan and personalize their learning more effectively, and assess and report on their progress more meaningfully.
- Teachers know each other better. They give each other moral support, plan students' programs collaboratively, and share ideas and insights about issues concerning individual students, as well as ones concerning academic material.
- The program becomes less fragmented, more coherent and more tailored to the needs of students whom teachers come to know well.

Such restructurings of high school organization to offer better care and support (as well as curriculum and assessment) for students are promising. But they are not perfect, and ongoing problems will need to be addressed by those who develop them.

One problem is that of maintaining effective liaison with 'feeder' schools. As the Inner London Education Authority (1988) reported in England, where several 'houses', clusters or cohorts exist in a secondary school, there is not always one teacher with whom primary/elementary or junior high colleagues can liaise. Solicitous attention therefore has to be given in restructured schools, to establishing and maintaining clear arrangements for liaison with feeder schools.

A second problem emerged in our own evaluation of schools endeavoring to establish core groupings of students in mini-schools or sub-schools in grade 9. Several schools we studied had placed grade 9 students in mixed ability groups that followed a common curriculum with a small team of teachers. Teachers tended to like this reform. It reduced the numbers of students with whom they were in contact. It enabled them to know their students better, care for them more effectively, plan their work more appropriately, and assess and report on their progress more meaningfully and extensively. These findings fit the existing literature very well.

Most students saw things rather differently. They felt condemned to repeating a grade 8-like experience: denied opportunities for greater challenge and wider choices and the general *rite de passage* which they expected secondary schools to provide. They reported becoming tired of 'the same old faces'. One interview response captures many students' perceptions:

Interviewer: Do you like this system of staying with the group the whole year?

Student: Actually, no, because you don't get to meet new people. I mean, even if they are nice or whatever, you have to stay with them the whole year. You basically get tired of people after a while, you know. If you changed classes and met different people, you kinda have to broaden your horizons with other new students, you meet new people and you can have the ability to learn with other people and see how they learn, you know. Because like in our class, everyone has a partner, more or less where they stay with that one person. (Hargreaves *et al*, 1993, p. 109)

These responses are salutary. They point to the fact that students are among the most powerful protectors of the past — wanting to preserve traditional differences between elementary and secondary schools, and the enduring patterns of classroom life with which they are familiar and indeed used to managing and manipulating (Rudduck, 1991). Change is a problem for students as much as it is for teachers — which indicates the importance of involving students early in any innovation. At the same time, it may be that many mini-school reforms have yet to strike the right balance between *community* and *monotony*. The challenge that remains here is to create an experience for early adolescents that is sufficiently common, caring and inclusive so as to counter the traditional problems of fragmentation and impersonality of secondary schooling, while incorporating enough elements of choice and diversity, and enough changes and challenges in the program and the strategies of teaching and learning, to convey to students a substantial sense of progression from the upper elementary years.

Conclusion

One of the most fundamental reforms needed in secondary or high school education is to make schools into better communities of caring and support for young people. Historically, large high schools have either neglected these needs, or channeled them into specialized systems of guidance and pastoral care that leave the academic system and prevailing patterns of classroom learning intact, that have little time for the personal needs of most students, and that tend to develop exaggerated reactions to the problem few (through systems of punishment, therapy or behavior management). Some specific innovations like mentoring or peer-assisted learning can counter these tendencies to some extent, but in the end, it is care in the classroom, in the routine relationships among teachers and students that matters most. Attending to these needs requires more fundamental restructurings of high school life to allow classroom teachers of early adolescents to know and care for their students better and vice versa. This calls for smaller numbers of contacts for teachers with students, more team-based and interdisciplinary approaches to teaching and learning, stronger classroom-based roles for guidance and special education teachers to enhance the integrity, flexibility and human resources of the teams, and more use in classrooms of other personnel such as student teachers, adults in the community, and senior students working in peer-assisted learning to make the teams productive and viable.

Once the necessity of these restructuring measures is appreciated, care and support are no longer self-contained and specialized areas, treatable with specific solutions that leave the prevailing academic priorities of the school untouched. They rebound on, and have ramifications for, the entire way in which curriculum and assessment in secondary schools or junior high schools are delivered.

6   Curriculum Problems

Three Problems of Curriculum

In previous chapters, we saw that what is now commonly believed to be a major crisis in secondary education is in many respects a crisis of community — of students feeling detached from their peers, their teachers and their schools. There is also another side to this crisis of secondary education — a crisis of curriculum. The secondary school curriculum has failed to engage or honor the interests of many students, particularly those who are less strong in academic achievement. For too many students, secondary school is 'just boring' and they cannot wait to leave. Whatever disagreement there may be over how to define a 'dropout' or how to calculate the dropout rates (Lawton *et al*, 1988), one of the reasons students leave secondary school early is their disenchantment with the curriculum and how it is presented.

Goodlad's (1984) study of 525 high school classrooms in the United States found that a typical class witnessed a lecture format that was generally divided into five activities — preparing for assignments, explaining/lecturing/reading aloud by the teacher, discussing, working on assignments and taking tests. In her study of eight high schools, Metz (1988) also noted the universal nature of high school classrooms with little variability among buildings and room set-ups, sequencing of subjects taught, texts and methods of instruction. Cuban's (1984) historical analysis of American education shows that high schools have essentially remained unchanged since the turn of the century in such areas as length of class periods, duration of program and subject specialization. He found that even such elements as furniture arrangement, grouping of students and the amount of physical movement students are allowed within the classroom, have seen few changes. Junior high schools have not fared any better. In his study of twelve American junior high schools, Tye (1985) concludes that:

> According to student and teacher reports and according to observation data, junior high school students in classes in all subjects in our sampled schools spent large amounts of time listening to the teacher. In addition to this, the most common activity, they also wrote answers to questions a lot and often took tests or quizzes. Less often, they wrote reports, read or were involved in discussion. In short, they were almost always involved in passive and traditional activities. Activities such as simulation and role-play were non-existent.

David Hargreaves (1982) likens the cumulative effect of this sort of experience to viewing lots of old television shows, sometimes even reruns. Tye (1985) compares it to watching long Andy Warhol movies of extraordinary tedium which portray banal events like a haircut in protracted, uninspiring detail. Tye concludes that much of junior high school life is like this for the student — a typical six-period day is like an interminably long film running 330 minutes.

Given this kind of context, we can begin to understand some of the difficulties that students with different talents or configurations of abilities, experience in secondary school; especially those who are underachieving or at-risk. But does this mean that their 'more able' peers are any better placed or that the presentation of the curriculum is any more interesting and motivating for them? When the able achieve, we naturally tend to assume there is no problem. Yet there is evidence that, many able and successful students are equally disillusioned with the quality of their school experience. In a large study of Scottish secondary schools, Gray and his colleagues (1983) administered a questionnaire to over 4000 secondary students who had taken their 'highers', a university-based examination taken towards the end of secondary schooling. Students were asked to rate ten different study methods or types of teaching-and-learning activities in terms of the frequency with which they had encountered them and in terms of their enjoyment of them. The most common single method of study was 'exercises, worked examples, proses, translations' (72 per cent), followed by 'having notes dictated to you in class' (60 per cent), 'using duplicated notes' (49 per cent), and 'reading' (47 per cent). The least encountered methods of study were 'practical activity' (17 per cent), 'class or group discussion' (14 per cent), and 'creative activity' (12 per cent), yet these were listed among the most enjoyed methods.

In a longitudinal case study of successful students entering the English 'sixth form' (approximately grades 11–13), Thomas (1984) found that, despite being 'warmed up' on entering this status passage by teachers' promises of intellectual excitement and university-style tutorial relationships, the presentation of the curriculum and structure of learning were much the same as earlier in their secondary school career. Generally, teachers dictated, gave out worksheets and demonstrated experiments. Many teachers of these able students were what Thomas called 'tedious talkers' who conducted long monologues from the front, giving students little opportunity to participate. She describes how, because of the absence of any real participation, these teachers would try to generate enthusiasm by creating 'imaginary participation', punctuating their monologue with responses to imaginary questions and inserting phrases like: 'No really, this is true' or 'I know you'll not believe this but . . .'.

Among academically successful students, conformity is easily mistaken for commitment. Hard work is frequently interpreted as a proxy for interest. Yet many successful students are not so much enthusiastic as bored, indifferent, insouciant or instrumentally focused on getting their paper certificates.

High-achieving students in secondary school, it would seem, are often motivated not so much by the quality of teaching or fascination for the material itself, but by the inner drive or need for achievement that psychologists like McClelland (1987) have documented. This motivation is a product of these students' cultural background. Their need for achievement is so strong, it will supersede even the most unnurturing educational environment. Secondary schools that have many students of this kind, and that take their motivation for granted, are not successful or effective schools. They are merely cruising. According to Stoll and Fink (1996), cruising schools

> appear to possess many of the qualities of an effective school. They are usually located in higher SES areas where the pupils achieve often in spite of teaching quality. League tables and other rankings based on absolute achievement rather than 'value added' often give the appearance of effectiveness. If, however, schools are to be effective for all children, we must raise the ceiling as well as the floor . . . Schools which are smugly marking time and not seeking to prepare their pupils for the changing world into which they are going, are doing them a disservice.

Dropout rates are highest among students not of low ability but among those who fall in the 'average' range of measured intelligence (Lawton *et al*, 1988). With dropout rates increasing even among more academically proficient students (Wehlage and Rutter, 1986), there are signs that this inner need for achievement may no longer be sufficient to carry them through. The kinds of curricula and teaching strategy in secondary school that have been a problem for the less academically proficient student may also be becoming problematic for the more academically proficient one. Perhaps secondary schools fail to retain students because they never really engaged them in the first place.

In broad terms, there are three ways in which secondary schools and their curricula often fail to engage students in the intrinsic commitment to learning. We describe these as:

* the problem of relevance
* the problem of imagination
* the problem of challenge.

The Problem of Relevance

In a Newfoundland study of secondary school students and their experience of school, family and community life, Gedge (1991) found that the students from working-class communities, whose life and work were mainly focused around fishing, found little in their experience of secondary school to excite or interest them. Home and work life offered more interests and rewards. While these students' parents valued education in the abstract, and the opportunities it could create, their sons and daughters saw no value in education as they experienced it in the concrete, day-to-day routines of the schools. Connell and his colleagues (1982) found similar patterns among working-class youth in Australia.

One interesting finding of Gedge's study was that teachers rated these students, their behavior and their ability lower than did the students themselves, their parents, and other people in the community who knew them. Similarly, in Ontario, Canada, Karp (1988) found that when dropouts, their parents, employers and teachers were asked to rate the dropouts in terms of qualities like responsibility, curiosity and ambition, only their teachers viewed them negatively. This could be because their teachers were overly harsh and critical, but it is more likely the result of accurate observations of how these young people behaved in the context of their schools and classrooms. This is an important insight. What can appear like a generic problem of the students and their background, may well be a very specific matter of those students' response to their experience of secondary schooling and its curriculum. As King and his colleagues (1988) point out, it is curriculum that is responsible for much of what we call the dropout problem. ' "Dropout" students feel that "what they are studying is not worthwhile or interesting enough to justify persevering in the face of difficulties" ' (Radwanski, 1987).

We know this because students do not display these responses equally in all areas of the curriculum. Gedge (1991), for example, notes that the working-class students he studied responded much more positively to their English classes, classes which engaged more dynamically with their own experience, than they did to other areas of the curriculum. In Australia, Power and Cotterell (1981) also found that transferring students adjusted more readily to their English curriculum than they did to many other subjects.

Students' adverse experiences of the secondary school curriculum are partly a product of narrow conceptions of what should constitute that curriculum. They also rest on undifferentiated views of how young people learn and of what will be required of them in the world they will enter as adults. Recent theories of intelligence and research about the ways young people learn have helped expose the restrictiveness of traditional curriculum offerings. In *Frames of Mind*, Gardner (1983) has challenged the notion that intelligence is a fixed, unitary trait. When intelligence is seen as singular and immutable, curriculum becomes defined as a ladder with simple entry-level learning and schooling for the less talented at the bottom and complex skills being introduced only at later levels for those with more intelligence. This conception of intelligence not only ranks students on single, simplistic scales. It also privileges some kinds of knowledge over others in a hierarchy of status and value (Wolf *et al*, 1991).

Gardner (1983) proposed a broader understanding of thoughtfulness and intelligence and isolated seven independent dimensions of intelligence that make up the talents of human beings. The perspective of multiple intelligences emphasizes that all learners, across ages and grades, construct knowledge within their own particular framework (Wolf *et al*, 1991). Students may be stronger in some aspects of intelligence than others. All aspects need cultivation if student achievement is to be encouraged and recognized. Recognizing this diversity of intelligence and learning styles among students makes relevance even more critical for learning.

Relevance is also important from the future-oriented perspective of the world that young adolescents will inhabit as adults. If one goal of schooling is to prepare students for their future, there is already an enormous gap between the knowledge and skills they will need and what schools currently provide (Schlechty, 1990). Anticipation of future demands has been at the root of the outcomes-based education movement that tries to link desired and measurable outcomes of learning to the skills that students will need beyond school (Spady, 1994). This is not to say that the curriculum should be uncritically based on (often exaggerated) corporate claims about our economic and technological future. If current trends are a reliable indicator, much of the work awaiting future high school graduates will be semi or low skilled service work in jobs that are temporary and insecure (A. Hargreaves, 1994; Livingstone, 1993; Barlow and Robertson, 1994; Lash and Urry, 1994). The positive forces of flexibility must not be overestimated. Even so, opportunities for gaining access to more highly skilled, flexible work assignments will be enhanced by granting every-one access to them. Moreover, an education that encourages criticism of and reflection on our social and technological future will lead young people to question and challenge, and help create their own future.

If one problem for potential 'dropouts' is their continual exposure to a *watered-down academic curriculum* (Hargreaves, 1982; Adler, 1982; LeCompte, 1987) that is fragmented, and engages little with students' interests, enthusiasms, talents or future lives, the principle of relevance clearly warrants inclusion on any secondary school curriculum reform agenda.

The Problem of Imagination

Relevance is not the only important principle of learning missed by an overly didactic and watered-down academic curriculum. In a challenging analysis of the principles of curriculum planning, Egan (1988) argues that *imagination* is one of the most neglected elements of curriculum planning. Commonly placed on the sidelines, treated as a frill, or confined to particular areas of the curriculum like English or drama, imagination, says Egan, should form one of the central principles of curricular planning. The curriculum, he argues, should be seen not as a set of objectives to be reached, but as a set of stories to be told. Storytelling, in fact, should be at the heart of teaching, not in terms of what the teacher actually says, but in terms of how the learning is structured.

Egan justifies this view by noting that what often interests young people is not their immediate world at all — not the local community or the pollution in the lake. What often interests them, rather, is an imaginative world of fantasy — as a momentary reflection on the popularity of video games or role-play games like *Dungeons and Dragons* will testify. Through this fascination with the world of imagination, Egan continues, young people have a fundamental grasp of basic general structures of thought and an understanding of concepts like the conflict between good and evil, the contrast between light and dark, and the basic structure of 'stories' themselves as ways of arousing dramatic interest in apparently insoluble problems and irresolvable conflicts, that can finally be resolved.

The importance of storytelling as a principle of curriculum planning, argues Egan, is in the use of the world of fantasy and imagination as content for study, and in the use of the basic properties of storytelling as a structure for planning. In the first case, he suggests, links to the fantastic as a starting point for learning can be made in many other areas than English. Social studies is one obvious case, but science too can appeal to young people's sense of wonder and fascination with fantasy. The worldwide popularity of Stephen Hawking's (1988) book, *A Brief History of Time*, illustrates how the public's interest in even the most esoteric aspects of physical science can be secured by appealing to people's imaginative fascination with the nature of time. How much more interesting to approach the seemingly mundane topic of 'light' in physics through discussions about time or stories about time travel than through pinhole cameras and prisms. As a starting point for learning, imagination is one of our most underused resources.

The capacity to harness the power of imagination in Egan's second sense is also under-exploited. As we shall see, the curriculum is too often presented as a fact, not as a problem. Curriculum material is treated as content to be covered without indications of any uncertainty that it may engender. Particularly in subjects like science, there is little sense of the conflict, excitement, anticipation and ultimate satisfaction in scientific discovery. One survey of high school science teachers indicated that teachers saw themselves primarily as providers of content (Beaton *et al*, 1988). The survey also noted a limited range of teaching strategies and methods of evaluation.

Egan's overall argument adds a second powerful ingredient to the ways of engaging student interest in the curriculum. Relevance is the most popularly voiced mechanism for doing this. But as Egan points out, the principle of relevance can sometimes degenerate into mediocre, descriptive studies of or tedious topics on self, family and community (also Woods, 1993). *Imagination* is an equally important principle of learning right across the curriculum and should also be taken into account in curriculum reform.

The Problem of Challenge

In a study of five United States school districts, Firestone and Rosenblum (1987) reported that 'deals' were frequently made between teachers and students where low academic standards were traded for quiet. Cusick's (1983) case studies of three American high schools revealed a proliferation of 'easy' course offerings in order to 'help' students meet formal requirements. Meanwhile, teachers

developed personal relations with students that reduced disciplinary problems and kept them in school. Similar findings are reported by Goodlad (1984)
and by Tye, B. (1985). In research on school effectiveness, having high but
achievable expectations of students is one of the most consistently cited
factors associated with positive student outcomes (Purkey and Smith, 1983;
Mortimore *et al*, 1988). Conversely, low expectations are often associated with
negative outcomes.

Absence of challenge is a third way that secondary schools often fail to
engage their students' interests and involvements. By challenge, we mean what
is in everyday language often understood as mastery. We do not mean mastery
in Bloom's (1971) sense of 'mastery learning', where mastery is defined in
terms of particular educational objectives that students are expected to cover
and achieve. Mastery in that sense really means only coverage or completion.
What we have in mind is something more like the dictionary definition of
mastery: 'evident skill, superior dexterity'. Mastery here is something substantial and significant, not just something completed. It is a process of facing
and overcoming immense personal challenges — the kind of engagement
that Csikzentmihalyi (1990) describes as 'flow'. 'Flow' is a state of concentration so focused that it amounts to absolute absorption in an activity and is the
necessary ingredient for optimal experience and quality of life. According to
Csikzentmihalyi, much of what we label juvenile delinquency is motivated
by a need to have 'flow' experiences not available in ordinary life. He main-
tains that as long as a significant segment of society has few opportunities to
encounter meaningful challenges, and few chances to develop the skills necessary to benefit from them, we must expect that violence and crime will attract
those who cannot find their way to more complex 'flow' activities.

This kind of challenge within secondary education can sometimes be
seen in out-of-school settings. In a review of programs of outdoor and residential experience (including community and cooperative education programs),
Hargreaves *et al* (1988) point to the significant sense of challenge and achievement that many academically less-able students face when climbing a rock face
or dealing with a crisis in the workplace. These encounters with real and not
contrived challenges often have dramatic effects on student self-esteem and
attitudes to school. Sadly, these are usually short-lived, as the particular experience is forgotten and the more ordinary classroom routines of secondary school
take over once more.

Some schools get around these difficulties of follow-through, by trying
to make school learning approximate more closely to challenges in real life.
Woods (1993) uses the term *verisimilitude* to describe this way of challenging
young people, and documents cases of what he calls 'critical events' in teaching and learning where children feel that their learning is exciting and 'real'.
In one case, a class of children undertake an archaeology project with a
real archaeologist and learn about the excitement (and toil) of discovery. In
another, a class of children write, illustrate and publish their own book which
is then successfully marketed in regular bookstores. Other works have advocated

similar orientations to teaching and learning. One of the nine common principles of Theodore Sizer's, *Coalition for Essential Schools*, for example, is that of diploma by exhibition, which is 'awarded upon a successful final demonstration of mastery — an exhibition of the central skills and knowledge of the school's program' (Sizer, 1992). An important collection of cases describing restructured schools also documents examples of how learning can be organized in more 'real life' ways (Lieberman, 1995).

Whatever approach is taken, it is clear that a key issue for secondary schools in reforming the curriculum is not just how to generate higher expectations in the diffuse sense that effective schools advocates once called for, but also how to build regular experiences of real and significant challenge into students' experiences of the secondary school curriculum.

The Subject-Based Curriculum

Secondary School Academic Orientation

Current initiatives to restructure secondary education worldwide arise out of concerns that students have not been properly prepared either for the world of work or for post-secondary studies. Universities, colleges and employers have perceived that fundamentals of literacy, basic skills and 'proper attitudes' have not been acquired by students leaving secondary school. These perceptions may in part reflect real changes in standards and expectations. But undoubtedly they also reflect shifts in the secondary school population (Barlow and Robertson, 1994). There is great cultural and linguistic diversity among our students now. For example, in all the school districts in Metropolitan Toronto, over 50 per cent of the students are categorized as English as a Second Language (ESL). Another issue is the increasing number of students who stay on at school, as entry into the full-time workforce is socially delayed. Consequently, as Noddings (1992) puts it, what was once taught to a few is now taught to everyone. The elite curriculum is now the curriculum for all. This extension of the academic curriculum has not taken place without adjustment — a process that many writers explain as *watering-down*.

In their large-scale study of secondary education, Gray *et al* (1983) explain that this watering down of the academic curriculum has, in many respects, occurred for the best of reasons — allowing as many students as possible to have access to high-level qualifications. The entry of more and more students into such programs is spurred by the pursuit of equality of educational opportunity. It is also fueled by what Dore (1976) calls 'credentialism'. Credentialism occurs when high numbers of students become qualified for an occupation at a particular level. The requirements for the occupation are raised and become inflated. The pursuit of qualifications becomes ever more frantic, increasing the emphasis on educational qualifications in a ratchet-like process. This credentialism cannot continue indefinitely. There comes a point when the difficulty of achieving qualifications becomes too great, when course requirements become overwhelming. Students are then likely to drop out from school physically, or tune out from their schooling mentally.

Reasons for Persistence of the Academic Curriculum

Beneath the continuing dominance of academic curricula, much deeper processes are responsible for subject specialization, departmentalized structures, and their resistance to change in secondary schools. These processes are all connected with what we described in chapter 3 as the academic orientation of secondary schools. In their comprehensive summary of changes in European education Wake *et al* (1979), point out that there is growing awareness that both the existing content of secondary education and the arrangement of it are either outdated or no longer important in contemporary life. They also note, however, that changes do not come easily.

McPartland *et al* (1987) refer to a 'subject-matter orientation' in high schools through which teachers perceive themselves as experts in particular subjects. They note that teaching practices tend to follow a continuum, from 'pupil orientation' at the elementary level to 'subject orientation' at the secondary level. Corbett *et al* (1987) argue that subject specialization is considered very much a 'sacred norm' at the secondary level. As Emile Durkheim (1956) suggested many decades ago, tampering with such norms can create a sense of panic among teachers, as they hold the 'sacred' to be unquestionably true.

Although these 'sacred' norms of schooling appear timeless, 'natural' or 'divine', they are, in many respects arbitrary, developed for other purposes in another time. Yet the longer they persist, the more timeless they appear. They then become fixed as a set of strategies that guide and limit our arrangements of schooling and our attempts to change them. Tyack and Tobin (1994) refer to this phenomenon as the *grammar of schooling*. Like language, they argue, schooling has a fundamental grammar. The grammar of language frames how we can speak. The grammar of schooling frames how we can educate. Each grammar has its origins. But once established, each grammar becomes highly stable, slow to change. Tyack and Tobin support their claims through an historical investigation of five educational reforms in the United States. Two of these — the graded school (with its batch processing of age-graded cohorts) and Carnegie units of course credits that have constituted the criteria for high school graduation and university entrance, — became institutionalized decades ago, and now form the contemporary grammar of schooling. Three other educational changes — the Dalton Plan, the Eight-Year Reform and Flexible High Schools — enjoyed only temporary or localized success because they contravened the fundamental grammar of schooling. In a way they were nonstandard, localized dialects of change, used only for a short time or on the margins of educational life.

A number of factors contribute to the strength and persistence in secondary schools of this fundamental 'grammar' with its emphasis on academic special-ization and departmentalization:

- *Teacher recruitment*: Teachers training for secondary education are more subject-oriented than their colleagues training for elementary education (Book and Freeman, 1986; Lacey, 1977).
- *Teacher identity*: Throughout their education in secondary school, university and beyond, teachers become attached to their subjects, developing loyalty toward them. Subjects become a major part of their identity (Bernstein, 1971; Siskin, 1994). To challenge their subject and its integrity is to challenge that identity.
- *Subject histories*: There is an extensive literature on the histories of school subjects (for example, Tomkins, 1986; Goodson, 1988; Goodson and Ball, 1985). It reveals that school subjects create not just intel-lectual communities but social and political communities as well (Hargreaves, 1989). School-subject boundaries have in many ways been defined arbitrarily. What counts as a subject and as valid content for that subject shifts over time, as different communities and traditions fight for influence within it (Ball, 1983). This process has been thoroughly documented even for subjects like mathematics (Cooper, 1985). The same kinds of processes are evident in contemporary struggles be-tween the 'literature' and 'communication' branches of the English curriculum. With respect to the establishment and defense of subject boundaries, Goodson (1983) describes the irony of geography, which was initially resisted by teachers of other subjects on the grounds that it was 'not a real subject'. Geography, in turn, then resisted the later establishment of other subjects like environmental studies, on the grounds that *they* were 'not real subjects'.

    In practice, most current secondary school subjects are a legacy of the early twentieth century — a time when working class students were beginning to take advantage of secondary education opportun-ities. The United States Committee of Ten's deliberations of 1893 and the English Secondary Education Regulations of 1904 were the key curriculum landmarks of the time (Goodson, 1988; Hargreaves, 1989; Tomkins, 1986). The establishment of Carnegie units in the 1920s consolidated the preeminence of academic subjects in the secondary curriculum of America (Tyack and Tobin, 1994). These academic defi-nitions of the secondary curriculum limited working-class aspirations. Subjects which were devised, developed and established largely to serve the interests of the middle and upper classes came to be seen as the valid definition of secondary curriculum for all. In this sense, today's 'natural' curriculum is, in many respects, an historically specific one that does not meets the needs of all students (Wake *et al*, 1979).

- *Department politics*: In secondary schools, subjects are normally taught in departments. These departments have territories to defend and resources to protect. They compete with each other for rooms and cupboards, favorable timetable slots, compulsory curriculum status and student numbers (Goodson and Ball, 1985). They also provide career routes for their members (Siskin and Little, 1995). Subject departments are highly politicized. This is one of the reasons why curriculum integration and staff collaboration across departments is so hard to achieve in secondary schools (Hargreaves *et al*, 1992). Not only are identities threatened but interests too.

- *Student entry into post-secondary institutions:* Subject-based qualifications can be 'cashed-in' by students for career and further educational opportunities. They are a kind of 'cultural capital' (Hargreaves, 1989). Universities are powerful gatekeepers of the academic curriculum in secondary schools. To challenge the academic curriculum is therefore seen as a threat by universities as well as by (usually more advantaged) parents who wish their children to go to these universities.

- *Subject status:* The school curriculum is divided into what might be called 'high-status' and 'low-status' knowledge areas (Young, 1971). 'High-status' knowledge is academic, theoretical and usually has compulsory status, large time allocations, high timetabling priority and attracts many students. 'Low-status' knowledge is non-academic, practical and has lower time allocations, lesser timetabling priority and attracts fewer students. The difference between high-status and low-status knowledge is chiefly a difference between rigor and relevance.

    Teachers, schools and subject associations are well acquainted with the implicit rules underpinning these differences of subject status. They try to raise the status of their favored subjects by making them more theoretical and academic. Many developments in physical education and family studies can be explained in these terms (Hargreaves *et al*, 1992; Little, 1993). The cost of improving a subject's status, though, may be the loss of that very relevance which was the source of its attraction for less academically oriented students. In this way, we can see that the dominance of academic values in schools affects developments not just *across* subjects, but *within* them too.

- *Overcrowded curriculum:* Because of the strength of the academic curriculum, and of subject interests within it, whenever schools are required to take on new mandates such as AIDS or drug education, the curriculum is treated like an old, familiar bookcase. New books are continually added but none are taken away (Gray *et al*, 1983). Additions are made to the existing structure but the structure is not altered to accommodate the changes. The result is overcrowding, clutter and lack of coherence (Wideen and Pye, 1989).

- *Content-laden curriculum:* Secondary school curriculum is designed to 'cover' the required subjects and to be sure that the information is provided to students. Consequently, teachers must teach to the intellectual middle of the class (Carroll, 1990). The subject-based curriculum tends to create classes which are more content-focused than process-focused, geared to teaching subjects not students. Curriculum documents themselves reflect this emphasis as Pratt (1987) found in a content analysis of 100 school board curricular guidelines from across Canada. There is evidence that strong content orientation may have adverse effects on the quality of teaching. In a study of teachers' sense of efficacy and its relationship to student achievement, Ashton and Webb (1986) found that there was a strong and significant relationship between teachers' low sense of efficacy (their felt capacity to improve student achievement, irrespective of students' backgrounds), their preoccupation with covering content, and their reliance on safe, undemanding teaching methods.

Impact of the Academic Orientation

Academic subjects and the academic orientation of secondary schools are heavily institutionalized both historically and politically. Buttressed by the universities and seen by many parents and communities as 'real learning' or 'real school' (Metz, 1988), they have a pervasive effect on the character of secondary schools as a whole and on their capacity to deliver effective and appropriate services to all their students. There is nothing inherently wrong with academic learning and academic subjects, and much that is praiseworthy about them, but the extent of their influence on the curriculum appears to have had a number of far-reaching negative consequences:

- lack of balance, breadth and coherence in the overall curriculum;
- tendency to focus on content more than on teaching methods or skill requirements for the future, adversely affecting the quality and diversity of teaching;
- creation of a curriculum with low relevance which can be unduly difficult and dispiriting for many students;
- fragmentation of student experience, preventing sustained engagement with curriculum, teachers and even peers;
- balkanization of secondary schools and departments, making it difficult for the schools to respond as a whole to outside influences and changes, and to establish cross-curricular themes and objectives (Hargreaves and Macmillan, 1995).

Many restructuring initiatives are designed to challenge the 'grammar' of secondary schooling; to loosen the stranglehold that overcommitment to an academic orientation has had on it and on those students who have not been served well by the academic, subject-based curriculum. One possible vehicle for creating such a shift is to organize the curriculum in a different way — around a common core of content or a common set of learning outcomes.

7 Outcomes and Integration

Common and Core Curriculum

Criteria for Justifying a Common or Core Curriculum

A common or core curriculum can take many forms and be developed according to many criteria. There is no single justification for it. Many arguments have been advanced in favor of such a curriculum. Some compete, some are complementary. The particular kinds of common or core curricula that are developed usually reflect the criteria that are used to justify their creation. We have derived six such criteria that have been used as a rationale in various jurisdictions which have moved towards a core curriculum.

Equality of opportunity: This justification is common in most of the countries of Western Europe (Wake *et al*, 1979). Premature streaming or tracking, or premature choice among courses can injure students' later life chances. A common or core curriculum is seen as a way of leaving options open until as late as possible and thereby helping equalize opportunities among classes, cultures and genders (Hargreaves, 1982; ILEA 1984; Adler, 1982; Boyer, 1983).

Educational quality: One commonly stated aim of school systems is bringing all students up to a basic level of competence by a particular grade so they can function fully as citizens in society (Radwanski, 1987; Sullivan, 1988; Government of Newfoundland and Labrador, 1989). High expectations are usually attached to these minimum standards in basic skills.

Transmission and development of the culture: A common or core curriculum is sometimes seen as a vehicle for transmitting and developing common values, knowledge and other learning considered important in the dominant culture. Although 'sub-cultures' are recognized, the need to develop a unified culture through a common or core curriculum is seen as important if people are to live together harmoniously and productively. (Barrow, 1979; Lawton, 1975; Williams, 1961). Hargreaves (1982) relates common or core curricula to the development and restoration of community and proposes that community studies form a key part of it. Griffiths (1980) insists that the rejuvenation of national cohesion will be achieved through a common or core curriculum taught to all students.

Educational entitlement: A common or core curriculum promises access to fundamental forms of knowledge that can enable students not only to reach a minimum level of competence but also to develop fully as 'well-rounded' human beings. While this criterion was a powerful component of curriculum reform in Britain in the early 1980s, it was ultimately dropped for safer goals of consistency between schools, basic competency in learning and a focus on academics. Building a common or core curriculum on the basis of educational entitlement involves recognizing different kinds of intelligence (Gardner, 1983), forms of knowledge (Hirst, 1975) or areas of educational experience. In Britain, Her Majesty's Inspectorate (1983) outlined eight such areas of educational experience. These were: the aesthetic and the creative, the linguistic, the physical, the social and political, the ethical, the mathematical, the scientific, and the spiritual. All students, the Inspectorate stated, should have access to these essential areas of experience as part of a balanced education. The Australian Curriculum Development Center, in seeking to establish the basis for a core curriculum, defined it in terms of nine major domains 'through which human experience and understanding have been organized and represented' (Skilbeck, 1984). Those were arts and crafts, environmental studies, mathematical skills and reasoning and their applications; social, cultural, and civic studies; health education; scientific and technological ways of learning and their social applications; communication; moral reasoning and action, values and belief systems; work, leisure, and lifestyle.

Stimulating and recognizing achievement: Developing a curriculum that stimulates, recognizes and rewards a range of educational achievements, not just academic ones, in order to maximize the possibilities for success and build motivation among the student population, is another justification for a common or core curriculum. The assumption here is that student achievement is boosted not by giving less academic students more of what they are poor at, but by nurturing success through building self-esteem. By recognizing and rewarding neglected strengths such a common or core curriculum can develop the sticking power that students need to work on areas in which they are weak. In its review of problems of underachievement in secondary schools, the Inner London Education Authority (1984) identified four aspects of achievement:

- *Intellectual-Cognitive Achievement* is concerned with propositional knowledge which is easily written down, remembered and relatively easily assessed. Knowledge tends to be emphasized more than skill, memorization more than problem-solving. This aspect of achievement is strongly represented in the secondary curriculum and, in many respects, dominates it.
- *Practical Achievement* is concerned with the practical application of knowledge. It is more oral than written. It is most obviously present in non-academic subjects but can be developed anywhere in the curriculum. Practical achievement is somewhat more difficult to evaluate and receives less emphasis in the curriculum than propositional knowledge.

- *Personal and social achievement* is concerned with such skills as co-operation, initiative, leadership and ability to work in groups. While much of this aspect of achievement generally goes unstimulated and unrecognized in the conventional classroom, it is nonetheless revealed in other out-of-school settings such as outdoor education or work experience. While these are the skills that many employers increasingly value, they receive less emphasis in the curriculum and are considerably harder to assess.
- *Motivation* subsumes the other forms of achievement and is perhaps the most interesting. Teachers and schools often assume that motivation is something that students either bring with them to school or do not. You are lucky if you have motivated students to teach, unlucky if you do not. Motivation is usually assessed under the heading of 'effort'. Many schools, says the ILEA Committee, pay little attention to motivation. Some actually depress it. Yet the willingness and commitment to learn, says the Committee, is itself an achievement to be developed, something for which the school holds responsibility. Failure to develop achievement in this area will probably lead to failure in the other three. One of the ten common learning outcomes for grade 9 in Ontario, Canada embodies this principle of achievement in its outcome that students should 'use the skills of learning to learn more effectively' by setting goals for their own learning, evaluating their own progress and reflecting on their own and others' thinking (Ontario Ministry of Education and Training, 1995).

As with the criterion of educational entitlement, when the criterion of stimulating and recognizing achievement figures strongly in the justification for a common curriculum, a broad curriculum results, rather than one mainly focused on only one area of learning or aspect of achievement.

Support for other educational purposes: This justification aims to bring together and secure coherence among curriculum, assessment, teaching and learning, and support for students. A common or core curriculum defined in terms that extend beyond subjects, can support improvements in other aspects of schooling by offering enough flexibility for them to be restructured as necessary; whereas a departmentalized, subject-based curriculum makes such restructurings very difficult.

An example of this approach to a common or core curriculum and its integration with other educational objectives is outlined in the report of a task force of the California League of Middle Schools (Lake, 1988b). The report recommended that time should be provided within the curriculum to incorporate core courses, exploratory courses, and collaborative and self-contained teaching. According to the task force, such a core curriculum would meet the needs of junior high school students in transition. The 'core block' of time within the curriculum would enable educators to smooth transition by:

- providing extended time with one or two teachers who would know and therefore be able to support, assess and report on students well;
- creating a home-base for students which would improve the amount and quality of support they received;
- improving students' sense of belonging, self-esteem and attitudes toward school;
- fostering teacher collegiality through collaborative planning, team teaching and an interdisciplinary approach to instruction;
- allowing time and flexibility for increased variety in teaching methods;
- providing every student with access to the same learning experiences.

There are many examples of what curriculum programs organized in core blocks look like in practice (for example, Lieberman, 1995). Our evaluation of pilot projects in school restructuring describes detailed cases of core group organization — although as we described in the previous chapter, it also identifies the risks of this arrangement creating *monotony* rather than *community* if taken to excess (Hargreaves *et al*, 1993).

Structure of a Core Curriculum

According to Skilbeck (1984), there are three distinct ways of interpreting and organizing a common or core curriculum. It may be:

- a set of required subjects or subject matter embodied within a centrally determined syllabus to be taught to all students;
- a set of required subjects or subject matter determined by a school with courses and activities required for all students;
- a broadly outlined statement of required learning for all students, defined by both central and local bodies and interpreted by schools.

To these we would add a fourth way that has gained increasing attention and significance in recent years:

- a statement (detailed or broad) of required learning *outcomes* for all students, defined by both central and local bodies and interpreted by schools.

For Skilbeck, the main difference among these ways of organizing a curriculum is the amount of local control in the decision-making process. Our own additional definition points to another difference: focusing on what the outcomes of learning are (however they are achieved), instead of on the kinds of learning opportunities to which students will be exposed. Skilbeck's second definition appears not very workable, if one takes seriously the need for guarantees that every school's core curriculum should meet the goals of educational entitlement and development of the culture. It might, for instance, allow particular schools in all-white communities to neglect their responsibilities for developing multicultural understanding (Troyna, 1993). Leaving the organization of core curriculum *entirely* to individual schools can easily lead to inconsistency and inequality in the achievement of valued curricular outcomes.

The other three definitions are more workable in this respect. In reviewing, evaluating and developing these definitions, we will take into account how well each meets the criteria for a common or core curriculum we outlined earlier. To recap, these criteria are:

- equality of opportunity;
- educational quality;
- common culture and community;
- educational entitlement;
- achievement and motivation;
- support for other educational purposes.

1   *A common or core curriculum as a set of required subjects or subject matter* has been put forward in a number of countries and jurisdictions. It generally has the following sorts of characteristics:

- The common or core curriculum is made up of required subjects such as mathematics, English, science, modern languages, geography, history, creative arts, physical education and technology (as in the English and Welsh National Curriculum). In some cases, the categories of subject matter are defined somewhat more broadly in terms of humanities, fine arts, sciences and practical arts, but these still encompass traditional subjects. Groupings of categories such as these leave little room for curriculum emphasis outside traditionally defined subjects (Goodson, 1994).
- The curriculum tends to focus on academic content, although it may include some attention to attitudes, skills and experiences as well.
- Although cross-curricular work and some integration of subjects may be encouraged through the expectation that all subjects will develop more generic attitudes and skills in students, conventional subjects and subject contents still tend to predominate (Hargreaves, 1989).
- Common or core curricula defined in terms of subject matter can create temptations to pack the prescribed curriculum with detailed subject content, leading to overload for the students, overwork for the teachers and difficulty in achieving educational purposes beyond those of basic coverage (Helsby and McCulloch, 1996).
- Common courses of any kind can be seen as enhancing *equality of opportunity* because they expose everyone equally to the same materials and experiences. However, when defined as specific contents, this curriculum may be too inflexible to adapt to local contexts and to the lives and interests of different ethnocultural and racial groups. History,

literature and other subject contents are especially prone to such racial and ethnocultural bias (Troyna, 1993).

- The goal of *educational quality* is seen as being addressed by the increasingly common practice of attaching detailed standardized assessments to particular grade levels or 'key stages' of children's learning.

- *Culture and community* are achievable goals of a common or core curriculum but are more difficult to attain systematically within specific and segregated subject categories than in the much broader categories of subject matter.

- The limited breadth of subject or subject matter definitions prevents this model from meeting several of the possible purposes of a common or core curriculum we reviewed earlier. Limited breadth jeopardizes fulfilling the goals of *educational entitlement*, of recognizing multiple intelligences or different *aspects of achievement*, and of creating the necessary coherence and flexibility to support other educational purposes that benefit early adolescents in the areas of assessment, teaching and learning, and guidance.

2 *Common or core curriculum as a broad outline or framework defined by both central and local bodies and interpreted by schools*: Such a curriculum normally possesses the following characteristics:

- Curriculum is defined not in terms of subject knowledge, courses of study or detailed content, but in terms of multiple intelligences (Gardner, 1983) or broad areas of experience and human understanding (Her Majesty's Inspectorate, 1983; Skilbeck, 1984).

- Defining a common or core curriculum in terms of multiple intelligences or broad areas of experience meets most, if not all of the criteria for establishing such a curriculum. Compared with subject-based models, ones organized around multiple intelligences or areas of experience address two criteria particularly effectively — students' *entitlement* to a broad and balanced range of educational experiences; and their access to expanded opportunities for educational *achievement*.

- A common or core curriculum defined as a broad framework leaves sufficient scope for and flexibility in curriculum development and teacher development at the level of the school. School-based curriculum development and teacher development are vital to the success of curriculum and assessment reform (Hargreaves, 1989; Skilbeck, 1984; Rudduck, 1991). Teacher development, we have seen, in the form of close working relationships with colleagues, builds collective commitment to norms of continuous improvement which make teachers responsive to and interested in educational change (Little and Bird, 1984). Yet teacher development is inseparable from curriculum development (Stenhouse, 1980). Teachers are unlikely to collaborate unless there is something substantial for them to collaborate on; unless there are significant things within the curriculum for which they can take ownership (A. Hargreaves, 1994). A common or core curriculum that leaves considerable latitude in curricular judgments at school level is necessary for these important developments to take place (Darling-Hammond, 1995).

- Leaving curriculum development entirely to the discretion of the school can create indefensible omissions and inconsistencies. Yet we have seen that close prescription of content through written curriculum guidelines can create a culture of dependency among teachers, leading to preoccupations with coverage. How then can teachers and schools be helped to meet broadly defined curriculum guidelines in their own particular way? Andy Hargreaves (1989) suggests that systems of inspection, support and review, administered at the level of the school district can ensure that schools sincerely try to meet the requirements in the common or core curriculum framework. Through the process of school-based curriculum development, such systems can help teachers to address the broad guidelines in their own particular way as they suit their own context. School district consultants and administrators might usefully undertake this role, diverting some of their time and energy from committees for writing detailed curriculum guidelines which currently appear to restrict many of the opportunities for curriculum development in schools. Or school-based review can be a review of teachers by their peers. But without broad orienting curriculum frameworks, without the pressure and support of inspection or review, and without professional cultures of teacher collaboration which make school-based planning and curriculum meaningful, school-based curriculum development is likely to prove patchy, wasteful and inconclusive.

3 *Common or core curriculum as a statement (detailed or broad) of required learning outcomes for all students, defined by both central and local bodies and interpreted by schools.*

- An outcome-based curriculum is defined by what students will demonstrate successfully at the 'real' end of their schooling not just the end of the week or year, (Spady, 1994). This approach shifts the focus from objectives derived from content or textbooks to desired changes in the students (King and Evans, 1991).
- In a curriculum defined by outcomes, high expectations are set for all students; time and teaching methods are variable (Spady, 1991).
- This model addresses many of the criteria for a core curriculum. It focuses on entitlement of students to a broad set of experiences and requires that students receive expanded opportunities to ensure educational achievement, while reinforcing success for all and allowing considerable latitude for local needs.
- It does this by establishing the ends in clear and vivid terms but leaves interpretation of the ends and the content that comprises them solidly in the hands of the classroom professionals.

- Just like the prior model, this one suffers from the possibility of omissions and inconsistencies in program delivery. However, the focus on results and using the outcomes to organize curriculum, holds the promise of establishing coherence and integration of larger ideas and competencies rather than subject content and low-level skills. It is not yet clear how well this theory works in practice.

- An outcome-based curriculum runs the risk of missing the mark of its lofty goals and deteriorating into unimaginative, narrowly defined content outcomes that limit learning rather than extending it. This could leave teachers trudging their way through endless miniscule outcomes rather than actively creating conditions for teaching and learning within outcomes that are more broadly defined.

- Similarly, if prescribed learning outcomes are too numerous or defined in too much detail, teachers will become overwhelmed by the effort required to implement them all and integrate them into their practice.

- In some places, this model has generated considerable controversy in both a moral and a political sense. Attempts to establish broad statements of outcomes for students have sparked great debate about the role of schools in defining values; about whether the outcomes are mandates or guidelines; about who gets to judge and about what the sanctions are for failing to meet them. For some conservatives and members of the religious right, outcomes-based education is the devil incarnate (Zlatos, 1993).

Summary

A common or core curriculum can take many forms and be developed according to many criteria. From the point of view of helping students adapt more positively and effectively in the long run to secondary school, it is important that the curriculum is broad and that it recognizes a wide range of educational achievements. This suggests a curriculum organized not around specific subjects and subject matter, but around broad frameworks of educational experience or common learning outcomes. It also suggests a role for school district consultants, inspectors or teacher evaluators working closely with small groups of schools, to help them meet these broad guidelines, and ensure they are endeavoring to do so sincerely.

A common or core curriculum of this kind is likely to avert and even counter the demotivating effects of the present subject-based academic curriculum. It is also likely to leave schools and teachers sufficient scope and flexibility to develop the substance of their own curricula, creating a culture of confident teachers who are committed to change and improvement. This kind of broadly defined, yet locally developed curriculum offers an important chance of superseding the traditional alternatives of centrally imposed and school-based models of curriculum development — models which have hitherto enjoyed little widespread success in breaking the stronghold of academic influence on secondary education.

Integrated Curriculum

An increasingly popular strategy for creating effective education for early adolescents is curriculum integration. The strategy is recommended by many proponents of middle schools for instance (for example, Beane, 1991). Integration is an attractive proposition for those who want the curriculum and the way students experience it to be less fragmented. But integrated curriculum and interdisciplinary studies also experience a great deal of criticism. Integration is often attacked for reducing standards and destroying rigor by subjecting children to blended subjects in a 'mish-mash' of ill-conceived curriculum offerings. The concept of curriculum integration is as elusive as it is attractive. Curriculum integration has many different meanings, can be pursued for quite different purposes, can vary immensely in practice and can have very different results. The meaning of curriculum integration and the value placed upon it cannot be presumed. Our discussion of curriculum integration therefore addresses the various meanings that can be attached to it, the different purposes to which it can be directed, the sorts of social and educational conditions that give rise to these purposes, and the consequences and realities of integration in practice.

The literature on curriculum integration is a wide one. Curriculum integration has been reviewed and analyzed at different levels of the educational system: for instance, in the context of elementary education (Pappas *et al*, 1990; Williams, 1980), middle schools (Kasten *et al*, 1989; Quattrone, 1989), secondary education (Watts, 1980), and adult education (Dickinson *et al*, 1980); in special education (Hamre-Nietupuki *et al*, 1989; Gire and Poe, 1988; Kersch *et al*, 1987) and in multicultural settings (Haase, 1980). It has also been investigated in the context of a range of different subjects including language arts (Norton, 1988; Duncan, 1987; Allen and Keller, 1983; Goodman *et al*, 1987; Stahl and Miller, 1989), science and mathematics (Shainline, 1987; Friend, 1984; Hunter, 1980); social studies and humanities (Atwood, 1989; Kaltsounis, 1990; Craig, 1987; Heath, 1988; Berg, 1988; Cardinale, 1988; Wolf, 1988; Rudduck, 1991); vocational and career education (Greenan and Tucker, 1990; Stevens and Lichtenstein, 1990; Rutgers, 1981; Gire and Poe, 1988); computers and information technology (Komski, 1990; Brent *et al*, 1985); ecology (Jewett and Ennis, 1990); and broader core programs (Hairston, 1983).

The most common accounts of curriculum integration are descriptions of particular initiatives. These are often written by the people responsible for developing the initiatives and presumably also for their success or failure (for example, Mansfield, 1989; Hunter, 1980). There is usually some element of evaluation in these accounts, but understandably it tends to be light.

A second set of accounts of curriculum integration is more conceptual and philosophical. This sort of literature reaches back as far as the earlier part of the century in some cases (Northwestern Educational Service District 189, 1989; Barnes, 1982; Betts, 1983; Conklin, 1966; Connelly, 1954; Dressel, 1958; Hirst, 1974; Pring, 1973; Richmond, 1975). Often, these conceptual analyses build frameworks or typologies of the different forms that curriculum integration can take (for example, Case, 1991; Drake, 1991; Fogarty, 1991).

A third set of accounts consists of studies of the interpretation and consequences of curriculum integration in practice (for example, Weston, 1979; Olson, 1983; Musgrave, 1973; Hamilton, 1975). These evaluations of what curriculum integration actually looks like and what effects it has in practice are least common in the literature. Our discussion of curriculum integration and its relevance for early adolescents draws on and analyzes these different kinds of literatures to determine what different possible forms integration can take, what the advantages and disadvantages of these different forms are and what happens with efforts to bring about curriculum integration in practice.

Meaning and Purpose of an Integrated Curriculum

One essential condition for any successful innovation is that the meaning of the innovation should have *clarity* (Fullan, 1991). Curriculum integration is no exception. A common problem with curriculum integration is that its meaning is often vague, unclear, ambiguous or even vacuous. Werner (1991a and 1991b), for instance, has found widespread vagueness in discussions of integration within policy documents surrounding recent educational reforms in British Columbia in Canada. Confusions have abounded, he says, about whether integration refers to the integration of time, teachers, students or curriculum. The scope and ambiguity of this approach to defining integration has permitted many teachers to review their practice and 'discover' examples of integration they are already doing that can be contained within the broad definition of the policy prescription. Curriculum integration, in this sense, has often supplied new rhetorics for justifying existing practice rather than conceptual levers for introducing new ones. It hasn't really changed anything. For Case (1994), policies advocating curriculum integration are often little more than slogans. The resulting practice can, as Brophy and Alleman (1991) point out, be 'ill conceived' (p. 66). They remind us that 'curriculum integration is not an end in itself but a means for accomplishing basic educational goals'. Clarifying the meaning and purpose of curriculum integration is therefore extremely important for both conceptual reasons and practical ones.

There are three broad ways in which the meaning of curriculum integration has been laid out within the literature: as one side of a dichotomy, as points on a continuum and as part of a multidimensional typology.

1 *Integration vs. Specialization.* Although there are earlier accounts of the meaning of curriculum integration (for example, Dressel, 1958), one of the most conceptually sophisticated analyses is Bernstein's (1971) discussion of the classification and framing of educational knowledge. *Classification* refers to 'the degree of boundary maintenance between contents'. *Frame* refers to 'the degree of control teachers and pupils possess over the selection, organization, pacing and timing of the knowledge transmitted and reviewed

in the pedagogical relationship'. Particular combinations of classification and framing produce different kinds of curriculum or what Bernstein calls *educational knowledge codes*. Bernstein describes the two major kinds of knowledge code as *collection code* and *integrated code* curricula.

- *Collection code* curricula are characterized by strong classification and strong framing. Boundaries between contents or subjects are strong and teachers have little opportunity to transgress them. Students tend to have little control over what is taught. A subject-based, academic curriculum is very much a collection code curriculum. This is so whether the curriculum is highly specialized, with small numbers of subjects taken by a select few, as in the later years of British secondary schooling, or rather generalized with many students choosing from a wide range of subject options and credits, as in the North American system.
- *Integrated code* curricula are characterized by weak classification and framing. Boundaries between contents or subjects are weak and blurred. Students have much more discretion over what is learned. Individual teachers, however, may have less discretion, as they have to collaborate with colleagues from other disciplines over what is taught.

The meaning that Bernstein attaches to integration is quite precise. Integration does not mean abolishing subjects or indulging in vaguely conceived themes. It entails *subordinating* previously insulated subjects or courses to some *relational* idea, which blurs the boundaries between the subjects.

Curriculum integration may take place within subjects or across them. What is essential is that there is a high level relational principle. For example, genetic and cultural codes can provide a basis for integrating sociology and biology. Loosely constructed topics and themes are insufficient. As Case (1994) suggests, superficial references to 'natural connections' and 'natural fits' of the kind that are common in the literature, should be avoided (p. 84). There are several implications of Bernstein's rigorous and robust conception of integration:

- There must be high ideological consensus among the teachers participating in integration.
- This high-level agreement *reduces* discretion among teachers over what and how they teach, but *increases* the discretion of students over what and how they learn.
- Contributing subjects must be linked at a high conceptual level, not through low level pragmatic themes (for example, 'railways'), or contrived and contorted connections between quite distinct areas of study (for example, writing modern advertising signs in hieroglyphics to form a spurious connection between media studies in English and studies of Egyptians in history!).
- Clear and distinctive criteria of evaluation should exist.

- 'Integration reduces the authority of the separate contents, and this has implications for existing authority structures'. Curriculum integration threatens existing structures of power and control inside and perhaps even outside education.

Bernstein's theory has largely been supported by subsequent studies of subject department politics and by histories of school subjects. These have shown how and why strong classifications of the curriculum emerge and persist. Bernstein's theory has helped clarify our understandings of integration. It has also proposed how the interest in integration arises under certain kinds of social conditions. Particularly intriguing here is Bernstein's suggestion that interest in integration emerges when there is a crisis in society's 'basic classifications and frames'. Such a crisis involves a questioning of and shift in society's hierarchies of status, its patterns of control, and its distribution of rewards. As the social boundaries in society become problematic, so too do the subject boundaries in curriculum. While an academically dominated subject-centered curriculum helps to reproduce patterns of social advantage from one generation to the next, any instability or shift in those structures of advantage, be this in politics, in the economy or in social life more generally, often brings with it parallel shifts in how we organize and manage the curriculum. In this sense, the emerging interest in curriculum integration as we enter the postmodern age and all its rapid changes is not hard to understand.

Similarly, while the emergence of curriculum integration can be precipitated by wider social change, such integration can in turn pose challenges to the existing social order. This happens when curriculum integration extends beyond isolated experiments with the urban poor or with middle class groups who embrace alternative lifestyles, to being a policy requirement for all children, of all backgrounds and abilities. Integration also provokes challenges to the existing order when it is not confined to younger children but becomes a requirement for secondary school children, who are closer to the exit gates of school that lead to university and occupational selection. When it affects almost all children, including older children, curriculum integration begins to threaten society's 'basic classifications and frames', its structures of power and control, and the recognized forms of knowledge through which the powerful perpetuate their advantage. Breaking down the barriers between school knowledge and non-school knowledge by promoting greater relevance, and between high status academic subjects and lower status practical ones (by recognizing different forms of achievement and intelligence), threatens the advantages of those groups who have traditionally benefited from an academic, *collection code* curriculum. It is usually at this point that integration is attacked by conservative politicians and middle class parents' groups, through criticisms that integration lowers standards, destroys 'real subjects', and exposes students and teachers to a 'wishy-washy' curriculum of 'blended subjects' (Delhi, 1995).

Integration fails and policy reverts back to more traditional curriculum categories, not just because there has been a failure to achieve clarity to define integration properly but also because integration threatens existing structures of power and control. Curriculum integration is therefore a political issue as well as a philosophical one. This insight is one of Bernstein's most significant contributions.

Notwithstanding such insights, Bernstein's theory also has its problems. One of these is its strict either/or nature. It establishes a clear dichotomy between integration and non-integration (see also Shoemaker, 1989). This creates a value polarity. It suggests that integration and non-integration are equivalent to good and bad practice respectively. They are seen as mutually exclusive. Thus, when Bernstein's theory has guided empirical study or curriculum practice, failure to meet all criteria of the integrative ideal has been interpreted as 'failed' or 'false' integration, or even 'disguised collection' (Walker and Adelman, 1972). Such dichotomies make distinctions that are bald and simplistic. Curriculum integration and subject specialization are not absolute, mutually exclusive alternatives. What is more important is defining the kind of curriculum integration that people want, the purposes for which it is designed, and how well it fits the setting in which it is to be used.

2   *The Continuum of Integration.* Some analyses of curriculum integration see it not as one half of a polarity, but as an arrangement of points along a continuum. Fogarty (1991) for example, has constructed a continuum of curriculum integration with ten models arranged along it. At one end of the continuum are models organized around single disciplines such as *the fragmented model* with its *periscopic* vision that takes a narrow focus on a single subject within an arrangement of separate and discrete disciplines. In the middle, are models that integrate across several disciplines such as *the shared model* with its *binocular* vision where two disciplines share overlapping concepts and skills within a framework of shared planning and teaching between these disciplines. Or there is *the webbed model* of integration which is *telescopic* in nature and which captures an entire constellation of disciplines at once. Further along the continuum are models that achieve integration not within material but within learners themselves. One example is *the immersed model* which is *microscopic* in nature and which filters all content through the lens of students' interests and expertise. At the other extreme of the continuum is *the networked model* of integration which is *prismatic* in nature because it creates multiple dimensions and directions of focus, among networks of learners who themselves direct the integration process.

Drake (1991) uses another continuum to describe the phases through which she and a group of other educators passed while trying to create interdisciplinary curricula. At first, the curricula were conceived in *multidisciplinary* terms as the contributions of particular subject areas to an agreed theme were identified. In a second, *interdisciplinary* phase, the team found 'there were fewer distinctions across subject areas than we had thought' (p. 21). Connections existed more through the theme than through formal relations between the subject areas, although units of learning were still broken down into subject-related parts. In the final interdisciplinary phase, subject area labels were abandoned altogether to 'let the activities stand by themselves' (p. 22) and to enable the team to identify 'natural connections'.

The continuum is a popular device for representing variations in educational practice. It allows finer discriminations to be made than straight polar opposites allow. This is certainly true for curriculum integration. There is much more to integration than its being good or bad, true or false, authentic or disguised.

A continuum of curriculum integration holds out the promise of charting and pushing progress towards ever more sophisticated interpretations and implementations of integration. But sometimes, the urge to measure and manage can obstruct the search for meaning. This can happen with educational continuums in two ways. First, quite complex and disparate behaviors may be clustered clumsily together into a single stage, level or point on the continuum for the sake of simple and convenient measurement, when in practice the specific behaviors often don't belong together at all. For example, it is conceivable that an integrated approach to curriculum can have content filtered through students' interests, while students choose that content in subject specialist ways!! In terms of how far students control the integration of their knowledge, this would put the stage of integration at one end of the continuum. In terms of how integrated the subject matter itself is, the degree of integration would fall towards the other end. One single continuum of curriculum integration does not allow these differences to be captured at any single point. The urge to monitor how well schools and teachers are progressing along the continuum of integration can obscure these subtle but important differences between different aspects of integration. Reviewing efforts to develop programs of interdisciplinary study in Scotland, Munn and Morrison (1984) concluded that the variations among these efforts were so complex and specific to the places they were developed, that it would be impossible to create any real continuum of curriculum integration along which they could be arranged.

A second point is that educational continuums often embody implicit values where movement along the continuum is construed as growth or progress towards a better state. However, progress along a continuum does not guarantee continuation towards progress. Given the many different kinds of curriculum integration, more integration is not always better. Sometimes it can be worse. When articles promoting integration talk about the need for teachers and administrators to let go of old categories and the security of boundaries, a quasi-therapeutic or evangelical language is used which implies that abandoning subject specialization is like withdrawing from addictions or casting out sin. Such language makes the continuum of integration a prescriptive rather than a descriptive one, and destroys the possibilities for achieving deeper understanding, subtle definition and a less doctrinaire approach. It also understandably alienates most subject teachers.

3   *Typologies of integration.* The final pattern through which understandings of integration have been constructed is that of a typology. Typologies permit integration to be arranged along many different dimensions. One useful typology has been developed by Case (1991). The first dimension of this typology consists of different *forms* of integration. These are integration of:

- content (for example, environmental studies);
- skills/processes (for example, dealing with writing skills in social studies);
- school and self (i.e., relevance);
- underlying principles that underpin all the curriculum (for example, principles of Catholicism).

Then Case describes two *dimensions* of integration. These are:

- horizontal (between contents at any one time); and
- vertical (within contents over time, for example, from one year to the next).

Case's typology also lists four *objectives* or *purposes* of integration. These are to:

- address important issues that cannot always be neatly packaged in existing subjects;
- develop wider views of their subjects among students;
- reflect 'the seamless web' of knowledge;
- increase efficiency and reduce redundancy of content.

Based on our research of pilot projects in school restructuring for early adolescents (Hargreaves *et al*, 1993), we would add one other purpose to Case's list. In this study, we discovered that where secondary schools tried to forge closer collaboration among teachers, they found the existing schedule or timetable and the departmental structure of school subjects too obstructive. Teachers couldn't arrange meetings within the timetable, so squeezed them exhaustingly into after-school time instead. This was wearing and made collaboration prone to fade over time. Therefore, one further purpose of curriculum integration is to:

- bring teachers together, by bringing material together.

Case goes on to outline four *modes* of integration. He does not place them on a continuum, though. They are simply different types of integration — none being better or worse than any of the others. The four modes are:

- *fusion* of formerly separately taught elements (for example, English and social studies);
- *insertion* of one element into a larger set (for example, novel study into history classes);
- *correlation* between elements that remain separately taught (for example, reference to hypotheses in history and science);
- *harmonization* of different skills, concepts, attitudes etc., across separately taught elements (for example, empathy).

Last, Case notes that integration can be organized and orchestrated in different places. In this sense, there are three *loci* of integration:

- national, state or regional;
- school or district;
- classroom.

Case observes that the items on the dimensions of this typology are not always compatible (for example, vertical and horizontal integration needs are often in conflict), stronger realizations of them are not always worthwhile (for example, some contents may best be confined within existing subjects rather than contrived across them), and not all combinations of different items necessarily lead to curricular coherence.

Case's typology and others like it, acknowledge the complexities of integration in practice. Moreover, they do not subordinate the need for complex meaning and careful description to a singular continuum along which teachers' 'progress' can be measured and controlled! However, typologies of integration only explain what kinds of integration might be possible. They do not explain how and why particular aspects of integration usually cluster together in particular ways, nor what it is that accounts for these patterns. They do not explain why some patterns of integration are common and some are not; why some are easy and some are hard. These questions can only be answered by looking at research on the realities of curriculum integration; on how integration is actually implemented in practice.

Integrated Curriculum in Practice

Curriculum reform policies and implementation plans are often put together in ways that assume relatively ideal and easily replicable school conditions where the reforms will be carried out. Yet the world of schools is far from ideal. It is messy, unpredictable and highly variable. Nor can this complexity be broken down easily into discrete variables that can be described and controlled as specific 'implementation problems' (Ball and Bowe, 1992). Sometimes the problems or circumstances are local, specific and idiosyncratic. For example, there may not be enough laboratory resources to share among teachers trying to develop team-taught integrated science. Or there may be too many part-time teachers involved in the integrated curriculum initiative, so that it is hard to get everyone together to meet (Hamilton, 1973 and 1975). Some problems and circumstances are more widespread. They point to challenges of implementing integration that apply across many settings. We want to draw attention to some of these most common implementation problems that beset curriculum integration, and to identify safeguards that can either offset these problems or at least mitigate them. In doing this, we draw on a number of key research studies of implementing curriculum integration. Among our chief sources are Weston (1979); Olson (1983); Munn and Morrison (1984); Skelton (1990); Rudduck (1991); Werner (1991a); Siskin (1994); Lieberman (1995); and Tyack and Tobin (1994). We have also drawn on our own research study of efforts to restructure education for early adolescents in Ontario, Canada (Hargreaves *et al*, 1993). Drawing on this work, it seems to us that the most common problems of implementation are:

- *Co-existence of more conventional and specialized curriculum requirements at a higher level of the school or educational system.* This can reduce teachers' commitments to integration and pressurize them to adjust their practice towards more conventional academic norms. In part, this problem calls for collective fortitude in resisting these pressures. It also points to the need to include universities, university defined knowledge and university entrance requirements in educational reform agendas. There is also a need for more teachers in high schools to work in both the lower and upper ends of the school or to be cross-appointed between high schools and middle schools to help build understanding between them.
- *Persistence of traditional patterns of assessment and assessment requirements.* This leads to teacher anxiety about the results and accountability of integration. Movements towards more authentic assessments such as performance-based assessments may ease these pressures, but only if the political and public desire for more and more standardized test scores is curtailed. Teachers cannot be expected to solve this problem themselves. Policymakers and administrators must have the courage to do so, and universities must be prepared to consider redefining their own criteria for entry.
- *Parental pressure for traditional academic standards and subject-based qualifications.* Parents want something that looks like 'real school'. Fears that integration will subject their children to lowered standards can be averted by communicating clearly and early to parents' groups what integration will involved and why it is necessary, and by increasing the flow of reports and other communication to parents about their own children, so they can be reassured regularly that standards are being maintained. Our own evidence from studies of schools attempting restructuring indicates that schools which involve

parents with them in the uncertainties of change achieve much more empathy and support from parents than schools that discuss and create change as an insulated group of closeted professionals who only inform parents once all the decisions have been made (Hargreaves *et al*, 1993).

- *Presence of staff who have developed long-standing attachments to their disciplines.* This can create resistance to integration. Using recruitment opportunities to attract some staff with varied subject backgrounds or even with some elementary experience can loosen the subject identities a little and provide the beginnings of an administrative solution. It can prevent what Hunt (1987) calls a 'hardening of the categories'. But for teachers with well established subject identities, especially sensitive approaches to implementing integration are also required, of the kind we review below.

- *The importance for personal identity of maintaining senses of boundary.* Seemingly trivial changes in responsibility for content can amount to major transformations in personal identity. Proclamations by some advocates of integration that boundaries should be dissolved and subjects abolished are idealistic and irresponsible. Senses of boundary are central to personal identity and ego strength (Fuller, 1969). Abolishing all boundaries can ultimately lead to abdication of personal responsibility (because it is no longer clear where one's responsibilities end) and to loss of purpose and direction (for there are no longer any limits, any clear definition to one's goals). The point is not to demolish subject boundaries or to dissolve them. The point is to redefine them so they are appropriate for current educational purposes and to soften them, so that people can communicate and move more easily across them. Integration, we have seen, is not always desirable and can be achieved within existing subjects as well as across them. What matters is that we revisit and revamp school subjects (perhaps even inventing some new ones) to see how well they fit our purposes, and that we find ways of making connections between them where justified and necessary.

- *Excessive speed of implementation.* Subject traditions are strong shapers of teachers' identities. Identities change slowly. Moves towards integration therefore also need to proceed slowly so they do not cause too much discomfort. Integration can begin with just two or three teachers or subjects rather than with the entire curriculum. It can be contained at first within one grade level, or one part of a teacher's load, rather than affecting the whole school or everything a teacher does, all at once.

- *The danger of interdisciplinary courses or programs balkanizing staff into 'insiders' and 'outsiders'.* Resentment can occur among those who feel excluded from or marginalized by experiments in integration. This difficulty can be offset by teachers in the interdisciplinary program spending at least some of their time outside it, working with other teachers and students elsewhere in the school. More generally, continuous and concerted efforts to reach out from the program to other staff, informing them about the program and asking for help to make it work, will keep teachers talking across the borders so they can understand one another's practice better.

- *Problems of bureaucracy and work overload.* It can be difficult for teachers of different subjects to meet, plan and work together in school time. Integrated programs need time for teachers to plan and review their joint work. This requires a little seed money, however modest, from the district or the school-based budget, so that at least part of the planning can take place in the regular workday. Shrewd scheduling also helps where it grants teachers in different subjects common planning times. More ambitiously, as we shall see in the final chapter, needs for teacher planning and other shared work can be built into new mini-school structures of curriculum integration and of education for early adolescents more generally.

- *Risks of burnout.* Teachers can become overwhelmed by the continuing need to prepare new materials, assessment instruments etc. Integration is no use if only teachers with extraordinary commitments and extraordinary lives can live up to it, and if it can only be developed in isolated, exceptional schools that attract such teachers. Again start-up money and creative scheduling can lessen the risks of ordinary teachers being overwhelmed. So too can slowing the pace and narrowing the initial scope of innovation to manageable (though not mediocre) levels (for example, beginning with one grade level, two or three subject areas, or only part of teachers' teaching responsibilities).

- *Threats to teachers' careers.* Involvement in integration can undermine teachers' chances of promotion to other schools where such schools value subject specialist experience. This problem will only properly be solved as integration expands from individual and atypical school experiments to changes that affect whole systems and the patterns of promotion within them.

- *Need for a clear sense of practicality.* Improvements in learning and in student performance are essential if the commitment of most teachers to integration is to be secured. As with most other innovations, integration must have clear and visible pay-offs for classroom learning if teachers are to accept it (Fullan, 1991). Integration that is ill-conceived, that makes contrived and contorted connections, or that is reduced to low level project work on badly thought-out themes, offers teachers few hopes of improvement with their own students.

- *Need to create a culture of school collaboration.* This is an essential context for curriculum integration. When teachers throughout a school work mainly alone and are unaccustomed to mutual help and support, special programs that call for collaboration, such as mentor programs with new teachers (Little, 1990a) or interdisciplinary programs in lower secondary school, can look exceptional by comparison and be seen as deviating from the norm. Needing help in these exceptional circumstances can then come to be perceived as unusual. It may even be seen as indicating weakness and deficiency. Teachers may therefore come under pressure to withdraw from collaboration over time towards seemingly 'stronger' positions of autonomy and independence. In this sense, integrated curricula and interdisciplinary programs must be seen by teachers and administrators as part of a long term effort to create school-wide collaborative cultures where teachers work together as a matter of course (Fullan and Hargreaves, 1991; A. Hargreaves, 1994). Our own research indicates that reforms for early adolescents are more likely to be successful where such collaborative cultures already exist because they support and encourage cooperation and risk-taking among teachers (Hargreaves *et al*, 1993).

Conclusion

This chapter and the previous one have reviewed the impact of patterns of curriculum on the capacity of schools to meet the needs of young adolescents. Secondary schools are places where subjects, their identities, their interests and their departmental organization prevail. School subjects are not just intellectual communities. They are social and political communities too. Most school subjects have their roots in turn-of-the-century categories which were defined and designed to meet the needs of secondary education for an academic elite. They persist partly for reasons of historical inertia, but also because of the ways secondary school teachers' identities and allegiances are formed through them, because of departmental politics which protect and sustain them, and because of the pressures of universities and other influential groups whose interests are served by preserving them. Subjects have become central to the organization of secondary schooling. They have become part of the basic grammar of schooling. They form one of the most sacred parts of its culture.

The subject structure may have some appropriateness for the latter years of secondary school, although we should note here that, as a collection, secondary school subjects are less bold, diverse and innovative than the range of subjects offered in higher education. The appropriateness of traditional subject structures for young adolescents is more questionable. Conventional subject structures skew the curriculum towards the academics, in a way that can be demotivating for many less able students, who find such work unnecessarily difficult and remote from their experiences. Conventional subject structures also tend to balkanize secondary schools into separate and sometimes competing departments. This can create serious obstacles to developing shared educational goals and establishing consistency in teaching style and in expectations for students. Subject-based secondary schooling can also fragment time and space for students in school, undermining their security and leaving them with little sense of 'home'. For these reasons, a conventional subject-divided curriculum seems poorly suited to the needs of early adolescence.

Developing a common or core curriculum has been seen as one way of addressing this problem, but views differ regarding why a common or core curriculum should be established and about the criteria which should be used to define any particular version of it. From the point of view of young adolescents, three criteria seem to us particularly important. A common or core curriculum

- can give students access to a broad and balanced curriculum, creating more possibilities for relevance, imagination and challenge in their learning;
- can widen our definitions of achievement and increase students' opportunities to succeed;
- can allow greater flexibility in scheduling and teaching arrangements by establishing teaching teams dealing with 'core blocks'. This curriculum can increase collegiality and consistency among teachers, improve the quality of guidance and care for students, and allow teachers to experiment with new patterns of teaching with smaller groups or over longer timeframes.

A core curriculum organized predominantly around conventional, high-status school subjects is unlikely to meet these key criteria. Such a curriculum will only reinforce the priorities of the academics and of narrowly defined forms of intellectual achievement in secondary schools. Relevance will be harder to establish, motivation more difficult to develop. Students' experiences will tend to remain fragmented as balkanization in secondary school persists. Curriculum reform in the transition years, must therefore address the most sacred norm of secondary schooling — its organization around high-status school subjects.

Varieties of core curriculum were reviewed that sought to overcome these difficulties. These curricula were organized around broad areas of human experience and understanding to which all students had an entitlement. They were broad and balanced, they defined achievement widely, and they allowed and encouraged the development of curriculum integration. These curricula are best defined firmly but broadly as in the most sophisticated kinds of outcomes-based education. They should set clear directions and expectations but leave considerable scope for local development, especially at school level. Less attention should be paid to writing detailed, content-filled guidelines beyond the individual school, and more to developing systems of support and review to help ensure that schools meet the broad criteria in their own ways. The scope offered for school-based curriculum development within the broad guidelines should respect the discretionary judgment that is at the heart of teacher professionalism, should allow teachers the flexibility to respond effectively to their students' needs within communities of great diversity, and should offer real opportunities for collaboration and collegiality among the teaching force.

These developments will not be achieved without difficulty or resistance. In the face of such difficulties, clear and robust definitions of commoness and integration are called for. Maintenance and improvement of high standards is essential. Communication with parents, students and other groups who may feel threatened by the loss of familiar categories and the end of 'real school' is imperative. Courage and fortitude in the face of resistance of those groups who have traditionally prospered from the academic curriculum, and its high-status subjects, and who may see their children's marginal advantages threatened by the passing of that curriculum, will also be required.

A common curriculum with greater integration between and beyond subject areas is essential to creating more effective education and better futures for all early adolescents. This need not mean that subjects be abolished. But they should be revisited and reinvented. Subject boundaries should also be significantly relaxed and new school subjects such as psychology, anthropology and astronomy should be created where necessary. Curriculum reform of this kind will be controversial. It will question assumptions, challenge identities and threaten the interests of those who benefit from the existing curriculum order. Equity is not easy. Equity with excellence is more difficult still. We must not falter in facing this profound curriculum challenge. Curriculum reform must be a top priority in school change efforts directed at young adolescents, no matter how many boats it rocks.

8   Assessment and Evaluation

Assessment is the tail that wags the curriculum dog (Hargreaves, 1989). Often, we view assessment as something that *follows* learning, that comes *after* instruction (Burgess and Adams, 1985). However, as Broadfoot (1979) argues, assessment commonly has a 'backwash' effect on the curriculum and on the processes of teaching and learning that go on within it. Assessment therefore operationalizes our educational goals as much as it reflects them (Murphy and Torrance, 1988). Any changes in educational assessment should, in this sense, be planned in accordance with changes being proposed for curriculum. Curriculum and assessment reform should be undertaken together, with planned coherence. Otherwise assessment reform will simply shape the curriculum by default (Hargreaves, 1989).

If our educational goals promote a broad range of outcomes and recognize a wide variety of educational achievements, these goals should be reflected in an equally broad assessment policy (Leithwood *et al*, 1988). Given the power of assessment to shape curriculum, teaching and learning, imbalances in assessment will likely create imbalances in curriculum, teaching and learning. Some types of assessment like written examinations and standardized testing are commonly criticized for their negative effects on curriculum, teaching and learning (for example, Hargreaves, 1982; Haney and Madaus, 1989). This has led some to advocate abolishing particular assessment strategies which are seen to have these effects (for example, Whitty, 1985). But assessment overall cannot be abolished. It is a constitutive part of teaching. Teachers assess all the time. They monitor the progress and response of their students continually in the ongoing flow of classroom events. Scanning for facial expressions, checking students' work, asking questions to test understanding — teachers undertake this kind of informal assessment as a routine part of their job (Jackson, 1988). Without it, they would scarcely be teaching at all. Assessment cannot be abolished, but it can be reformed. In view of our earlier argument, it seems sensible to suggest that the driving force behind assessment reform should be the goal of meeting our curriculum and teaching objectives more effectively.

Assessment fulfills many purposes. These include accountability, certification, diagnosis and student motivation. No single assessment strategy (for example, standardized tests or portfolios), can meet all these purposes (Haney, 1991; Hargreaves, 1989; Broadfoot, 1979). Some assessment strategies, like portfolios, that are useful in stimulating student motivation are poor as devices to meet the demands of public accountability. Equally, some strategies, like national tests or examinations that provide accessible and concise information to external publics, are not particularly helpful as tools to aid diagnosis of individual-student problems. We are more likely to meet the range of assessment purposes, therefore, by using a wide *range* of assessment strategies. The corollary of this is that if we invest in a narrow range of assessment strategies we will fulfill only some of our assessment purposes at the expense of the rest.

Developing and deploying a wide range of assessment strategies is commonly criticized as taking up excessive amounts of teacher time (Stiggins and Bridgeford, 1985; Broadfoot *et al*, 1988). The burden of additional assessment demands on the teacher can seem particularly great where assessment tasks, such as paper-and-pencil tests, are administered separately from the rest of the curriculum. Yet we know that teachers assess their students informally all the time as an integral part of their teaching. If a wider range of assessment strategies are to be developed and deployed, and if these are not to make excessive demands on teacher time, these new assessment strategies should become part of the learning that goes on in the classroom, not something administered or marked like stacks of students' books, when the learning is over. Integrating new assessment strategies into curriculum and learning is one of the greatest practical and conceptual leaps to be made in assessment reform. In short, we base our review of educational assessment on the following principles:

- that assessment reform and curriculum reform are closely interrelated and should be undertaken together;
- that broad curriculum goals should be reflected in broad assessment goals;
- that educational assessment cannot be abolished — it can only be reformed;
- that educational assessment fulfills diverse purposes which cannot be captured properly in any single assessment strategy — only in a wide range of assessment strategies;
- that assessment should be an integral part of the learning process, not something administered once the learning is over.

We will elaborate on these points in the remainder of this chapter by clarifying the nature of educational assessment, outlining its main purposes and describing the specific types of assessment that teachers can and do use in their own classrooms. We will then examine traditional patterns of assessment and their implications for teaching and learning. Finally we will discuss a range of alternative assessment strategies along with some possibilities and problems in their application.

Definitions of Assessment

Assessment, according to Bloom (1970), is one of three aspects of the testing enterprise, the other two being measurement and evaluation. Bloom defined assessment as an 'attempt to assess the characteristics of individuals in relation to a particular environment, task, or criterion situation'. Satterly (1981) defined assessment more widely as 'a term that includes all the processes and products which describe students' learning' and Wood and Power (1984) expressed the need to separate the term 'assessment' from 'measurement'. Student evaluation, on the other hand, is defined as the process of assessing student progress towards stated educational objectives and includes making value judgments (Stennett, 1987). In this chapter, assessment will be defined as the processes used to describe and discriminate what students learn at school.

It is reasonable for those involved in the learning process to want to understand its outcomes (Murphy and Torrance, 1988). Therefore, by definition, good assessment is not only an essential part of teaching and learning, but is also inseparable from teaching itself (Shipman, 1983).

Assessment can be differentiated in terms of what teachers assess — the *process* of work (how the student sets about collecting, organizing, and interpreting the information), or the *product* (the presentation of the ideas and the quality and quantity of the work). Usually, precedence is given to the assessment of finished products, since assessment is commonly viewed as an attempt to quantify outputs, within a product-oriented view of learning (Shipman, 1983).

Depending on *why* assessment takes place, it can be diagnostic, formative or summative. *Diagnostic* assessment is conducted to identify whether or not a student is having difficulties or to isolate the nature of a student's understanding, in order to make decisions about placement or program modifications. Much of this type of assessment is done informally and continually. Informal assessment takes place as the teacher interacts with students in the classroom, interprets students' answers and responds to them by modifying his/her teaching style, adapting the topic or changing the curriculum.

The terms *formative* and *summative* assessment are used respectively, to distinguish between continuous assessment throughout the course of instruction, with its prime purpose of improving teaching and learning, and assessment that occurs once the teaching is over and aims at assessing what has been achieved. As with the process-product distinction, the emphasis is on how assessment will help the teacher identify the learners' problems and provide immediate support, as compared to describing final performance (Scriven, 1978).

Finally, assessment can be differentiated in terms of its point of reference. *Criterion-referenced or outcome-referenced* assessment records students' attainment of specific curricular goals. It matches students against a standard. The advantage of this method is that it enables teachers to identify by how much a student has exceeded or fallen short of the predetermined level of performance so that appropriate help can be offered (Rowntree, 1980). When the comparison is made against peers and not specific standards, the assessment is called *norm-referenced*. Broadfoot (1979) argues that the predominance of norm-referenced assessment, which is of little help to teachers in improving their teaching, reflects the competitiveness which characterizes our society. In addition to these two widely discussed reference points of assessment, there is also a third, less widely discussed one — *ipsative or self-referenced assessment*. Derived from the Latin *ipse* (meaning 'self'), this pattern of assessment is one where one's performance and achievements are measured neither against any norm or average, nor against pre-set criteria, but against one's own past performances and achievements.

One of the problems in transferring to secondary school is the puzzling dip that occurs in some students' grades when they may move from being assessed by ipsative referencing in elementary school, to norm- or criteria-based referencing in secondary school (ILEA, 1984). This common problem points to the importance of establishing consistency in assessment practice according to the point of reference, especially as students move from one institution to another. To sum up:

- assessment has been defined as the processes used to describe and discriminate what students learn at school;
- assessment can assess the process of work, or its product;
- assessment can be diagnostic, formative, or summative in nature;
- assessment can be criterion-referenced, norm-referenced, or ipsative in character;
- because inconsistency in assessment practice can lead to confusion and disappointment as students transfer between schools, establishing clarity and consistency in the point of reference for assessment is an important priority.

Purposes of Assessment

Educational assessment serves a number of different purposes. Four of these are widely discussed in the literature: accountability, certification, diagnosis and motivation.

Accountability

In the eyes of the public, assessment can legitimize the existence of a given educational system and communicate to society how far its expectations for schooling are being met. Since taxpayers invest money in education, they want to make sure that their money is well spent. As the proportion of taxpayers who do not themselves currently have children in school rises, so too does the demand for educational accountability to the general public. The quality of work brought home or communicated by students themselves is not itself sufficient for this wider public. Instead, the public requests generalized and measurable criteria of accountability. Schools in this view have to produce 'goods', which in educational terms amount to bringing students up to a certain level (Broadfoot, 1984).

This pressure for accountability is not new. It was expressed in the nineteenth century, in England, for instance, when schools were 'paid by results' for bringing students up to specific measurable standards. Even today, in the Netherlands, state grants are only given to schools whose students can demonstrate minimum competence in numerical and other basic skills (Maguire, 1976).

Certification

This is perhaps the most commonly recognized purpose of school assessment, especially in the later years of secondary education (Broadfoot, 1979). Certification attests to students' competence in a particular area of learning upon completion of their school career or a major stage of it. This competence is demonstrated by apparently fair and objective tests or examinations usually given by teachers. The results of this assessment are compared to the performance of other students, thereby ranking students against predetermined criteria and sometimes against each other. The major aim of this ranking is to allow the two 'major consumers' of the educational system, namely employers and higher education institutions, to select those they think have performed satisfactorily (McLean, 1985).

Like accountability, certification has grown in importance over the years as a key purpose of assessment. Its expanding influence upon systems of assessment and systems of education more generally is attributable to what Dore (1976), in his international review of assessment trends, calls qualification inflation or 'the diploma disease'. This process involves an escalation of qualification requirements for the same job over time, even though the skill requirements of the job itself remain relatively static. In the pursuit of fairness within a system where formal equality of opportunity prevails, more and more students take examinations, tests, and other assessments at higher and higher levels in order to maximize their chances of success. As greater numbers of students attain success at each level and the pool of eligible candidates for particular jobs expands, the 'gatekeepers' of those jobs raise their standards to shrink the pool and gain better quality applicants. Gatekeepers of parallel jobs do the same so as not to get left behind in the status stakes, resulting in inflation. The immediate effect of this inflation is the opening of higher level programs to increasing numbers of students, and the linking of other formerly non-certified programs to credentials in order to give them greater public credibility. Overall, certification comes to exert an ever-widening influence, becoming one of the most powerful purposes of educational assessment.

Educational Diagnosis

Assessment allows the teacher to evaluate the learning process, to identify students' levels of understanding, to locate problems and to offer individual help or adjust the program accordingly. This kind of assessment has value not only for external publics interested in accountability or recruiting competent personnel, but also for teachers, so they can help their students by adjusting their program and improving their teaching. Assessment, in this sense, improves the quality of teaching and learning (Rowntree, 1980).

Student Motivation

Most obviously, assessment motivates by the 'carrot and stick' principle where students are willing to commit the effort necessary to perform a task because they are going to be rewarded for it (Natriello, 1987). Motivation can also be created by student achievement being officially recorded and recognized (Munby, 1989). Where students are involved in the assessment process, assessment can motivate by helping create more responsibility among students for their own learning (Burgess and Adams, 1985). Assessment can also have indirect benefits for student motivation by leading to improvements in curriculum and teaching, and in the quality of the learning that students experience (Hargreaves, 1989). Using assessment for motivation is a two-edged sword, however. Stiggins (1988) points out that scores or grades are not motivating for low achievers who protect themselves by being less persistent and less motivated.

In a general sense, accountability and certification are important and unavoidable purposes of educational assessment. But from the point of view of this review the key purposes of assessment are those that address the needs of early adolescents in the transition years. Diagnosis and motivation are in this sense the prime purposes of assessment from the particular standpoint of student needs. If these needs are indeed paramount in a practical as well as a rhetorical sense, then the first priority for assessment reform must be that the purposes of diagnosis and motivation are properly met.

Our review of assessment strategies is conducted from this standpoint. It is not a review of the advantages and disadvantages of different patterns of assessment in general. We assess assessment, rather, from the standpoint of the needs of young adolescents. Different patterns of assessment will therefore be considered in terms of their capacity to enhance or depress student motivation, to improve or inhibit effective diagnosis, and to recognize and stimulate a broad or narrow range of educational achievements and experiences.

Traditional Patterns of Assessment

Historically, the most dominant and publicly visible forms of assessment have been standardized tests, external examinations and tests and examinations conducted by teachers. In a review of literature on evaluation processes in schools and classrooms, Natriello (1987) concluded that 'the dominant technique for collecting information on student performance is some form of testing', be this at the national, state, district, or classroom level, where teachers rely extensively on their own tests (Herman and Dorr-Bremme, 1984; Wilson, 1989).

Effects of Traditional Assessment

In all Western industrial societies, examinations began as a means of securing entrance to certain elite professions, thus controlling recruitment to membership in them (Broadfoot, 1979). From the beginning, therefore, examinations were part of a sorting and selection process which emphasized particular products of education. Two types of examinations have dominated the literature in recent years; minimum competency and grade-specific examinations (Nagy, Traub and MacRury, 1986). Competency tests have been widely used in the United States. Although they were originally introduced to protect the interests of students whose needs were being neglected, there is considerable discussion about their fairness and impact on educational programs (Corcoran, 1985).

In addition to externally set examinations and standardized tests, teachers also use their own paper-and-pencil tests extensively as a basis for grading student performance (Gullickson, 1982). In fact, Stiggins and his colleagues (1989) found that teachers rely on their own classroom assessments as the primary source of information about student achievement and prefer to develop their own assessments. Several studies of evaluation practices in Canadian schools found that teachers prefer to make up their own tests (Wahlstrom and Daley, 1976; Anderson, 1989; Wilson *et al*, 1989).

Traditional patterns of examination and assessment have the following features in common:

- they are predominately applied out-of-context, once the required learnings have been completed;
- they are usually paper-and-pencil tests;
- they are usually norm-referenced or criterion-referenced;
- they provide the basis for scores or grades which can be used as measures of performance at individual, school, district, state/province/or national level.

The arguments for and against public examinations were put most eloquently if a little quaintly almost eighty years ago by the Board of Education

(1911) in England. Many more recent evaluations of the effects of examinations and similar patterns of assessment have added considerable detail but little further substance to these concisely expressed arguments.

The good effects of examinations on the pupil are that:

- they make him (sic) work up to time by requiring him to reach a stated degree of knowledge by a fixed date;
- they incite him to get his knowledge into reproducible form and to lessen the risk of vagueness;
- they make him work at parts of a study which, though important, may be uninteresting or repugnant to him personally;
- they train the power of getting up a subject for a definite purpose, even though it may not appear necessary to remember it afterwards — a training which is useful for parts of the professional duty of the lawyer, the administrator, the journalist, and the man (sic) of business, and secretary;
- in some cases they encourage a certain steadiness of work over a long period of time; and
- they enable the pupil to measure his real attainment by:
    (i) the standard required by outside examiners,
    (ii) comparison with the attainments of his fellow-pupils, and
    (iii) comparison with the attainments of his contemporaries in other schools.

On the other hand, examinations may have a bad effect upon the pupil's mind by:

- setting a premium on the power of merely reproducing other people's ideas and other people's methods of presentment, thus diverting energy from the creative process;
- rewarding evanescent (quick to disappear) forms of knowledge;
- favoring a somewhat passive type of mind;
- giving an unfair advantage to those who, in answering questions on paper, can cleverly make the best use of, perhaps, slender attainments;
- inducing the pupil, in his preparation for an examination, to aim rather at absorbing information imparted to him by the teacher than at forming an independent judgment upon the subjects in which he received instruction; and
- stimulating the competitive (and, at its worst, a mercenary) spirit in the acquisition of knowledge.

The good effects of well-conducted examinations upon the teacher are that they:

- induce him to treat his subject thoroughly;
- make him so arrange his lessons as to cover with intellectual

thoroughness a prescribed course of study within appointed limits of time;

- impel him to pay attention not only to his best pupils, but also to the backward and the slower amongst those who are being prepared for the examination; and
- make him acquainted with the standard which others and their pupils are able to reach in the same subject in other places of education.

On the other hand, the effects of examinations on the teacher are bad:

- insofar as they constrain him to watch the examiner's foibles and to note his idiosyncrasies (or the tradition of the examination) in order that they may arm his pupils with the kind of knowledge required for dealing successfully with the questions that will probably be put to them;
- insofar as they limit the freedom of the teacher in choosing the way in which he shall treat his subject;
- insofar as they encourage him to take upon himself work which had better be left to the largely unaided efforts of his pupils, causing him to impart information to them in too digested a form or to select for them groups of facts or aspects of the subject which each pupil should properly be left to collect or envisage for himself;
- insofar as they predispose the teacher to overvalue among his pupils that type of mental development which secures success in examinations;
- insofar as they make it the teacher's interest to excel in the purely examinable side of his professional work and divert his attention from those parts of education which cannot be tested by the process of examination.

Persuasive though this document is, and useful as it is for stimulating debate about the benefits and drawbacks of traditional patterns of assessment, it should be remembered that it was written at another time when the range of available assessment strategies was considerably narrower than today. With the availability of other assessment strategies, many of the claimed 'good' effects of examinations are not exclusively attributable to examinations alone. Students can be required 'to reach a stated degree of knowledge by a fixed date' by having to prepare presentations for a Science Fair, for instance. Similarly, 'the risk of vagueness' in student writing can be lessened by formative assessment of a series of drafts, as in the writing process that is now widely used in elementary and secondary school English programs. Equally, many of the alleged adverse effects of examinations also occur in teacher tests.

While much of the research discussed here concerns the effects of examinations, our concern is not merely with examinations but with other traditional patterns of assessment such as standardized tests that share many features in common with conventional examinations — patterns of assessment which are, by and large, decontextualized, paper-and-pencil ones and administered on completion of a unit or program of study. We will consider the effects of these traditional patterns of assessment on the curriculum, on the teacher, and on the student.

Curriculum Effects: Discussion of the effects of traditional patterns of assessment on the curriculum has centered on two views: narrowing of the curriculum and emphasis on tested subjects. Although most examinations occur at the end of a student's school career, they have been criticized for influencing the curriculum long before that terminal point (Broadfoot, 1979). The concern here is that examinations can come to dictate the curriculum (Nagy, Traub and MacRury, 1986). In a critique of the secondary education system in Britain with its domination by academic values and preoccupations, Hargreaves (1982) claimed that the public-examination system gave the message to students that only examined subjects had real importance and that only knowledge, skills and abilities that could be easily measured, especially in a written test, were valuable. More than this, he argued, examinations systematically screened out the everyday experience of many young people from the curriculum. In music, for instance, emphasis on the intellectual-cognitive side of the subject, on ability to interpret notation within a broadly classical frame, excluded many young people from enjoying and succeeding in the subject at school. The traditional assessment of music converted a potentially accessible subject into an inaccessible, unattainable one for many students by emphasizing its intellectual-cognitive components. Bresler (1993) has detected similar effects among music students at university.

Traditional patterns of assessment tend to privilege intellectual-cognitive aspects of achievement and the subjects in which these forms of achievement are preeminent. They only recognize a fraction of the multiple intelligences described by Gardner (1983). By narrowing the curriculum and the possibilities for achievement in this way, traditional patterns of assessment, which dominate a school's assessment system, narrow the possibilities for success and tend to create a curriculum skewed toward the academics, remote from students' everyday lives, and demotivating for many of those students we call 'less able'. The multiple choice format of standardized tests also emphasize low level skills of recognition and recall rather than higher-order thinking skills. In a national study of uses and perceptions of educational testing among principals and teachers in the United States, Herman and Dorr-Bremme (1984) found that increased testing led to more emphasis on instruction in basic skills. Basic skills, it was found, consumed more teaching time and more educational resources, particularly in schools catering to students from poorer socioeconomic backgrounds. In this context, less easily tested subjects like social studies, received less emphasis (Rimmington, 1977).

Where traditional patterns of assessment dominate, it is not likely that breadth in curriculum and teaching objectives will be achieved, and it is most likely that students will be exposed to a demotivating, academically skewed curriculum, remote from their experience, at a vital point in their development.

Teacher Effects: The effects of traditional assessment on the teacher have

been documented extensively in the United Kingdom where public examinations are an important feature of the educational system. The effects of such
examinations on the teacher have been claimed to be overwhelmingly negative (Mortimore and Mortimore, 1984). In a survey of secondary schools Her
Majesty's Inspectorate (1979), found that:

> the work attempted in the classroom was often constrained by exclus-
> ive emphasis placed on the examination syllabus, on topics thought to
> be favored by the examiner and on the acquisition of examination
> techniques.

This dominant teaching style, the Inspectorate observed, was 'uncritical,
unstimulating, and unsound'. In their study of Scottish secondary school leavers,
Gray and his colleagues (1983) also found that traditional teaching methods
predominated in student recollections of their experience. Gray *et al* concluded
that 'one may infer that many felt there had been a conflict between studying
for interests sake and studying for examination success'.

Traditional assessment patterns can also undermine innovation at the level
of the classroom. In separate studies of the Schools Council Integrated Science
Project in Britain, both Olson (1982) and Weston (1979) found that teachers
failed to adhere to project guidelines and persisted in teaching from the
chalkboard and in encouraging students to revise — practices which teachers
attributed to the constraints of examinations. Evaluations of how new mathematics programs were implemented in California elementary schools showed
similar effects. Teachers found it hard to give proper emphasis to the projects
recommending problem-solving approach to mathematics, given that their students' mathematical performance continued to be assessed by standardized tests
that placed a premium on basic skills (Darling-Hammond, 1990).

The constraints of examinations and standardized tests are not always
ones to which teachers adhere reluctantly. Many teachers embrace examinations with enthusiasm, seeing in them a key resource for motivating their students at a point when enthusiasm might otherwise be waning (Sikes, Measor and
Woods, 1985). In a profession riddled with teachers' uncertainty about how
well they are achieving their goals, favorable standardized test scores offer
some teachers reassurance about their effectiveness.

The effects of traditional assessments on teachers are not always consistently positive or negative. In an interesting and carefully devised study
Hammersley and Scarth (1986), for example, raised some provocative questions about the widely alleged negative effects of public examinations on
teaching and learning. They compared assessed and unassessed programs taught
by different teachers. They also compared the same teachers teaching different
programs — some examined, some unexamined. They were therefore able to
study variations in teaching by teacher and by the status of the program as
examined or not examined. The researchers found no significant variation in
patterns of teaching between the examined and unexamined courses. However,

close inspection of the study reveals that the measure of teaching effects they chose was one of quantity and proportion of teacher-initiated talk. Arguably this is an inappropriate or insufficient criterion for differentiating between teaching styles. Other criteria, such as the amount and type of groupwork or group discussion, may have yielded different results.

For some teachers, examinations are a constraint; for others they are an opportunity; but for most, they are simply there — a taken-for-granted 'fact of life' to which their teaching is routinely directed (Scarth, 1987). Much the same can be said for North American teachers' attitudes to grading and testing, especially when they themselves set those assessments. In a survey of teachers in South Dakota, Gullickson (1982) found that 89 per cent of elementary teachers and 99 per cent of secondary teachers relied on some kind of testing, and most tested at least weekly (95 per cent) or bi-weekly (98 per cent). Stiggins (1988) revealed that teachers typically spend a third or more of their professional time involved in assessment-related activities. Testing forms a significant part of the school culture. For half the teachers surveyed in Gullickson's (1984) study, these tests provided the primary basis for grading students. Herman and Dorr-Bremme (1984) found that a typical tenth grade student spends around one-eighth of their time in English and mathematics completing tests. Traub and Nagy (1988) found that 12 per cent of class time in a sample of grade 13 calculus classes in Ontario, Canada was devoted to testing. Gullickson's (1982) and Herman and Dorr-Bremme's (1984) research raised important questions about the quality of teacher-made tests and their backwash implications for teaching and learning (supported by Stiggins, 1988; Crooks, 1988; Wilson, 1989). Teacher-made tests, it was found:

- emphasize short answer and matching items;
- rarely are essay-type examinations;
- mainly require students to recall facts and terms;
- rarely ask students to translate or apply knowledge;
- are mainly limited to lower-level cognitive understanding;
- are not continuously improved by teachers in any systematic way following analysis of the quality of the items;
- are often illegible or do not assign clear directions.

Clearly, many of the criticisms commonly leveled at examinations concerning their effects on the teacher and the quality of learning that he/she offers the student, are equally attributable to classroom testing and grading. Abolition of examinations or standardized testing provides no panaceas for assessment reform.

Crooks' (1988) comprehensive review of the impact of classroom evaluation practices on students draws attention to teachers' lack of formal training in educational measurement techniques and to the likelihood that, because teachers do not follow important assessment procedures, they may often produce reports for students that are unreliable and invalid (supported by Stiggins and Bridgeford, 1985).

Testing and grading, whether internally devised by the teacher or externally imposed by the system, are deeply embedded in the culture of our schools and exert a powerful grip on teachers and their approaches to teaching. It appears that traditional practices of testing and grading are currently given excessive weight within the overall structure of student assessment and that the goal of providing a learning environment better suited to the needs of early adolescents will be met more effectively through the development of wider, more flexible, and more balanced structures of assessment.

Student Effects: The British Board of Education Report of 1911 argued that examinations rewarded the reproduction of knowledge, passivity of mind and the competitive spirit among students. In the United States, Bloom (1970) suggested that in their desire to beat traditional assessment systems, students resort to cramming and memorization. Many writers have commented that traditional types of assessment in the form of tests and examinations do not promote the critical and independent thinking that higher education institutions want (Makins, 1977; Entwistle, 1981). There is a danger, then, that traditional forms of assessment can create attitudes among students toward their learning of a cynical, calculating, instrumental nature. Deutsch (1979) notes that explicit evaluation systems can lead mark-oriented students to limit their work to what is being assessed. Achievement-conscious students may even influence their teachers, drawing them back to safer ground when their digressions and explorations appear to divert the students from their examination goal (Atkinson and Delamont, 1977; Turner, 1983).

One of the prominent effects of examinations on students — more so than tests, perhaps — is anxiety. These effects can vary depending on the student. Some students experience mild forms of anxiety that encourage them to be more competitive and perform better (Ligon, 1983). Others experience high levels of anxiety that can have debilitating effects (Sarason, 1983). Thus, anxiety can either enhance or actually prevent students from showing their true skill level. Fear of failure is one aspect of test anxiety. The actual failure itself may have very damaging effects on students' self-concept and self-worth (Mortimore and Mortimore, 1984) with high school dropout, rebelliousness, and low self-esteem as possible effects (Ratsoy, 1983).

Tests and examinations also have effects on motivation and learning habits. Students may be motivated to study for examinations and tests since they get rewarded with grades, However, evidence from studies of the impact of standardized testing suggest that motivation from such testing varies with student ability. There seems to be a curvilinear relationship between student performance and the levels or standards of a course. While high-ability students are challenged by subjects that have high standards, low-ability students may give up (Natriello, 1987). Moreover, the motivating value of credentials varies with the school's holding power over students in relation to labor-market opportunities. Where work is readily available without requirements for credentials, or where it is so scarce that credentials cannot be 'cashed in' (Hargreaves, 1989) then the extrinsic motivating power of credentials is diminished. In addition, the drive to enter more and more students for examinations presents increasing numbers of students with programs of increasing difficulty which may prove over time to be dispiriting and demotivating (Gray *et al*, 1983). Moreover, we must ask what it is students are being motivated *towards*. If traditional forms of assessment reward passive acceptance of prevailing knowledge, then students are motivated towards becoming passive learners, and towards valuing cognitive skills above all others.

This raises some important closing questions about values and goals. It has been observed that testing and grading reward excellence, help students set 'realistic' expectations (Ebel, 1980), and prepare them for a competitive society (Simon, 1972). Many people may value these goals and feel it appropriate that traditional patterns of assessment should help achieve them. But as we outlined earlier, it is important that our assessment practices conform with our broader educational goals for early adolescents in particular and for schooling more generally. The outcomes of traditional assessment patterns appear discrepant with such goals. Instead traditional patterns of assessment appear to affect students by:

- fostering an instrumental approach to learning, particularly among higher achievers;
- creating student anxiety, especially among the less able, and particularly in the context of 'one-off' examinations and tests;
- frustrating and demotivating the less able;
- promoting qualities such as individual competitiveness, which have a questionable relationship to broader educational goals.

Traditional Assessment Techniques and the Purposes of Assessment

How well do traditional patterns of assessment meet the different purposes of assessment?

Accountability: Traditional practices generally fulfill accountability demands since the marks and scores derived from tests and examinations permit comparisons among students, schools and systems. These forms of accountability have been addressed through international comparisons of students' achievements in subjects like science and mathematics. Such comparisons have both driven and justified new national goals and ambitions for education in many countries which see themselves through the figures as poor academic performers and poor economic competitors internationally. One of the newly-created National Educational Goals of the United States, for example, proclaims that by the year 2000, 'The United States will be the first in the world in mathematics and science achievement'. The Swedes, meanwhile, plan merely to be the best in Europe!! International test comparisons often do not compare like with like, however. One country may be driven by equity considerations to expose many older students to science and mathematics in learning. Another may only have a selected minority take these subjects (Barlow and Robertson,

1994). The accountability value of such comparisons, therefore, is often more symbolic than real.

Test scores have also been used for accountability purposes by comparing the achievement of schools, most controversially in the form of league tables of measured performance, so that schools can be ranked within a district or even within an entire nation as a basis for parental choice. This pattern of accountability has been pursued in a number of places such as Australia and England and Wales. Although this practice of comparing schools by their standardized test or examination results is appealing politically, it makes no allowance for the very different sorts of students for which those schools cater. Not only is this form of unweighted comparison profoundly unfair, but as Glatter (1994) shows in a study of schools in England that occupy very differing places in the league tables, the effects of those tables on teacher morale can be devastating. For instance, teachers who give solid commitment and thankless toil in schools within large, socially blighted welfare estates, still end up at the bottom of league tables where their efforts are publicly and shamefully exposed as amounting only to abject failure (compared to high-flying schools in more socially favored communities).

In response to these criticisms of crude league tables, subsequent efforts have been made to meet accountability demands by devising 'value-added' measures of school performance. Here, standardized test data are used to establish baseline measures of school performance, on which schools are then expected to improve over time. This practice compares schools against their own performance rather than the performance of others, and helps commit them to the goal of continuous improvement. In some cases, rewards such as additional funds are then allocated to 'achieving' schools that have improved their record, and sanctions or penalties may be applied to 'non-achieving' schools whose record has not improved or may even have worsened. Under the Kentucky Education Reform Act, for example, schools in the latter category have a 'distinguished educator' whose task is to begin to 'turn to school around' in less than two years, by identifying where the problems are and implementing appropriate solutions. The powers of distinguished educators are sweeping and include removing the principal, where necessary (Guskey, 1994).

Despite the advantages of value-added measures of assessment in encouraging schools to track their own performance over time, the attachment of rewards and sanctions to measured performance gives assessment such exceptionally 'high stakes' (*ibid*) that schools may be led to falsify data, intentionally depress baseline measures (to make subsequent 'improvements' easier), teach ruthlessly to the test and so on, in order to avoid negative outcomes and punitive consequences. There are also serious problems with comparing school-based improvement quotients without first adjusting their scores by intake measures to compare 'like with like' (Sammons, 1993). Even with all the problems surrounding value added and other standardized assessments, it is clear that the demands of public accountability are so great as to lead to their continued and increased use in years to come.

Certification: A second major purpose of assessment is providing students with some record of their educational achievements when they leave school. The major consumers of these certificates have traditionally been higher education institutions and employers.

Studies in Canada have found that grade 13 marks correlate quite well with first-year university average marks (Traub *et al*, 1977), and that universities still look at candidates' marks when deciding about admission (McLean, 1985). Nevertheless, even in the universities, there is some movement away from marks towards a more holistic appraisal of students (for example, information about students' extra-curricular accomplishments are often requested with the application to a higher education institution).

Similarly, employers are often more interested in personal qualities like commitment and responsibility than in high school marks (Broadfoot, 1986; McLean, 1985). Many feel that high school marks say nothing about students' commitment to work, and complain that 'most graduates have no common sense at all . . . and all they know is what they memorize from the book' (McLean, 1985). The Canadian Corporate Council of Education, for example, describes 'the combination of skills, attitudes and behaviors required to get, keep and progress on a job and to achieve the best results' as including the following:

- Self-esteem and confidence
- Honesty, integrity and personal ethics
- A positive attitude toward learning, growth and personal health
- Initiative, energy and persistence to get the job done
- The ability to set goals and priorities in work and personal life
- The ability to plan and manage time, money and other resources to achieve goals
- Accountability for actions taken
- A positive attitude toward change
- Recognition of and respect for people's diversity and individual differences
- The ability to identify and suggest new ideas to get the job done — creativity

And among 'those skills needed to work with others on a job and to achieve the best results', they list the ability to:

- Understand and contribute to the organization's goals
- Understand and work within the culture of the group
- Plan and make decisions with others and support the outcomes
- Respect the thoughts and opinions of others in the group
- Exercise 'give and take' to achieve group results
- Seek a team approach as appropriate
- Lead when appropriate, mobilizing the group for high performance. (Conference Board of Canada, 1991)

Those employers who do emphasize marks are usually ones concerned with jobs that require school-related work, such as banks, trust companies, and insurance companies. Therefore, the purpose of certification is only partly fulfilled by current assessment practices. As we showed in our discussion in chapter 5, there appears to be growing demand for certification of personal and social achievements or outcomes as well as cognitive ones, which current assessment practices are not meeting.

Diagnosis: Standardized tests and examinations, which chiefly supply terminal judgments rather than identifying specific points where assistance may be required, are not good diagnostic tools. Teacher-set tests are more helpful for diagnosing basic-skill needs and identifying gaps and shortcomings in factual, low-level cognitive learning (Crooks, 1988; Stiggins *et al*, 1989). But because they rarely focus on higher cognitive reasoning, such tests are not usually helpful in a diagnostic sense with regard to these areas of learning. Even more than this, because tests are at best loosely related to classroom tasks, what failure tends to indicate is failure at the test rather than failure at the task (Natriello, 1987).

Motivation: Motivation may be enhanced by the 'carrot and stick' principle of tests or examinations where high-achieving students are concerned. Low-achieving students, however, are prone to motivation problems arising from test or examination stress and from an excessively difficult, unbalanced program, skewed towards the academics. Broadfoot (1979) sums up the motivational problems incurred by traditional patterns of assessment this way:

> In our society . . . we choose to assess, mainly academic ability. We do not choose, by and large to assess in any formal way non-cognitive qualities such as effort, cooperation, leadership, responsibility or useful experience in extra-curricular activities such as school plays, social service units, outdoor pursuits or debating societies . . . Since assessment in such activities and abilities is not part of the formal assessment system, the influence of which permeates right through the informal assessment network, these activities do not provide an alternative source of motivation or self-valuation for pupils. In consequence, a potential source of motivation for non-academic pupils and a potential mechanism for the development of many personal qualities which most of us would regard as desirable for future members of society, are neglected.

One solution to the problem of motivation caused by underemphasizing non-academic achievements in the conventional sense, is logically, therefore, to assess them. It is to this issue of assessing, recognizing, and rewarding student achievement beyond the intellectual-cognitive domain that this chapter now turns, by reviewing alternative approaches to assessment and their implications. This review of alternative assessment, will also show how we are learning to assess more conventional 'cognitive' achievements, more 'authentically' and effectively.

Alternative Assessment Strategies

Recent years have seen the rapid emergence of a range of alternative assessment strategies. These have usually been developed to complement, rather than replace, more traditional patterns. What principles are behind this movement towards alternative forms of assessment? What needs do they address?

In the United States, the phrase used to capture these new directions in student assessment is 'authentic assessment'. Authentic assessment refers to forms of student work that reflect real-life situations and challenge students' ability to test what they have learned in those situations (Archibald and Newman, 1988; Wiggins, 1989; Sheppard, 1989). Authentic assessment:

- is based on actual performances of what we want students to be good at (for example, writing, reading, speaking, creating, doing research, solving problems);
- requires more complex and challenging mental processes;
- acknowledges more than one approach or right answer;
- emphasizes uncoached explanations and real products;
- has transparent criteria and standards;
- involves trained assessor judgment.

We will now review three of the major kinds of 'authentic' assessment and evaluate their implications for early adolescents' education. They are performance-based assessments, portfolios and personal records and records of achievement.

Performance-Based Assessment

Performance-based assessment involves assessing students in the context of classroom tasks. The tasks are designed to provide criteria and objectives that constitute a basis for the assessment. Students are assessed in the context of learning activities within the classroom. The assessment can be of a wide range of skills and knowledge — some displayed in pencil-and-paper form but others in practical, manipulative ways, or in social interaction with other students. Speaking and listening skills, presentation and organization skills, participation and leadership skills — these things are open to assessment just as much as skills displayed on paper.

Performance-based assessment has a number of distinct advantages over traditional patterns of assessment:

- It establishes a close relationship between assessment and classroom tasks. The criteria underpinning the assessment also lay the basis for developing the classroom tasks that are to be assessed. This is an important step in view of the commonly reported finding that teacher-designed tests and standardized tests have a loose relationship to the tasks students undertake in the classroom (National Institute of Education, 1979; Natriello, 1987). Performance-based assessment establishes a closer relationship between what is tested and what is taught.

- Because of the link between teaching and testing, performance-based assessment makes assessment part of the learning process.
- The establishment of a closer relationship between testing and teaching also encourages teachers to emphasize the skills being tested and the tasks being set.
- This 'backwash' effect of performance-based assessment can lead to higher order learning being assessed and being taught too.
- By being task-related, performance-based assessment has the capacity to recognize and promote a wide range of skills and achievements, including personal and practical as well as cognitive and intellectual ones. This broadening of opportunities for achievement can stimulate student motivation.
- Performance-based assessment also improves the diagnosis of student learning problems by observing these problems in context.

Through a survey of elementary and high school teachers in five school districts, Stiggins and Bridgeford (1985) documented the existing awareness and use of performance-based assessment among teachers. Their results indicate that 78 per cent of teachers report some use of structured performance tests, and almost half use them comfortably. This indicates that performance-based assessment is not an unknown or untried innovation and is already familiar to and actively used by many teachers. However, more detailed responses to questions about teachers' precise uses of such assessment indicate several areas of concern:

- The assessments are used more widely in some subject areas (especially those dealing with speaking and writing) than in others (especially mathematics and science).
- In 30–40 per cent of cases, the assessments are recorded in an unsystematic way. Scoring criteria are often not written down, judgments are frequently based on each single observation and teachers often keep only a mental record of the assessment.
- Teachers tend to develop these assessment criteria alone rather than together — creating possible sources of inconsistency and uncertainty in assessment policy. Isolation and individualism in teaching are often the source of uncertainty among teachers about their effectiveness — uncertainty which itself has been found to correlate with lower academic standards (Rosenholtz, 1989). Stiggins and Bridegeford (1985) found such uncertainty in their own study among teachers who develop and apply their assessment criteria individually. A stronger base of collegial planning for developing performance-based assessment therefore seems warranted.

- In a third of cases, performance criteria are not shared with students. This is a common difficulty with teacher-designed tests more generally (Natriello, 1982). This is often responsible for students' dissatisfaction with the assessment process, since they feel they have misunderstood the criteria on which they are being assessed. One advantage of standardized tests and public examinations is that the criteria of assessment are public and in that sense fair. If criteria of assessment are not shared with students, then students do not know how to perform well and the assessment becomes private and unfair. While this may offer some protection to students prone to anxiety, it also makes it difficult for them to achieve and may be responsible for dips in motivation if they feel they have been assessed unfairly or inappropriately (Natriello, 1982).

- Teachers commonly report problems with time in developing and applying performance-based assessments, feeling this interferes with actual teaching time. Some of the concerns about time raise important resource issues, especially where time for collegial development of performance-based assessment is concerned. This might be an appropriate focus for professional development days, for instance. Time to administer the assessment also requires a conceptual leap — that this assessment is part of learning, not additional to it. But observing the activities of one group may still require that another teacher sometimes teaches the rest of the class. This is more difficult to achieve in isolated classroom settings with short bursts of time devoted to specific-subject learning. More integrated learning settings where teachers teach together, of the kinds described in previous chapters, are likely to provide the flexibility required for performance-based assessment.

  Teachers might also use some of their preparation time to assess and work with individuals and small groups, while a covering teacher takes responsibility for the rest of the class (A. Hargreaves, 1994). This strategy could be justified if the balance of assessment demands was to shift away from the paper-and-pencil tests and batch-marking of assignments that currently consume a great deal of preparation time, especially at the secondary school level. If one of the purposes of preparation time is to evaluate students' work and if some of the burden of assessment is to shift toward evaluating that work in the context of classroom tasks, then use of some preparation time for performance-based assessment in the classroom would be appropriate. For that case to be made effectively, however, there needs to be a genuine shift in the balance of assessment priorities; not simply an addition of performance-based assessment to the existing assessment load.

- A final difficulty not mentioned by Stiggins and Bridgeford (1985), but an emerging concern in current research on the implementation of active learning (Neufeld, 1991), is that there are dangers in over-assessment, in multiplying teachers' responsibilities for effective, structured observation. Many moments in the classroom need to be left relatively loose to enable teachers to provide care, to settle their class for a story, or to console a particular child. Such actions are an essential part of the teacher's work, especially at the elementary school level (Fullan and Hargreaves, 1991). Evidence from Neufeld's study suggests that the time demands of performance-based assessment can lead teachers to 'steal' time from elsewhere — particularly the 'slack' time where they provide care for their students. Care, we have argued, is an important human quality that students still very much need in early adolescence. Overscheduled classrooms can become as frantic and fruitless as overscheduled families. This suggests that while performance-based assessment has important advantages, it is best used in moderation, as part of a broad repertoire of assessment strategies.

Portfolios and Personal Records

Portfolios are widely used among elementary school teachers and in certain secondary school subjects, like English, as a way of collecting and selecting students' work to communicate their achievements to themselves, their teachers, and their parents. In Britain, a number of secondary schools have used systems of what are known as pupils' personal records for similar purposes. These records typically provide students with opportunities to record experiences and achievements significant to them, in a continuous way. The records are usually owned by the students but may be shared and discussed with teachers if students wish. They are normally written in scheduled time devoted for this purpose. They may be written on blank sheets of paper, in response to optional prompt words or key questions, or on a series of cards with titles like 'Hobbies' or 'Working With Other'. It is usual for personal records to be compiled in files or folders and for pictures, examples of work or other materials, of importance to the student to be added to the collection. On leaving school, the records are the students' property, and can be shown to potential employers if they wish (Stansbury, 1980).

There are some differences between portfolios and personal records. Portfolios tend to collect together samples of student work from across the curriculum, demonstrating a range of experiences and achievements. Personal records tend to have more of a personal and social emphasis and are often compiled in scheduled time, but may also be used in connection with work experience/co-op education (Further Education Curriculum, 1982) or outdoor and residential experience (Hargreaves *et al*, 1988), to document and reflect on the experience in which the student has been involved. Notwithstanding these differences between portfolios and personal records, however, they also address a number of common purposes:

- They seek to motivate less able students by providing them with 'something to show for their efforts' beyond what might otherwise be a dispiriting set of grades and marks.
- They provide students with opportunities to declare their identity, to document and display things of importance to them — another source of motivation.
- They offer students opportunity to reflect upon their experiences and achievements in and out of school and thereby to take more responsibility for those experiences and achievements.
- They stimulate and give some form of recognition to outcomes and achievements beyond the academic domain.
- They provide more rounded evidence of student competence and success to external publics like parents and employers.

Some of the limitations and drawbacks of portfolios and personal records are:

- They are not themselves a form of assessment. They simply supply a record, a wider range of evidence, as a basis for educational assessment. Assessment is involved in selecting items to be included in a portfolio or personal record. Assessment is also involved in judging the quality and characteristics of portfolios and personal records. But these things themselves are not forms of assessment as such.
- Portfolios and personal records may be of value for the individual student, but they cannot easily be collated at a group level. They are too cumbersome, too divergent in form and compiled under too many different circumstances for that.
- Portfolios tend not to be helpful for accountability purposes — they are hard to score especially in ways on which evaluators can consistently and reliably agree (Koretz, 1994), and they are unwieldly to process for large numbers of students and schools. This is not an argument against portfolios, but does point to their limitations from the point of bureaucratic accountability to the system.
- Because of their cumbersome nature, personal records in particular have been found to have less value for employers than first hoped, thus detracting from some of their motivational benefits (Swales, 1980).
- Portfolios can have adverse as well as positive backwash effects on how teachers teach. There can be actual or felt pressure to value or teach only those things that can be displayed or exhibited. Important learning that is more private and contemplative, or less glossy and glitzy may be given less emphasis. Teaching and learning may become like living a particular life to have the right kind of resumé. Superficial imagery may diminish rather than enhance the substance of learning.

In summary, personal records and portfolios can provide evidence of a wider range of student achievements than conventional assessments often allow.

These portfolios and personal records can be a source of pride for the student and provide opportunities for reflection on learning and achievement. They can be valuable in communicating student achievements and learning activities to parents but are less successful in this respect where employers are concerned.

The process of compiling and reflecting on portfolios and personal records can itself be a valuable kind of formative assessment, providing a basis for dialogue between students, teachers and parents about progress. The key value of portfolios and personal records, then, may well reside less in the products themselves than in the formative processes of assessment which organize the ways in which they are compiled. Some process of summarizing these voluminous records succinctly would also appear to be helpful — both from the point of view of external clients like employers in search of usable information that can be scanned relatively swiftly, and from the point of view of students themselves who will be stimulated to reflect on their achievements as they are called upon to summarize them. This leads us to our third alternative pattern of assessment: records of achievement.

Records of Achievement

Records of achievement, formerly known as 'pupil profiles', first emerged in Scotland in the 1970s as ways of documenting and describing the qualities, skills and achievements of students destined to leave school without any other certificates or qualifications (Scottish Council for Research in Education, 1977). The records were meant to provide employers with useful, succinct information about students' qualities and achievements and to enhance students' self-knowledge motivation, and goal-setting.

By the 1980s, many locally developed schemes for records of achievement had sprung up to the point where, with ministerial encouragement, records of achievement were advocated for use in all English and Welsh secondary schools by the early 1990s (Department of Education and Science, 1984). Although such records currently take many different forms, in practice all of them provide a method of presenting broad yet succinct information on students' abilities, skills and achievements across a range of assessments (Murphy and Torrance, 1988). The distinctive features of records of achievements are:

- They document a range of student outcomes and achievements within and beyond the academic domain — whether in the form of tick-the-box grids of qualities, item banks or checklists that list skills and achievements, or descriptive prose statements of actual achievements which signal underlying personal qualities.
- They present this information in a sufficiently succinct form that can be used and interpreted easily by parents, employers and other clients.
- They are compiled not on a one-off basis at the end of the student's

schooling but through a process of continuous one-to-one review of progress throughout secondary school. The final school-leaving record is but the last in a series of statements that a student develops in consultation and negotiation with his/her teacher over the course of his or her education. The formative process of review is at least as important as the final summative statement. It is a way of monitoring and reflecting on progress, securing greater student commitment to learning, improving educational diagnosis and stimulating changes in curriculum and teaching to meet student needs.

• Many of the assessments, particularly those of personal and social achievements are not just documented by teachers *about* students, but developed by teachers and students together through one-to-one conferencing. Records of achievement are designed to involve students in the assessment process and thereby in the learning process, too.

In one particularly sophisticated version of records of achievement, the Oxford Certificate of Educational Achievement (1984), the Record was divided into three components — E, G and P. The 'E' component documented all publicly recognized qualifications and certificates attained by the student, including public examination results, music and swimming certificates, and first aid awards. The 'G' component documented the outcomes in terms of skills, knowledge and attitudes attained to particular levels in a number of subject areas — which were documented through performance-based assessment. Lastly, the 'P' component consisted of a succinct prose statement which recorded personal and social achievements and experiences in a positive way, following periodic discussions between students and teachers who knew them well over the course of their schooling. This certificate and the processes underlying it were meant to capture and stimulate the diversity of experiences and achievements that are formally valued within secondary education.

Records of achievement have been designed and developed to fulfill a number of educational purposes, although there is considerable argument as to whether these purposes are complementary or contradictory (Hargreaves, 1989; Broadfoot *et al*, 1988):

• They recognize the whole range of students' achievements, not just academic ones.
• By recognizing other achievements, they stimulate greater emphasis to be given to them in the curriculum. If you assess and record something, you have to teach it, too!
• By widening the definition of achievement, they provide greater opportunities for genuine, not contrived success.
• They help students develop self-awareness and independence by giving them opportunity to declare and record things of importance to them.

- They encourage students to take more responsibility for their own learning by involving them in the assessment process.
- By providing teachers with more detailed information about their students, they improve teachers' capacity to diagnose student learning needs effectively.
- When these records are compiled within subject areas, they integrate assessment into the learning process itself, giving teachers helpful information and students constructive feedback to improve performance.
- By providing feedback on student response to the curriculum and the way it is taught, they stimulate teachers to generate changes in curriculum and teaching *of their own volition*. They stimulate teacher-based and school-based change in curriculum and teaching as teachers become more aware of and seek to respond to their students' needs.
- When used in the context of home-room time, they provide students with the right to periodic reviews of progress and personal development with one teacher who knows them well. They provide content as well as a context for personal care to be given to students by their home-room teachers.
- When used in the context of school subjects, they can organize and give coherence to the reporting system. They can move reports away from highly condensed and stylized summaries of progress, written at infrequent intervals, often under conditions of great stress. These reports can be replaced by periodic statements at the end of each unit of work which are discussed with students and sent home to their parents along with examples of work done on that unit, all at the same time. In this way, the formative process of assessment involved in records of achievement can be used to supply parents with a continuous flow of information about their children's progress, perhaps also including opportunities for parents to respond in writing or in person to that progress (or its absence) where appropriate.

At their best, records of achievement can integrate assessment with learning, with personal care, and with the reporting system, involving students, their teachers, and their parents as partners in the continuous process of learning.

Records of achievement are not without their difficulties. Every solution brings with it new problems and records of achievement are no exception. Some of the key areas requiring attention are:

- *Professional Development Needs.* Just because teachers can teach classes does not mean they know how to counsel and conference with individuals. In our own evaluation of secondary schools paying attention to alternative forms of assessment and reporting, teachers said it was often presumed they would already know how to write new anecdotal reports, yet they found writing such reports immensely challenging (Hargreaves *et al*, 1993). The skills of conferencing, anecdotal report card writing, and other new kinds of assessment 'literacy' need focused attention in professional development training for teachers.

- *Student Development Needs.* Students also need to develop effective skills in conferencing and self-evaluation. It cannot be assumed they already have them. Clumsiness, gaucheness and rudeness from students must be expected in the early days of records of achievement as students brag, feel shy, underestimate themselves, lack discretion, speak too bluntly and commit all kinds of personal gaffes. Possession of the personal, social and reflective skills required for effective conferencing and self-evaluation should not be seen as essential prerequisites for implementing records of achievement, however. They are in part also an outcome of records of achievement.

- *Time Crunches.* Compiling records of achievement, especially through individual conferencing can take inordinate amounts of time. The time crunches involved in implementing records of achievement can, however, be mitigated to some extent. Peer assessment can sometimes supplement teacher assessment, for instance (Munby, 1989). More importantly, for this system to be workable, the kind of core grouping arrangements described in chapter 5 seem almost essential, reducing the number of students per year with which a teacher has contact to a reasonable number. Within such a core grouping system, flexibility of time can also be created by other members of the teaching team releasing one teacher to work with individuals while they take charge of the rest of the group.

- *Temptations of Control.* Sometimes, what is recorded and assessed can be proxies for behavioral control and classroom management that suit the teachers' interest, rather than providing opportunities for students' own developmental needs. For instance, systems we have seen that rate students in how well they 'can bring books and equipment to class' tend to be seen by students not only as controlling, but also as trivial and demeaning (Hargreaves *et al*, 1993).

- *Dangers of Surveillance.* Records of achievement widen the areas of student performance and development that are open to assessment. Not just performance, but emotions, behavior and personal relationships are all now subject to evaluation, appraisal and intervention; to the teacher's all-seeing eye. Of course, a chief aim of records of achievement is to recognize, reward and record achievements in the personal and social domain. This means that teachers will need to know what happens there if they are to do their students credit. But there are times when this proper concern can extend to unnecessary invasions of privacy. There is a sinister side to students being open to assessment wherever they go, whatever they do (Hargreaves *et al*, 1988). For these reasons, it is essential that rules and understandings are clear about what can and should be recorded. That the ownership of the record of achievement rests ultimately with the student may also be a vital protection against invasions of privacy.

These difficulties are real. They may well explain why, in our evaluation of secondary school restructuring pilot projects in Ontario, Canada, we found that while student assessment was one of the most frequently chosen initiatives on which schools wished to focus (83 per cent in all), almost all the schools developed new systems of judgment where students remained objects of assessment and evaluation rather than creating assessment systems that made students participants in the process (Hargreaves *et al*, 1993). Indeed, we found that efforts at alternative assessment could sometimes turn into gridlocked processes of highly detailed and unending judgment — ones which continued to exclude students from decisions about the learning process and which consumed immense amounts of teachers' time. Much has yet to be achieved in terms of involving students more widely in self-evaluation and in evaluation of their courses and curriculum. Yet such developments would be welcome because there is good evidence to suggest that they can bring great benefits for student motivation and teacher enthusiasm as teachers learn more about their students and become more involved with them as partners in the learning process (Broadfoot *et al*, 1988).

Summary

This chapter has pointed to the importance of establishing a broad and balanced range of assessment strategies in order to capture the many different purposes of assessment, such as those of accountability, certification, student motivation and effective diagnosis. We have reviewed literature which suggests that some assessment strategies are more widely used than others and that these, in the form of grades, tests and examinations, recognize, reward and give emphasis to intellectual-cognitive achievements above all others, narrowing possibilities for success and creating threats to student motivation.

We then described and reviewed a range of alternative assessment strategies including performance-based assessment, portfolios and records of achievement which recognize, reward and give emphasis to a wider range of achievements. These alternatives increase the likelihood of boosting student-motivation. Such alternative strategies used in conjunction with existing ones, we suggested, also help provide an environment of care and support for the early adolescent, they improve the quality of teacher diagnosis, and they integrate assessment more effectively with the learning process and the reporting system. This gives greater coherence to the young adolescent's education and helps schools in their efforts to meet the needs of young people at this important stage of their development.

Many of the alternative assessment strategies described are already widely used. But they are often developed and used by teachers in isolation, and the criteria are not sufficiently shared with students. Assessment drives the curriculum. If the needs of young adolescents are to be met by a coherent, relevant program and by a caring system of help and support among a community of teachers who know these students well, the assessment system should be planned to support the required programs and the required processes of care. We have seen that inflexible assessment systems undermine many of our curriculum and guidance objectives. School reform efforts provide important opportunities to change that, to develop an assessment system that is primarily designed to support the curriculum and guidance needs of early adolescence. Integrating the different aspects of schooling such as curriculum, assessment and student support, matters greatly for how well students in the transition years are educated. Together, these things provide an essential context for how effectively transition years students can be taught. These issues of teaching and learning are the focus of our next chapter.

9   Teaching and Learning

If schools are going to be transformed to meet the needs of early adolescents, curriculum and assessment reform are only part of the puzzle. Ultimately, the only curriculum and assessment that count are the ones experienced by the student — the curriculum and assessment in use. How do teachers and students transform resources, timetables and ideas into teaching and learning? As we, and many other writers, have mentioned, changing grouping patterns, school organization or curriculum outcomes is unlikely to have any major positive impact on classrooms or students unless there are changes in how teachers teach as well (Leithwood *et al*, 1988; Slavin, 1987c; Epstein, 1990).

Teaching, like all other human endeavors, is not static. The process for shaping the next generation is evolving, along with the society as a whole. The nature and role of teaching are inextricably tied to the expectations that we have for our students, to our understanding of the way that humans learn and to our beliefs about how adults, particularly teachers, can guide young people in their learning. We have already discussed many of the increased demands on our society and its young people. As a number of authors have told us very eloquently — schools of the future are going to have to bear little resemblance to those of the past (Schlechty, 1990; Fullan, 1993) and teachers will have to teach very differently (McLaughlin and Talbert, 1993). This may be hard to accept when little in our basic school structures has changed for a century or more. Nevertheless, the forces of change impacting upon our schools seem to be reaching a critical mass and schools, like countries and corporations, are finally beginning to contemplate fundamental restructuring. At least part of the impetus for school reform comes from a recognition that the modernistic model of specialization and standardization that has been rejected in other organizations and workplaces is also being questioned in education. It is no longer sufficient for schools to provide students with basic skills. In addition to the foundation skills of literacy and numeracy, students generally, not just a few, will need to attain more sophisticated skills like complex, critical thinking, novel problem-solving, weighing alternatives, making informed judgments, developing flexible identities, working independently and in groups and discerning appropriate courses of action in ambiguous situations (Earl and Cousins, 1995; Peterson and Knapp, 1993). The challenge for schools is to capitalize on new teaching methods and learning environments that are built upon what we now know about human learning and development, in order to prepare our adolescent students to cope with the increased demands the society that lay ahead.

Students in these years of transition need to experience and have access to more of the emerging strategies of teaching and learning. We have seen that young adolescents are very active physically, emotionally and intellectually as they try out their growing bodies and abilities. They are highly aware of the importance of human relationships and are consequently, preoccupied with the struggle for social engagement. They are insecure and unsure of their power and capacity to adapt to and succeed in the larger world. Yet researchers have shown repeatedly that the teaching which young adolescents have typically experienced demands passive absorption rather than active engagement; puts intellect and cognition above emotions and care; subordinates real life and relevance to textbook coverage and academic content and denies students independence in the interests of control.

As we understand more about how people learn and what makes teaching effective, we are also finding better ways to address the needs of young adolescents as they encounter a world in turmoil and trauma. This chapter describes some emerging and influential conceptions of how children learn; it explores their implications for teaching and classroom practice; it also look at how well these strategies can help prepare young adolescents for their changing social realities in a complex and uncertain post-modern world. We have no wish to make teachers feel guilty by defining a 'perfect' set of teaching strategies, which turn out to be unworkable in their classrooms. Creative teaching strategies will not 'take' well where standardized testing requires teachers to teach otherwise, where teachers work in isolation within their own classes, or where the timetable limits teachers to short lessons with too much time spent on starting and clearing up and no flexibility to work beyond the bell. The familiar scenario of exhorting teachers and 'in-servicing' them in new teaching strategies, when implementation is impossible because the structures of schooling remain unchanged, is a sad one of repeated failure. Structural and cultural change in schools that serve young adolescents are imperative for successful change in classroom practices. All the same, teaching and learning won't improve unless there is a clear image of what better practices look like and unless there is an understanding of the principles which make such teaching and learning work well. So, while we don't itemize an endless list of alternative teaching and learning strategies, we do want to address the principles teachers should adopt when they consider pedagogical alternatives.

Learning for Understanding

The human species is the only one that can reflect on its own existence. The mystery of the human mind and how it works has therefore fascinated us for a long time. Even with this centuries-old interest, it is sobering to realize how little we really know about human learning and how difficult it is to translate new knowledge into practice.

Throughout this century, the dominant conceptions of how learning works have been incremental and behaviorist. Schools have operated as if learning can be separated into specific, discrete skills and facts that can be acquired bit by bit, in an orderly fashion (Cole, 1990). Traditional school practice has been a matter of assimilating, usually by rote, drill and practice of correct procedures and facts, and the rules and content of the disciplines in order to strengthen correct mental bonds and habits (Peterson and Knapp, 1993).

In the past thirty years, however, a quiet revolution in the social sciences has challenged the model of learning underpinning our schools. Cognitive psychologists have proposed a constructivist view of learning that sees it as not linear but interactive. They hold that there is a real world that we experience but the meaning we give it is imposed by us, rather than existing in the world independently of us. There are many ways to structure the world, and there are many meanings or perspectives for any event or concept (Duffy and Jonassen, 1992). Working on the principle that things should make sense and constructivists have suggested that learning is a process where students take in information, interpret it, connect it to what they already know, and, if necessary, reorganize their understanding to accommodate it (Shepard, 1991). This means that students construct their own understanding based on new experiences that enlarge their existing knowledge. Gardner (1985) describes it this way:

> . . . human subjects do not come to tasks as empty slates: they have expectations and well-structured schemata within which they approach diverse materials . . . the organism, with its structures already prepared for stimulation, itself manipulates and otherwise reorders the information it freshly encounters. (p. 126)

One of the profound discoveries that has occurred as part of this exploration of learning as construction is the surprising ignorance and shallow understanding of ideas, knowledge and concepts that students have, not just in one discipline, country, or level of school, but everywhere the studies have been done (White, 1992). Students may be able to reproduce information they have memorized but they are much less competent when operating under novel conditions that require them to apply it. In *The Unschooled Mind* Gardner (1991) argues that learning for understanding involves much more than producing a 'correct' response. When an individual has learned something so there is deep understanding, that person can take knowledge, concepts, skills and facts and apply them in new and appropriate situations (Gardner, 1994). Schools are full of examples of students who can plug numbers into a formula, but cannot use the formula to solve a problem they have not encountered before; who study physics at university but believe that where there is no air, there is no gravity; who can express a complex phenomenon they have studied in school but give only simplistic answers when something complex happens in the real world. Gardner (1991) describes what he calls 'the five-year-old' or 'unschooled' mind that is developed without any formal education. It is a wonderful mind which has theories about everything it encounters — theories of matter, life, self, others, etc. Unfortunately, many of the ideas that are deeply engraved into our minds from early experience are wrong. As Gardner (1994) evocatively puts it:

> . . . in school the engraving gets covered with a very fine powder — the stuff that school is trying to teach. If you peek into the mind in school, it looks pretty good because you just see the powder. But beneath the powder, the engraving is unaffected. And when you leave the school and slam the door for the last time, the powder blows away and the initial engraving is still there. (p. 27)

Without commitment to genuine understanding, shallow learning remains until the need for it passes (for example, when the examination is over) and it can be discarded. 'School knowledge' helps one to progress in school but its relation to life beyond school is not well understood by the student, and perhaps not even by the teacher. People derive their everyday views from experience, and even though the views may not be accurate in relation to school knowledge, they often serve their holders very well (White, 1992). Little wonder that much of what is taught in schools is not retained by students.

But, aspiring to learning for understanding conjures up a whole new image of the pieces in the teaching/learning puzzle. If the adults of tomorrow are going to have deep understanding, the teaching of today must contain many more pieces, intricately connected to one another. In particular, this kind of teaching recognizes many kinds of knowledge, intelligences and learning styles; sees prior knowledge as a critical starting point for acquiring new knowledge; focuses on higher-order learning and thinking; gives attention to the social and emotional nature of learning; ties learning to real life and provides a genuine role for students in their own learning. Researchers world-wide are exploring each of these pieces to try to understand the many different facets of this more complex, differentiated and inclusive conception of teaching and learning.

Different Forms of Knowledge, Intelligence and Ways of Learning

Leinhardt (1992) draws attention to different kinds of knowledge and skills that we expect students to develop. Within each discipline, there is a unique arrangement of facts, concepts, notations and patterns of reasoning.

Learning for understanding involves connecting information and transporting general principles across disciplines in all kinds of ways; some well tried and familiar, others more novel and imaginative. Students need to have both kinds of knowledge — actions and skills, as well as concepts and principles, so they can connect strategic action with specific content knowledge, in situations that, for them at least, are new and challenging. They need a knowledge base with interconnections in their head, strategies or routines to access the knowledge during problem-solving, and dispositions or habits of mind that move them to draw on their various intellectual resources as each situation arises (Prawat, 1989).

When we value many forms of knowledge, this calls into question our most basic beliefs about the nature of intelligence. Gardner (1993) has challenged the view that intelligence is unidimensional and immutable. We do not arrive in this world with a fixed amount of intelligence and no single scale can capture all the various forms of intelligence. Gardner defines intelligence as the ability to solve problems or fashion products of consequence in particular settings. He has identified seven intelligences (so far): musical, bodily-kinesthetic, logical-mathematical, linguistic, spatial, interpersonal, and intrapersonal. In his view, we are all born with the potential to develop a multiplicity of intelligences that can be taught and learned. Although these intelligences may begin with raw ability, they can be developed and nurtured through instruction and practice. Each of us has our own unique pattern of intelligences that we are constantly developing and routinely using in endless combinations. Schools, however, have concentrated largely on only two (logical-mathematical and linguistic) and undervalued the rest. For the most part, schools have accepted a singular concept of intelligence that emphases ranking above accomplishment; what is easily measured above messy complexity; individual above group learning; and tracking (or streaming) above heterogeneous grouping of students. This attention to relative position on a fixed scale has obscured our capacity to see that all students learn and to identify each student's unique level of understanding, rather than just his or her relative position. The capacity for thoughtfulness is widespread, not just the exclusive capacity of those who rank high. Mobilizing multiple forms of intelligence is one way that society can unlock our human diversity to accomplish a broader range of goals (Wolf *et al*, 1991).

The term 'learning styles' captures many theories about the different ways students approach and interact with material in order to understand it. There are references to cognitive styles (Messick, 1969), mediation abilities (Gregorc, 1979), conceptual styles, learning types (McCarthy, 1980) and learning style elements (Dunn and Dunn, 1982). Basically all these theories contend that people see and make sense of the world in different ways. They consider different aspects of the environment; approach problems from different perspectives; rely on different cues; and process information in different but personally consistent ways. It is this combination of how people perceive and how they process that forms the uniqueness of learning style, an individual's most comfortable way to learn. Any group of young adolescents, will contain a wide spectrum of different styles of learning — those who need to touch, taste and smell things; the talkers who seem to only be able to think out loud; or the quiet child who takes the book away and ponders the ideas before speaking. Each of them explores their world in their own characteristic terms. For the most part, schools have neither honored the existence of different styles of learning nor have they attempted to tailor teaching activities to these different styles. Although proponents of learning styles believe that it is important for teachers to pay attention to the unique styles of their students, they routinely caution against misusing learning style concepts, by turning these ideas into stereotypes to pigeon-hole individuals, or to match young people directly to educational environments that reflect their strengths. Rather, teachers should ensure that they use a range of teaching approaches to allow all students to benefit from opportunities to learn in ways that both capitalize on their strengths and try to mitigate their weaknesses.

Prior Knowledge

If students are going to construct their own understanding of new material and ideas, how and how well they do it is very much dependent on their prior knowledge. The impact of prior knowledge is not a matter of readiness or developmental stages of understanding. It is an issue of depth, interconnectedness and access (Leinhardt, 1992). The knowledge and beliefs held by a student are a complex network of ideas, facts, principles and actions that are more than building blocks of information. They can facilitate, inhibit or transform learning in productive or dysfunctional ways. When they are accurate, students' pre-existing beliefs about a topic facilitate learning and provide a natural starting point to teaching. Students' misconceptions, however, can distort the new learning in dramatic ways (Brophy, 1992).

If the constructivist model is a fair representation of how children learn, it is not surprising that they often have difficulty in school. Indeed, the mismatches between what children know and bring from their experience and what curricula assume they know are at the root of much underachievement. This is part of the problem of relevance. Not only do students find their schooling irrelevant to their lives, they also form distorted and confused understandings of the material in the curriculum because it is not consistent with or does not connect with their prior learning. This is particularly true as many classrooms include students from a wide range of backgrounds.

Higher order thinking

Once the exclusive purview of high-ability or gifted students, higher-order thinking is being recognized as necessary for all students, since all learning requires us to make sense of what we are trying to learn (Costa, 1991). As Resnick and Resnick (1992) describe it:

> ... the kinds of mental processes associated with thinking are not restricted to an advanced or 'higher-order' stage of mental development. Instead, thinking and reasoning are intimately involved in successfully

learning even elementary levels of reading, mathematics and other school subjects . . . Learning the three Rs involves important components of inference, judgment and active mental construction. The traditional view that the basics can be taught as routine basic skills, with thinking to follow later, can no longer guide our education.

This notion that thinking is not a product of, but a prerequisite for acquiring basic skills has spawned many theories and observations about the nature of thinking. Marzano (1992) has proposed that learning is the product of five dimensions or types of thinking: positive attitudes and perceptions about learning; thinking involved in acquiring and integrating knowledge; thinking involved in extending and refining knowledge; thinking involved in using knowledge meaningfully; and, productive habits of mind. These types of thinking do not function in isolation or in a linear order. They interact, bounce off one another, and roll around. Sometimes they work in concert, sometimes they create dissonance. This all happens at lightning speed, as the thinker grapples with the messy, indeterminate problems and decisions of real life in our uncertain world, where simply using a formula isn't sufficient.

In the same vein, Barell (1991) argues that a key outcome of schooling should be thoughtfulness. In his conception, thoughtfulness combines two aspects of our lives — intellectual or cognitive operations plus feelings, attitudes and dispositions. To be thoughtful is to be full of thought in a cognitive sense. It is also to be considerate and reflective in dispositional terms (Clark, 1996). The cognitive operations are attempts to search for meaning in complex, non-routine situations, to be adventurous with solutions or interpretations and, through it all, to attempt to make reasonable and worthwhile choices and judgments. Thoughtfulness integrates thinking with feeling. It is a union of heart and mind; an important component of the learning and development of young adolescents who are striving to find their identity and a place where they belong.

Perkins (1995) provides a number of examples of what he calls 'weak' thinking or reasoning. His research shows that when confronted with questions about everyday issues, people generally do not reason well, they make a whole range of logical errors, and they are prone to 'my-side' bias. This propensity is just as common among people with high IQs as all others. Although many of his subjects were cognitively capable of generating more balanced and extensive ideas when questioned further, until that point, they were content that they had thought enough about the issues and were satisfied with their answers. Quality of thinking is not a natural consequence of ability. Major shortfalls of thinking in school and in life often occur for students of all kinds as a result. All too often, we assume that high ability is synonymous with wisdom and good judgment. Instead, it is clear that all students need to learn how to use their minds well; to investigate, invent, challenge, reconsider, and sustain their attention to the task as they interpret the information around them and decide how to make sense of it.

Teaching and Learning as Social Phenomena

One of the most radical ideas to emerge from a constructivist approach to teaching and learning is their social nature. Psychology, as it has developed in Western cultures, has operated on the assumption that the proper object of study is the individual operating in a sociocultural vacuum. Because these approaches, grounded in individualism, have come to dominate psychology, few theories have explicated how mental processes are inherently linked to cultural, historical and institutional settings (Wertsch, 1991). Recent work in the area has been inspired by the noted Russian social scientist, Vygotsky, who theorized that human learning takes place in the social situations of people's lives. In his view, learning is not solitary nor is it prescribed by genetic or developmental preconditions. It happens as a result of activity in the external conditions of life. Young people learn by being and becoming part of the surrounding collective culture and by aligning their personal understanding with this wider cultural view (Davydov, 1995). When people interact with one another, they learn from the group and they influence the group as well. They are constantly in the process of creating and transforming their understanding as they share ideas among members of the group (Leinhardt, 1992). The collective knowledge of the group is greater than the knowledge of any single member, and has a powerful role in shaping the thinking, activities and skills of its members. Because learning in individuals is the product of the social context in which they live, and is mediated by the signs and symbols of the surrounding culture, students are potentially smarter in groups than they are on their own. They learn best when they learn how to think together — to challenge one another's assumptions and build new understandings. For teachers this offers many kinds of challenges. In their roles of director and guide of learning, teachers will need to use the social milieu in which young people live to construct understanding (Davydov, 1995). But groups of adolescents with all their energy, sexuality and bravado are often scary to teachers. Teachers may even have to struggle to overcome their own unresolved issues and sometimes are loathe to let go of their power and trust the group. At the same time schools include students who reflect many different social and cultural realms, each with its own history, values and language. Teachers need to find ways to bridge the differences and help students make connections.

Making Teaching and Learning Like Real Life

It should be clear by now that students are the architects, engineers and builders of their own understanding. But teaching and schooling have mainly not been organized to recognize and capitalize on how young people actually learn. Children's construction of their own understanding has taken place on shallow foundations, upon the unyielding rock of our existing schooling system. Young people, indeed all people, learn well by paying attention to their learning, monitoring their own understanding, capitalizing on their strengths and working on their weaknesses (White, 1992; Perkins and Blythe, 1994). Schools have to search for better ways to engage this kind of learning.

Learning can be particularly effective not just when it relates to life beyond school, but also when it is very similar to or an integral part of 'real life' itself. In chapter 6, we referred to Woods' (1993) concept of verisimilitude, where what he calls 'critical events' in teaching and learning, are close to and often integrated with other kinds of learning and achievement outside the school, and gain recognition within that wider world. Woods vividly portrays a school archeology project conducted in conjunction with a real (female) archeologist; the production by primary school children of a book which they wrote, illustrated and then commercially published for other children to read; an elaborate video constructed for and with the wider community, and other projects besides. In all the critical events that Woods described:

> The learning that takes place is real learning. It builds on (students') own needs and relevancies, and their existing cognitive and affective structures. There is a strong emphasis on reality, on a real problem or issues of importance or value, on constructing situations that are the same as those they purport to represent, on using real professionals, on collecting first-hand evidence and materials, on doing things oneself, on having a realistic aim.

Critical events in teaching and learning can achieve exhilarating 'peak experiences' and senses of real breakthrough and achievement for students (Woods, 1994). They are authentic achievement writ large. Creating them requires release from demands of content coverage and flexibility in scheduling and school structure more generally. But above and beyond these essential structural supports, successful 'critical events' also require a 'critical agent', 'a teacher, or teachers, with the issues, commitment, faith, skills and relationships to conceptualize and plan the project, orchestrate it, promote it and bring it to fruition, often in the face of considerable difficulties'. Such teachers, Woods continues, have strong commitment. They feel 'that teaching is central to their lives, that their identities are enhanced by their work, that it makes them feel "whole" and "themselves"'.

Verisimilitude, or making teaching and learning more like real life, need not always be so intense and dramatic. Many teachers of writing have long recognized that writing should have a purpose and an audience that give it more meaning and value than a disembodied school assignment (Barnes, 1976). Writing letters to newspapers, communicating with celebrities, constructing stories that are then read to younger children, and corresponding by electronic mail with young people in other cities and countries all add purpose and reality to the task of writing. Other examples of verisimilitude as a principle of learning include cooperative school-work education (too often confined to 'lower ability' vocational students rather than available to all), outdoor education, environmental science, sharing data collection and analysis by computer with other schools, learning politics through student courts, and so on. There are many ways to introduce the 'reality principle' into teaching and learning, some ambitious, others quite modest. Teachers, need not be daunted by the prospect of suspending an entire curriculum or changing their whole teaching, in order to experiment with them.

Assessment as Learning

Self-monitoring one's own knowledge and thinking, and self-assessment are at the heart of effective learning. For example, in order to read, students use their personal knowledge to construct meaning from the texts that confront them. They also use self-monitoring and self-correcting strategies to guide this process (Cole, 1990). Only when they realize that they don't understand something and have ways of fixing it can they move from reading words to comprehending ideas in text. This is also true of adults. How often have you read a paragraph, having understood every word individually only to realize at the end that you did not understand the ideas? This is self-monitoring. Presumably, then you reread, searched for more information, asked someone for clarification, tried to anchor the passage within the broader text or whatever other approaches might help you increase your understanding (Earl and Cousins, 1995). Learning is a search for meaning. It is impossible for anyone to learn without recognizing and investigating what they do and do not understand, what does and does not make sense. That is why we have emphasized assessment as an integral part of learning. Effective assessment gives students the tools to ask reflective questions and search for what they need to extend their learning.

Actively engaging students in learning also brings into play questions of motivation and attribution. What are the conditions that help students become their own best monitors and take a responsible and active role in what and how they learn? What is it that makes some students embrace challenges, while others avoid them? What motivates some to invest a great deal of themselves in learning, while others give only a little? Developing student motivation is a complex and dynamic process that depends on many conditions.

Students have different beliefs about why they succeed and fail (for example, ability, luck, effort, task difficulty). These beliefs influence their motivation. Sometimes, students' beliefs are deeply embedded in cultural values. In American society, for example, students who are 'bright' are expected to get it and those who are 'dull' are assumed to lack the ability for ever learning certain material. Asian societies, on the other hand, portray learning as gradual and incremental, to be acquired over a long time, with considerable effort and persistence (Stevenson and Stigler, 1991).

But motivation does not reside only in the student and the culture. Teachers can be key catalysts of student motivation (Brophy, 1987). As we mentioned earlier, motivation is a form of achievement in itself, not just something that students bring with them. Developing this achievement should be a key responsibility for schools. If, as Prawat (1989) proposes, learning can be presented as either a means to an end that gets the job done as quickly as possible or as a way to increase competence, with learning the end in itself, the way that teachers characterize learning can exert a strong influence on students' motivation. People who are engaged in their work are driven by four essential needs — for success, understanding, self-expression and involvement with or caring for others (Strong, Silver and Robinson, 1995). These provide an excellent basis for teachers to structure their work with young adolescents who are curious, imaginative, crave success and thrive on relationships with others.

Implications for Teachers and Teaching

Because teachers, just like their students, make sense of new information by integrating it into what is already known, we have chosen not to launch into a string of recommendations about worthwhile changes that teachers can make in how they teach. Instead, we want to review some of the realities of what it takes for teachers to change their practice before identifying a few promising practices that teachers might consider as they start to alter or expand their approach to teaching.

Teachers are the ultimate school reformers. Attempts at changing schools will have little or no impact on students unless they affect how teachers teach and young people learn. For this to happen, teachers have to construct their own understanding of various reform efforts. Just like students, teachers are influenced in their learning by their own approaches to thinking, their knowledge base, their pattern of intelligences, their ways of learning, the social milieu and their willingness and opportunity to engage actively in any new learning. If the needs for active learning and constructivist understanding among teachers are neglected by reform efforts, the consequences are as serious as when students' learning styles and learning needs are neglected in the classroom. Peterson and Knapp (1993) argue that:

> Teachers' enactments of suggested reforms are profoundly influenced by the theories and beliefs that they currently hold . . . they interpret reform recommendations in light of their existing assumptions and frames. If not privy to the underlying assumptions and understanding of the author, teachers may attempt to incorporate the 'new information' without reexamining their existing understanding. Educators who are expected to implement surface features of the constructivist reforms without being given time and access to consider and interpret for them-selves the assumptions and ideas about learning that underlie these reforms may miss the main meaning of the reform, while adhering to the letter of the suggested procedures. (pp. 137–8)

A vivid example of the considerable time, commitment and staff development that is required to change teachers' practices through principles of active learning and constructivist understanding emerged from some recent efforts to transform mathematics learning for students from memorization to deep understanding of how mathematics operates. It quickly became clear that such a move would require considerable learning for elementary school teachers. Just producing new textbooks and resources (teacher-proof or not) would not be enough. Most of the teachers of early grades only knew a little mathematics themselves and what they knew was routine and algorithmic, not deeply understood. They could hardly be expected to help children cultivate a deeper and more complex understanding of mathematics unless they learned a different version of mathematics themselves (Cohen and Barnes, 1992).

This example only gives a glimpse of the changes and dilemmas that teachers encounter in reform efforts. If they are going to 'teach for understanding', teachers must accept that their young adolescent students are thoughtful and interesting thinkers, who are capable of working actively and using their intelligences to extend and enhance their understanding. Considered this way, many teachers are faced with the prospect of adopting a whole new approach to teaching — of becoming guides, coaches, mentors and facilitators of students' learning by posing questions, challenging students' thinking, leading them in examining ideas and relationships and focusing on their conceptual understanding (McLaughlin and Talbert, 1993). This kind of teaching is much more difficult than filling up students with textbook content. Teachers not only have to learn new ways to teach. They must also unlearn and cast aside much that they had known and done confidently before (Cohen and Barnes, 1992). The challenge for teachers is that they must now learn to teach in ways in which they have not been taught themselves (McLaughlin and Talbert, 1994). Clearly, making changes of this magnitude will not happen quickly or easily and there are no silver bullets of simple success. Rather, teachers will wander and stumble, three steps forward and two steps back, as they try to assimilate and integrate these new ideas and turn them into manageable classroom practices.

There is no one right way. As Smith (1987) remarked, 'Any time you try to reduce teaching to a model, you're in trouble because models give us formulas, and formulas squeeze the life out of teaching'. Each of the items below describes a pedagogical strategy or approach that has arisen out of the constructivist tradition and that contributes to 'teaching for understanding'. This collection is not exhaustive and the approaches are not presented as models to be followed slavishly. Rather, they are promising options or useful tools that have been developed for teachers' use. If they are not implemented wisely and thoughtfully in ways that respect and appreciate the complexity of learning and the diversity of background, experiences and intelligences of the particular young adolescents being taught, they are just as likely to lead to superficial learning and misunderstanding instead of authentic learning and self-monitoring.

Using Cooperative Learning

Cooperative learning, where students work in small groups to investigate and share their learning, is a natural approach to teaching young adolescents. It capitalizes on their preoccupation with the social world around them and their dependence on the peer group. It creates a context for learning where students explore new ideas, examine their own positions and challenge their prior beliefs by examining them with other people. It provides a forum for them to establish a sense of personal identity and self-esteem, and be actively engaged in their learning. For these reasons, it is mentioned frequently as an appropriate strategy with heterogeneous groups of students in the middle years (Garcia, 1990; Lyman and Foyle, 1989). Many books and resources have been produced for teachers who are interested in cooperative learning (Garcia, 1990), and there is no reason to provide detail here. Rather, we want to note that just seating students at tables and instructing them to work in groups does not constitute 'cooperative learning'. Effective cooperative learning lessons are very carefully designed by the teacher to provide challenging, messy, real-life problems with multiple solutions and delineate how students in the group will work together in order to create the final product in a context where everyone has a role to play (Nystrand *et al*, 1992; Lyman and Foyle, 1989). The teacher designs the logistics that will shape how students work together. The teacher organizes the students, tasks and roles they will play by balancing personalities, skills and intended outcomes to produce the maximum amount of learning for all of the students. This planning allows considerable flexibility in the way the groups operate and causes them to confront real problems along the way. The structure is therefore both tight and loose. It both stimulates and permits students to use their minds together to construct their own knowledge, individually and collectively.

Teaching a Thinking Curriculum

If we accept that higher order thinking is essential for all students and that it can be taught and learned, classrooms for young adolescents are obvious places to emphasize and generate excitement about learning new and more sophisticated ways of thinking. The natural curiosity and rapid intellectual growth of students at this stage provide the springboard for them to attempt (and reach) new heights in thinking.

There are any number of books, kits and resources available to teach thinking using a wide variety of approaches. Although there has been debate about whether teaching thinking as an adjunct to normal classes is superior to infusing such teaching into the whole curriculum (White, 1992), the various approaches all operate on the belief that thinking can be improved with explicit instruction, practice and coaching. Costa (1991) describes a process of teaching *for* thinking, teaching *of* thinking and teaching *about* thinking. Rather than defining a prescribed program, he provides this threefold framework along with a wide range of questions, examples and resources to help teachers install a program for thinking. Marzano (1992) offers the same; a clear framework of five 'dimensions of learning' and a series of questions and examples to use when planning a unit of work. Barell (1991) provides a conceptual overview, examples and many detailed classroom strategies to enhance intellectual development. Other systems like de Bono's (1990) or Fogarty's (1994) offer more structured approaches to teaching thinking in classrooms. Regardless of the materials that are used, the common focus is on making a conscious effort to develop students' cognitive and metacognitive skills and help them become learners who are more responsible for their own learning.

Developing Student Independence

Since students must become critical thinkers and problem-solvers who can use their talents and knowledge in novel situations, they have to develop skills of self-assessment and self-adjustment. They cannot wait for the teacher to declare the right answer, but must develop facility and confidence in making their own judgments (Earl and Cousins, 1995). We have shown how developing independence is particularly important in early adolescence when students are leaving the safety of elementary school for the more impersonal realm of secondary school. But this is not a time to throw the lambs to the wolves. Instead, it is a time to encourage risk-taking, hone skills, extend horizons and celebrate success. As Purkey and Novak (1984) describe it, it is a time for invitational education where the teacher creates the conditions for learning by taking an 'inviting stance' and developing a sense of trust, engaging with students to draw them into the learning process.

Experiential learning is a powerful and exciting way to engage students in the world outside school. Cooperative education programs, job shadowing, outdoor education centers, volunteerism and extra-curricular programs all give students a chance to try their hands at the real life challenges of many worlds without committing too early to any one direction for the future. They can venture into the workplace, and the wide open spaces beyond the concrete jungle. The theater, sports, almost anywhere their imaginations can take them, offer experiential opportunities for learning, while still providing them with protection and support.

When teachers work to promote student independence, they are really teaching students to be responsible for their own learning and giving them the tools to undertake it wisely and well. The most effective strategies for increasing motivation have to do with treating students as capable persons, making material relevant by capitalizing on their knowledge and interests, and involving them in determining the goals, the learning methods and the criteria for success (Levin, 1994). When students are active participants in their own learning and in genuine self-evaluation, they increase their self-awareness and begin to understand errors, difficult problems and even failures as a natural part of learning and life (Earl and Cousins, 1995).

Providing Experiences that are Broad and Deep

Given the vast amount of available knowledge and the inherent differences among individuals, it is obvious that no one can learn everything and that it is folly to try and teach everyone exactly the same things or to teach things in the same way to everyone. Instead teachers must take advantage of the raw energy of young adolescents and engage them in a range of activities to tap their existing knowledge, extend their horizons and utilize all their talents and interests.

In '*The Unschooled Mind*', Gardner (1991) describes two institutions which help students extend their understanding of the world and the way people are — apprenticeships and children's museums. He attributes the potential power of these institutions to the educational wisdom that is embedded within them, not to their existence outside the school, and suggests a number of ways that their value can be created within schools as well. In an apprenticeship, the student 'hangs around' somebody who is an expert and a mentor and both observes and assists them as they use their knowledge-in-action. In a children's museum, students inquire, exploring, experiment, approach things in their own way and reflect about what is going on (Gardner, 1994). Within schools, Gardner's theory of multiple intelligences has been translated into a series of classroom based activities and materials (Lazear, 1991; Gardner, 1993; Armstrong, 1994) that are designed to become part of a teacher's repertoire.

The 4 MAT system, developed by McCarthy (1980) is another approach to planning teaching and learning that is designed to ensure that students with very different ways of learning are taught and learn in ways that are compatible with their learning style. She has used a 4-quadrant model to construct a framework for planning teaching and learning that identifies students who are primarily 'innovative learners', 'analytic learners', 'common sense learners' and 'dynamic learners'. This framework offers a wide range of activities that would be appropriate to each of them. Although she isolates these categories and provides teaching strategies associated with them, she is quick to point out that the intent is not to pigeon-hole students or limit their access to learning but to extend it by using all strategies with the whole class and ensuring that all students benefit by experiencing a variety of teaching approaches. These are only a very few examples of what is available to teachers who want to make learning meaningful and relevant by extending and enriching the experiences of students' experiences.

Using Technology

It is impossible to imagine the future without technology being even more powerful, user-friendly and transportable. Already, 5-year olds are more comfortable and knowledgeable about the workings of computers, microwave ovens and VCRs than most adults. Many young adolescents spend hours 'cruising the net' and have established contacts and developed interests far beyond the confines of their own community (Cummins and Sayer, 1995). Communities of learning need no longer be confined to the classroom but can now also be constituted through the virtual space of technology (Hargreaves, forthcoming). Technology is an accepted part of students' worlds that captures their imagination and frightens them far less than it does their teachers.

Teachers are increasingly making use of technology in the classroom. With technology, it is much easier to create rich learning environments where multiple intelligences and learning styles are addressed simultaneously. Computer technology, in particular, can provide access to more information more quickly. It can improve the composition, editing, illustration and professional presentation of texts (not least for those with motor skill difficulties). It can enable data to be collated, analyzed and communicated more easily.

It is important to note, however, that not all technology makes education better. If it is nothing more than adding pictures and sounds to words and numbers, technology is still based on a model of learning that sees the mind as a vessel to be filled. The value comes when students are more proactive in asking questions and acquiring information that can be used to solve problems. Used well, technology has the chance of allowing teachers to fulfill age-old dreams: to individualize teaching and learning, to create simulations that lead to the discovery of important relationships, to give students control of their own learning, to enhance motivation, and to organize and present any kind of information. Used badly, technology can limit knowledge, isolate students, and convert emotional and critical writing that requires a teacher's inspiration and intervention, to simple communication and clinical technique (Thornburg, 1994; Postman, 1992). As Stoll (1995) eloquently expresses it:

> All of us want children to experience warmth, human interaction, the thrill of discovery, and solid grounding in essentials: reading, getting along with others, training in civic values . . . Only a teacher live in the classroom, can bring about this inspiration. This can't happen over a speaker, a television or a computer screen. (p. 116)

It is important not to indulge an uncritical, euphoric love of all new technology, nor to be a Luddite, dismissive of all its possibly valuable effects. A constructive and critically selective relationship to new technology, like all new teaching methods is what we should most demand of ourselves and our colleagues.

There is also an important equity issue associated with the use of technology. In an age of resource scarcity, how can every child have access to the wonderful world of technology? Without a solution, the end result will be an increased gap between advantaged and disadvantaged students. Perhaps one day access will not be a problem and a computer link will be as commonplace as the telephone is today. But for now, teachers face the serious challenge of differential access.

Even with these problems, technology, perhaps more than any other single innovation, is a powerful resource for restructuring schools in profound ways. It should be used not just to do the old job better but to create experiences of learning that are completely new. We have only just begun to explore.

Dangers and Difficulties

Our brief glimpse of some promising methods has been designed to entice teachers and encourage them to explore the possibilities that these and other teaching innovations might offer. However, although we have highlighted some patterns of teaching and learning that appear to yield positive outcomes for learning and student growth, we want to conclude by cautioning against rapid and wholesale adoption of such methods. We issue this caution for the following reasons:

Obsessions with In-service Training

Teaching strategies are a tempting focus for change. In some ways, this is appropriate, for it is through these strategies that students experience the curriculum. But department heads, principals, and school system administrators are sometimes inclined to concentrate their change efforts too heavily on teaching strategies at the individual-teacher level, to the exclusion of other areas of reform. Although a sensitive and difficult task, improving teachers' classroom strategies is an attractive proposition for reformers. The norms it challenges are less sacred than those threatened by changes in curriculum or school subjects. Yet in many respects it is subjects and subject organization that support traditional patterns of teaching and make teaching so difficult to change. The working definitions of learning in many subjects support traditional patterns of teaching. And the fragmentation of the timetable that tends to come with a subject-based curriculum restricts opportunities for sustained project or theme work that would allow greater flexibility in teaching methods. The implication is that changes in teaching style and strategy cannot be undertaken effectively without parallel changes in other aspects of secondary schooling.

Changes in teaching, such as implementing cooperative learning, are often initiated through intensive programs of training directed at the skills and attitudes of teachers. In-service training programs, the use of school district co-ordinators, and the development of peer-coaching strategies to implement new methods are some of the approaches taken to such training. Yet, these training approaches presume that teachers persist with traditional patterns of teaching because they lack knowledge of alternatives, do not know how to use them, or are unwilling to try them (Hargreaves and Dawe, 1990). We have seen, however, that traditional patterns of teaching are not just a matter of individual-teacher preference. They are supported by other 'sacred' aspects of secondary schooling — in particular, its organization around academic subjects and, its continuing use of traditional patterns of assessment.

Unless these more 'sacred' aspects of secondary schooling are addressed, we would predict, on the basis of the evidence, that efforts to improve teaching by itself will be ineffective. At best, isolated efforts to implement new methods like cooperative learning will have a short-term impact, will take most effectively among those who are already committed and enthusiastic, and will be adopted in a few 'sympathetic' subjects only. At worst, they will be an expensive diversion of scarce resources which unwisely approach change and improvement as something rooted only in teachers' skills and attitudes, rather than in the 'sacred' structures in which teachers work.

Silver Bullets

When the value of new teaching strategies like cooperative learning is discovered, administrators and other change agents are often inclined to advocate and implement them too enthusiastically, quickly, and dogmatically. Research evidence suggests that the most effective approaches to teaching are those where teachers draw on a wide repertoire of strategies which they apply flexibly and selectively to different learning situations (for example, Galton, Simon and Croll, 1980; Mortimore *et al*, 1988). Changing teachers and their patterns of teaching is not like giving them frontal lobotomies. Most teachers do not change their entire approach to teaching after many years experience because of a few in-service training sessions or coaching in new teaching techniques. Nor should we expect them to change in that way. The use of a wide, flexible repertoire is more effective than overkill in a single strategy. It is even possible that overzealously insisting that reluctant teachers convert wholesale to new teaching strategies can make them less, not more effective (Hargreaves, 1994).

Moreover, research on teachers in mid-career suggests that, having already seen several major innovations come and go in their careers, many experienced teachers are sensibly reluctant to give their all one more time, and change their whole teaching approach around again (Huberman, 1993). But what these teachers *are* willing to do, given time and flexibility, is 'tinker around' with new methods and expand their repertoire a little.

In terms of the strategies most likely to be effective, and of the realities of teachers' careers, therefore, evidence suggests that it is advisable to encourage teachers to widen their repertoires and try out new methods. What is *not* advisable is advocating, still less insisting, that they swing to completely different styles of teaching, and become very different kinds of teachers.

Speed Kills

A final and related caution is that new patterns of teaching should not be implemented too quickly. Teachers, we have argued, are not just collections of skills and techniques. Teachers teach the way they do, not just because of the skills they have learned, but also because of the structures in which they work and the kinds of people they have become. Changing teachers involves changing people, and changing people is slow work (Goodson, 1992; Fullan and Hargreaves, 1991). This means that new teaching strategies should be implemented at a pace and with sufficient flexibility to allow teachers to adopt them and adapt to them at their own comfort level.

It is unfair, unrealistic and ineffective to expect or insist that teachers change their teaching dramatically, in a short space of time. But it is fair, realistic, and likely to prove more effective if we expect teachers to commit themselves to continuous improvement as a community of colleagues, and to experiment with new teaching strategies as part of that commitment. When seeking to improve strategies of teaching, we often commit ourselves enthusiastically to conversion, when extension would be a more practical and productive goal.

Conclusion

In this chapter we emphasize that, when everything is stripped away, schooling is about learning and teaching. But, not any kind of learning and teaching will do. If we are going to prepare young adolescents for the next century, their learning must go far beyond shallow learning and memorization of algorithms to deep, enduring 'learning for understanding'. This kind of deep learning is premised on very different views of knowledge, intelligence, learning outcomes, engagement of students and most particularly, ways of teaching.

Teachers are facing dramatic changes in their practices — to being guides, coaches, mentors and facilitators while students grapple with new ideas and struggle to make sense and construct a coherent picture out of all that surrounds them. At the same time, they are struggling themselves to integrate new theories and approaches with their own beliefs and experiences. The examples and dilemmas that we describe are already happening in many classrooms; but they are noticeably absent in many others. Without fundamental changes in teaching and learning as well as support systems, curriculum, assessment and school cultures, young adolescents will not be the beneficiaries of all that we know. So, 'getting there', is all important.

10 Getting There

The Need for Change

If we want a better deal for the teenagers of today and a better future for the world they will inherit tomorrow, there is no doubt that our schools need to change in fundamental and far-reaching ways. Too many of our students are turning away from schools physically, or tuning out of them emotionally and intellectually. When young teenagers yearn for greater independence, we tighten the screws of classroom control. When they are most in need of care and support to guide them through the turbulent years leading to adulthood, we focus on teaching subject matter, put away care with other childish things, and leave students' emotional needs to the peer group and the gang. Early adolescents need independence but we show them indifference. They need kindness but we crush them with control. They are brimming with criticism and curiosity, but we bludgeon them with content and its coverage.

In the days when many young people left school early, there were jobs for them to go to, and we expected little of students who were female, black or poor, these disparities were not so obvious or so great. But more students stay in school now, there are few other options open to them, and our expectations for all students are rightly higher. School matters more, to more students, more of the time. The pressure in schools is mounting, and there are no safety valves to release it. Today, if young people are sold short on their schooling, if it fails to engage them or frustrates the fulfillment of their needs, teachers are the first to know. Violence, disrespect for authority and the relentless grind of students' reluctance to comply with anything but the barest minimum of academic requirements, remind teachers daily of their students' resistance to what they have to offer.

The secondary schools or junior high schools of today face significant new challenges. These are not just vague, abstract, futuristic needs of a new century. Change is already occurring inside teachers' classrooms because change is everywhere outside them. Schools and teachers are caught up in a worldwide transformation of politics, economics, technology, culture, morality and everyday life. Family structures are changing, relationships are becoming more temporary and fragile, and children's selves and identities are more at risk. Teachers speak of there being many more social-work responsibilities in teaching today than there used to be (A. Hargreaves, 1994). Mounting problems of safety and violence only add to the onerous nature of these responsibilities.

The multicultural diversity of many urban classrooms is another changing reality for teachers. In a large school district where one of us is currently working on language-policy issues, over 50 per cent of the district's students are categorized as English-as-a-second language, and over seventy languages are spoken in its schools. These trends have already brought about profound changes in the materials that teachers use with their classes, in the choice of words and examples that make up teachers' classroom language, and in the very structures of teaching and learning that teachers use so as to allow children of different languages, cultures, and traditions to find a voice among their peers.

Important changes are also at work in the movement from a written to a visual culture within a world of greater technological complexity. As we have seen, new technologies pose significant questions for relationships between teachers and students, school and home, classroom life and the world beyond. Against all this high-tech imagery, the chalkboard and the overhead offer poor competition.

These forces of change are dissolving the boundaries between school and community (Elkind, 1993). Schools and teachers are no longer islands. Change is not just knocking on the doors of teachers' classrooms. It is right there in the classroom itself — in the changing lives of the young people who occupy it. This is the reality of what teachers and schools have to face.

Many teachers, it must be said, have already responded magnificently to these challenges. They have taken on more responsibilities, diversified and adapted their teaching methods, reviewed and expanded what they teach. But they have frequently had to do this in adverse circumstances, and these circumstances have taken their toll. Teachers have often changed alone, in their own classes, without being connected to the expertise, support, and planning ideas of their colleagues. They have worked in an isolated and individualized culture. They have also often had to make changes in and around existing structures — working against a structural grain of subjects, time periods, and single-teacher classes that are unsympathetic to their purposes. They have had to meet with colleagues in their own time outside the regular school day; to practice cooperative learning several times a day for fixed periods with different secondary school classes rather than having longer time frames and other teachers of other subjects alongside to assist them (Hargreaves *et al*, 1993); and to work administrative miracles so their schedules can be synchronized with other subject teachers with whom they want to team teach or develop integrated curricula.

Secondary schools and junior high schools are full of fine teachers working in terrible structures that diminish or defeat them over time. Struggling with change alone, inside existing structures, leads to guilt, exhaustion, perfectionism, and burnout (A. Hargreaves, 1994). It subjects teachers to the principle of what one secondary school teacher we interviewed termed 'implementation by stamina' (Hargreaves *et al*, 1993). As one innovative teacher in the same study put it, 'I don't think everybody should have to do this much work!', especially 'older teachers (who) are going to have an already fixed family, personal kind of life. And who wants to give that up?'

In this book, we have laid out an ambitious agenda of fundamental changes that need to be addressed and that some have already tried, in order to align today's secondary school and junior high school structures with the needs of their students and with the times in which they live. This agenda includes developing:

- processes and systems of *care and support* where every teacher takes responsibility for students' social and emotional well-being in addition to their intellectual development;
- a curriculum and a set of teaching strategies that engage all students by being *relevant, imaginative and challenging;*
- a broad curriculum framework of *common learning outcomes* (not detailed subject contents) that addresses multiple intelligences and forms of achievement within culturally diverse student populations, while giving teachers considerable latitude to decide on the particular curriculum contents that are best suited to their own student mix;
- *authentic and wide-ranging classroom assessment* that captures the diverse ways in which students can achieve, and that also enables teachers to respond swiftly to any problems of their students' learning which the assessments have been able to identify;
- *teaching for understanding* which utilizes a broad repertoire of teaching strategies that teachers are always seeking to improve and expand;
- *structures of schooling* such as mini-schools or team-based core programs which make teachers ready, willing and able to care for and relate to their students properly; to diagnose their learning needs and report on their progress knowledgeably; and to accommodate their multiple intelligences, and diverse learning styles sensitively.

The need for educational change is evident. The pressure for it to happen, from reformers across the world, is intense and unending. The agenda that we have laid out is not unique, or even unusual. Numerous reform proposals have embodied one or more of the principles within it. The problem is not how to imagine or aspire to structures and processes of schooling for young adolescents that are different or better. The problem, rather, is how to convert the aspirations embodied in our agenda, into living actuality in our classrooms and schools. It is implementation that repeatedly defeats us, not imagination. So what is it that is so difficult about educational change? Why is it so hard to convert aspiration into actuality? We have become much clearer in recent years about where the education of young adolescents needs to go. But getting there consistently eludes us.

The Difficulty of Educational Change

There are many reasons why educational change is so difficult, why 'getting there' can be so hard. Among them are that:

- the reason for the change is poorly conceptualized or not clearly demonstrated. It is not obvious who will benefit and how. What the change will achieve for students in particular is not spelled out;
- the change is too broad and ambitious so that teachers have to work on too many fronts; or it is too limited and specific so that little real change occurs at all;
- the change is too fast for people to cope with, or too slow so that they become impatient or bored and move on to something else;
- the change is poorly resourced or resources are withdrawn once the first flush of innovation is over. There is not enough money for materials or time for teachers to plan. The change is built on the backs of teachers, who cannot bear it for long without additional support;
- there is no long-term commitment to the change to carry people through the anxiety, frustration and despair of early experimentation and unavoidable setbacks;
- key staff who can contribute to the change, or might be affected by it, are not committed. Conversely, key staff might become overinvolved as an administrative or innovative elite, from which other teachers feel excluded. Resistance and resentment are the consequences in either case;
- students are not involved in the change, or do not have it explained to them, so they yearn for and cling to ways of learning that are familiar to them, and become the school's most powerful protectors of the past;
- parents oppose the change because they are kept at a distance from it. Alternatively, influential groups or individuals among the parents can negotiate special deals with the school that protect their own children from the effects of innovation (for example, by placing them in 'gifted classes' or allocating the best teachers to them);
- leaders are either too controlling, too ineffectual, or cash in on the early success of the innovation to move on to higher things;
- the change is pursued in isolation and gets undermined by other unchanged structures (for example, when common curriculum outcomes are juxtaposed with traditional report cards or standardized tests); conversely, the change may be poorly coordinated with and engulfed by a tidal wave of parallel changes that make it hard for teachers to focus their efforts.

These common causes of failure to bring about educational change are well documented in the change literature (for example, Fullan, 1991 and 1993; Berman and McLaughlin, 1977; McLaughlin, 1990; Rudduck, 1991; Miles and

Huberman, 1984; Louis and Miles, 1990; Sarason, 1990; Stoll and Fink, 1996). As a *technical* process of proper planning, design and structural alignment, and as a *cultural* process of building effective relationships of collaboration and consultation, educational change is something we now understand much better than a decade or more ago. Yet even with this impressive knowledge base and expertise about the technical and cultural aspects of educational change, too many change efforts remain disappointing and ineffective. Successful school change on a widespread basis continues to be infuriatingly elusive. Why?

One reason is that educational change is not just a technical process of managerial efficiency, or a cultural one of understanding and involvement. It is a political and paradoxical process as well. Throughout this book, we have shown that educational change proposals which promise to benefit all students in the transition years, threaten many entrenched interests. Privileged parents resist attempts at restructuring that appear to depart from the conventional kinds of schooling at which their children traditionally succeed (Oakes, Lipton and Jones, 1992). Subject teachers defend their departments (and therefore their subject identities and careers) against attempts to dismantle them for the sake of common outcomes and integration (Siskin, 1994).

People fear change not just because it presents them with something new, uncertain and unclear. The agenda of educational change is also a contested one. Education is the greatest gatekeeper of opportunity and a powerful distributor of life chances. In a socially divided and culturally diverse society, what education is and how it is defined, will always tend to favor some groups and interests over others. So attempts to change education in fundamental ways are ultimately political acts. They are attempts to redistribute power and opportunity within the wider culture. Generalized theories of educational change which concentrate on its technical and cultural aspects, tend to ignore these essentially political elements of the change process. This is a pity. For it is the political dimension of fundamental educational change that causes it to flounder most.

In the early stages of educational reform, political differences and divisions are not always evident. At first glance, the need for educational reform appears to be widely understood and appreciated. People seem to concur that schools aren't working. But they do so for different reasons. The consensus is deeply deceptive. At least two broad sets of arguments, interests and social constituencies appear to be involved here. Although they are not always mutually exclusive, they point to significantly different forces underpinning educational change. The coexistence of these forces carries important consequences for teachers, as we shall see.

One group sees that secondary schools are not what they used to be. The traditional subject curriculum remains but is increasingly watered-down to accommodate the seemingly more modest abilities of students who stay in school longer. As well as being diluted, the conventional curriculum also seems to be compressed by mandates to teach drug education, sex education and other social programs that squeeze academic subjects to the side. For this group, secondary schools have adapted to extraneous social demands and a more inclusive student population to the point where standards are at risk and existing structures can no longer stand the strain. In a recession where competition for jobs is severe, economically advantaged parents become educationally anxious ones. They are fearful that the changes which have already occurred in secondary schools will prejudice their own children's chances of success, and remove the marginal benefits they already enjoy, by diluting or destroying what it is they are good at (Delhi, 1995).

A nostalgic longing for basic skills and traditional subject standards, along with a neophiliac preoccupation with educational markets, school choice and new technologies are the unlikely bedfellows of this group's aspirations for reform. A return to basic skills and traditional subject standards restores the conventional curriculum and protects privilege. Support for school choice and educational markets enables these parents to find and form their own schools, or to influence existing ones with their vouchers and their values (Kenway *et al*, 1993). New technologies add a twist to this traditional tale by promising access to better learning and occupational success.

A second orientation to reform has been reiterated throughout our book. This emphasizes teaching for understanding, common and integrated curricula, and diverse forms of achievement and assessment, within smaller communities of care and support as the basis for success for *all* students. It is an orientation guided by concerns for equity, and by ambitions for young people's success whatever their background. This orientation does not presume that there is one traditional model of schooling that suits all. The challenge rather, is to reform the school system so it can engage with the cultures, backgrounds and learning styles of students with very diverse lives and needs.

In principle, the two orientations are discrete and contradict each other. In practice, however, the political pragmatism of large scale policy reform often brings elements from the two orientations together in policies that are meant to embrace compromise and consensus, but which lead only to confusion and contradiction. Teachers then become caught in a pincer movement of change demands.

The challenge for teachers who adjust to this particular context of change is to work within a world of paradox (Handy, 1994). Paradoxes — seemingly absurd or self-contradictory statements or states of affairs — are becoming more and more evident in education now, pulling teachers in different directions at the same time. Teachers are called upon to be integrated *and* specialized, standardized *and* variegated, local *and* global, autonomous *and* accountable, embracing change *and* continuity. It is hard to work with perpetual paradox, but essential that teachers and educational leaders do so (Deal and Peterson, 1994). This does not mean expecting all teachers to cope compliantly with any and all contradictions, however morally bankrupt or educationally indefensible some aspects of these contradictions might be. Teachers and others should take moral and political stands wherever policies are cruel, capricious or otherwise injurious to children. Much of the 'upbeat' change literature is sadly silent or curiously coy about these issues. But other paradoxes can be embraced and addressed positively and creatively, raising educators to more sophisticated forms of practice through *both/and* solutions instead of *either/or* ones (Deal and Peterson, 1994). Teachers can commit to traditions of change, plan for spontaneity, show skeptical commitment, affirm their strength by showing vulnerability, increase their power by letting go of it, and so on.

Most existing approaches to educational change offer only limited help to those struggling with the paradoxes we have described.

- *Effective schools* strategies might have given us good schools for the 1960s, but by themselves don't prepare children well for the 1990s (Stoll and Fink, 1996). Raising expectations for achievement; putting more emphasis on and giving more time to instruction; tightening up policy on discipline; creating a safe, orderly and supportive school climate; and strengthening school leadership might make conventional schools work better and improve their performance in test scores, basic skills and attendance. But schools that are effective in these conventional and restricted terms might not be at all effective at developing problem solving, cooperation, creativity flexibility and risk-taking. Moreover, the 'tight ship' patterns of organization that effective schools models produce may not be sufficiently flexible or inclusive of all staff expertise to respond swiftly and creatively to contradictory demands and constant change (Reynolds and Sullivan, 1987). For these challenges to be met, reform efforts must attack the fundamental structures or basic 'grammar' of schooling, rather than merely making those structures work more smoothly (Tyack and Tobin, 1994; Schlechty, 1990).
- *School improvement* efforts have taught us how to improve individual schools by promoting shared leadership, continuous problem-solving, high quality professional development that is linked to classroom practice, and processes of self-evaluation and school review. But we do not yet know what sustains improved schools over time and protects them against teacher burnout, staff turnover, leaders who leave or withdrawal of system support. Similarly, while we have learned a lot about how to create exceptional islands of improvement, we know less about how to construct archipelagoes and still less about how to build whole continents of successful change (A. Hargreaves, 1994). Improved schools are often treated by systems as a select *avant garde*, subject to special treatment, additional resources, extra discretion over hiring and firing of staff etc. These things are difficult to replicate in other settings. Indeed, the successful schools may even drain them of resources, personnel and attention.

    Perhaps the most fundamental flaw in extrapolating the principles of individual school success to effective system-wide change is that exemplars of individual school improvement often presume that principals can and should transfer teachers who do not share the school's mission to other schools (for example, Deal and Peterson, 1994). This may work reasonably well in the competitive corporate world from which it has been borrowed, because individual corporations are interested only in their own success, not in that of the corporate sphere more generally. But the principle does not transfer well to schools at all, where our interest should be not just in improving schools for our own students (whatever the costs to those in other schools), but improving schooling in general.

A final problem in school improvement is that most change efforts ultimately run up against the fundamental form and fabric of secondary schooling that are historically ingrained in its structures and procedures. As we argued earlier, change efforts usually run against the old structural grain, rather than with a new one. If we are serious in our struggle to create better schooling for early adolescents in a changing world, these fundamental structural questions have to be addressed.

- *Model schools* are an extreme case of the limitations of school improvement. As 'lighthouse' or 'showpiece' institutions, their innovative practices are intended to serve as exemplars for others to emulate. In practice, as Lortie (1975) cynically observed 'large school systems sometimes use new approaches in showplace schools while resisting their widespread adoption; this tactic can "cool out" enthusiasts until their ardor has waned' (p. 218). Even without such active deceptions, it is almost impossible for existing schools to match the resources with which new schools are normally blessed at their birth — most dramatically in terms of electronic hardware in showcase 'computer' schools, but more generally in terms of building space and design, textbooks and other resources. New schools also often have their pick of the best human resources who are drawn like magnets to the innovative environments which those working with a clean slate are usually able to offer. As Sarason (1972) recognized many years ago, creating a new setting is not like changing an existing one. New schools have the advantage of better resources and exceptionally motivated personnel. At the same time, being in the spotlight can put them under intense pressure to embellish their successes and disguise their mistakes (Hargreaves and Macmillan, 1995). It is easier for new schools to shine, but, all that glitters is not gold, and new schools are sometimes just 'too good to be true'. In any event, it seems, new schools have few positive change lessons to offer those who are struggling to bring about change with existing staff and materials in more mundane environments.

- *Exceptional leadership* suffers from some of the same afflictions as exceptional schools. In the form of charismatic, visionary or transformational leadership, it is often seen as the brilliant, heroic savior of schools that have found change difficult. Important as leadership is for any change efforts, these conceptions of leadership equate leadership with leaders, qualities with individuals, and create images of leaders as superheroes whom few of us could ever emulate. Though they are said to be effective at mobilizing team efforts, theoretically, these leaders are accorded all the individual credit. Charismatic qualities are attributed to visionary and transformational leaders, yet the concept of charisma is rooted in dictatorial leaders who inspired religious devotion or irrational allegiance within cults of personality and cared little for democratic ways (Gronn, 1995). These history-making heroes are poor models for democratic change.

More than this, there is evidence that visionary leaders are not timelessly so. Their charismatic qualities do not endure across time and place. Visionary leaders tend to move on to other places, leaving their loyal dependents behind with the intractable problem of institutionalizing the charismatic qualities in other people. Yet charisma is something that only exceptional leaders can by definition, possess (Tichy and Devanna, 1990). Equally, the transformational impact of such leaders is often only temporary. It fades as conditions change; as limits of life, health and patience mean that the higher levels of extra effort they have been able to extract from the workforce can no longer be sustained; or (as with many 'successful' innovators) as they themselves move on to more interesting things. In short, exceptional leaders, like exceptional schools, offer poor models for successful and sustained system-wide change. The success rests on atypical individuals who may actually be hailed by temporary and propitious circumstances rather than possessing generic qualities that can transform any organization, in any place or time (Gronn, 1995).

- *Mandated reform* is a popular priority for those who have become frustrated with waves of unsuccessful innovations or impatient with the grinding slowness of bottom-up change. However, imposed reform 'cannot mandate what matters to effective practice' (McLaughlin, 1990). Improvements in teaching and learning can ultimately only come about through skilled and discretionary judgments that teachers are able and willing to make in their own unique classroom circumstances. 'What matters most are local motivation, skills, knowhow and commitment' (Fullan, 1994, p. 187). These cannot be demanded. They can only be developed.

Darling-Hammond (1995) argues that what she terms 'old paradigm' policies of mandated reform have presented obstacles to rather than supports for positive educational change among diverse communities of teachers and learners.

The tendency of educational policy makers over recent decades has been to assume little knowledge, capacity or ethical

commitment on the part of school faculties, and to prescribe practices accordingly — to specify precisely what
schools should do and how they should do it. Although many
of these prescriptions conflict with one another . . . the top-
down approach is comforting to policy makers because it pre-
serves the illusion of control and the pretense of accountability.
(p. 160)

'Old paradigm' policy fails to deal with the problem that 'the complex,
contextually different determinants of good practice and of strategies
for change cannot be accounted for in the monolithic approach standardized policies require' (*ibid.* see also Corson, 1993). 'Old paradigm'
policy is hierarchical. It lodges design and development responsibility
within an administrative elite (with greater or lesser degrees of 'consultation'). It requires teachers to 'implement' (be the tools of) other people's system policies, rather than to develop their own. This paradigm
has a poor record of success because it is unable to deal with the personal commitments and local contingencies that are integral to teaching.

The difficulties of educational change can seem overwhelming. Educational change is hard because it is about transforming sophisticated relationships not simple behaviors, in complex classroom situations and organizational
systems, whose purpose and direction are politically compromised and contested. In the face of all this, the recurrent tragedy of change is that politicians
and administrators lurch chaotically from one change strategy to the next in a
desperate search for solutions. Teachers, meanwhile, become worn down by
endless change and also cynical and dismissive about the shifting demands,
and manic-depressive mood swings of political ideology with which they are
supposed to deal (Huberman, 1993). The sad consequence is that too many
teachers turn aside from change, when, they really need to embrace it more
than ever.

Principles of Change

Much of the existing literature of educational change offers only limited help
to teachers working in a world of paradox. We have seen that it either addresses
change problems of a bygone age that might have given us effective schools
for the 1960s but certainly wouldn't prepare children well for the 1990s. Or it
relies too heavily on 'pop-management' models of change in the corporate
world that transfer rather poorly to education where care is a paramount
purpose, and where change must succeed not in individual corporations at
the expense of others, but across the system as a whole. New guidelines for
creating better schools for young adolescents in our rapidly changing world,
will not arise from seeming certainties of set steps or stages through which
change efforts should proceed. Educational problems and circumstances are just

too complex and variable for that. But there do seem to be a number of important principles to which educators should attend if they want to improve schooling for young adolescents. There are also a few starting points that look like promising places to begin. We begin with six principles of successful school change for post-modern times.

Purpose

Many teachers enter teaching because they care about children in particular or contributing to social improvement in general. Often these purposes become submerged as teachers fall prey to daily classroom pressures and routines (Fullan, 1993). Teacher's purposes can also differ, leading to confusion and inconsistency for children and creating difficult or superficial staff relationships. Teachers and schools should therefore review and renew their purposes over time.

However, people cannot be given a purpose. Purposes are driven from within. Our study of secondary school work cultures and educational change in eight high schools, found that the teachers most likely to resist a newly legislated mandate to detrack or destream grade 9 were those in academically successful suburban schools (Hargreaves *et al*, 1992). For them, the mandate addressed alien agendas of student equity in multicultural communities within the inner city. Policy makers often impose purposes in this way. So do some school principals. As Fullan (1993) says, 'it is not a good idea to borrow someone else's vision' (p. 13).

However, while purposes are ultimately personal, not any purpose will do. Teachers whose only purpose is to transmit subject matter have no place educating early adolescents, for we have seen that care and support from all teachers is essential to widespread student success. Some commitment to teaching for understanding, however difficult this is to achieve, is also important, especially for teachers of 'other people's children' — children who often don't share the background, culture or assumptions of those who teach them (Delpit, 1994). In addition, while teachers should certainly take pride in their achievements, they should always beware of resting on their laurels. Being always open to new learning and ever eager to improve is a third fundamental purpose in a profession as demanding and complex as teaching.

All other educational purposes can be negotiable to a greater or lesser extent, but it is important that teachers engage in dialogue about them, and that their purposes are not 'all over the map'. Dialogue about, and coalescence of, purposes among teachers can secure a much smoother transition to secondary school for students, and more consistent learning experiences across different subjects once the transition is complete.

But the search for moral coherence can be overdone. Common missions that require complete consensus such as 'educate all children to their full potential' may become bland and vacuous because they must appease or appeal to so many different interests. At the same time, mission statements can become too fixed to enable sufficient responsiveness to changes in policy mandates, staff personnel or student populations. Similarly, strategic planning can over-commit teachers to particular goals for up to five years and leave no room for new purposes to develop as circumstances change, new developments arise, or changes occur in the local community. Not that we should dispense with missions, visions and planning altogether merely that in a complex and a fast moving world, missions will work better if they are temporary and approximate, do not require complete consensus, and are explicitly open to continuing renewal through inquiry, dialogue and review. If teachers keep reflecting, thinking and talking over time, their purposes about how best to educate early adolescents will become clearer.

Administration and Decision-Making

If teachers are to review and renew their purposes continuously, they must have sufficient scope to do so. Most educational policy inhibits these opportunities for renewal. Its languages and practices of implementation make teachers into mere tools of other people's purposes.

Insofar as is possible policy decisions should be determined at the immediate level where people will have to deal with them (Corson, 1993). In a complex, uncertain and highly variable world, planned change that follows systematic cycles of development, implementation and review is too inflexible and bureaucratic to respond to local circumstances (Louis, 1994). Moreover, detailed documents that freeze policies in text become outdated and are overtaken even as they are being written, by changing communities, new technologies, fresh legislation, research insights and unanticipated problems (Darling-Hammond, 1995). Like all written texts, written policies are also interpreted differently by those who read them. Passed through the prisms of teachers' purposes and perceptions, the black and white texts of educational policy become scattered into an array of colors and shades of interpretation. No written policy can be clear or literal enough to secure real consensus. Policy is therefore best established through communities of people within and across schools who create policies, talk about them, process them, inquire into them and reformulate them, bearing in mind the circumstances and the children they know best.

Public bureaucracies have tended to inhibit dialogue about and for development of policies close to the people, by imposing mandates and procedures with which teachers must comply. Movements towards market systems of individual school choice and site-based management might release schools from bureaucratic interference, but they also risk cutting teachers off from new ideas and outside expertise; not least those that are available in each other's schools. Some systems, such as England's in the wake of the 1988 Education Reform Act, where individual school management has been established alongside detailed prescriptions for curriculum and testing, leave teachers with not much freedom, but most of the blame!

The challenge is to create structures across schools that transcend the old oppositions between competitive markets and controlling states. For Giddens (1995, p. 15) these involve providing material conditions and local organizational frameworks that help people engage in dialogue and make their own decisions. Networks, professional development agencies, school review teams, data gathering and inquiry, as well as relationships with university faculties of education, can all stimulate and support teachers as they talk, learn, reflect and improve together.

Culture

Before collective action and dialogue can take place, certain relationships must be built among teachers and others. These relationships form the *culture* of the school. To develop or alter these relationships is to *reculture* the school (Hargreaves, 1991; Fullan, 1993).

We have seen that two kinds of cultures among teachers have traditionally prevailed. In *cultures of individualism*, teachers have worked largely in isolation, being sociable with their colleagues, but sharing few resources and ideas, rarely visiting one another's classrooms, and engaging only occasionally in planning or problem-solving together (Little, 1990b). In *balkanized cultures*, teachers have worked in sub-groups like subject departments that are relatively insulated from one another, and that struggle competitively for resources and principals' favors (A. Hargreaves, 1994). Both individualism and balkanization fragment professional relationships in schools, making it hard for teachers to build on one another's expertise. They also stifle the moral support necessary for risk-taking and experimentation.

Reculturing the school to create collaborative cultures among teachers and with the broader community reverses these dynamics. It helps teachers build on existing expertise, pool resources, provide moral support and create a climate of trust in which problems and setbacks can be aired and successes celebrated. Collaboration brings together the human resources necessary for dealing with complex and unanticipated problems. It can enable teachers to interact more assertively with their surrounding systems and the multiplicity of reasonable and unreasonable reforms that come from them. Through its renewal of fundamental purpose, collaboration can provide the resolve to adopt external reforms, the wisdom to delay them and the moral fortitude to resist them, where appropriate (Wideen *et al*, 1996). In these ways, collaborative cultures can make the paradoxes of the post-modern age psychologically meaningful and politically manageable for teachers.

Structure

Cultures do not exist in a vacuum. They are rooted in *structures* of time and space. These structures shape relationships. They frame the possibilities for interaction. Cultures of teacher individualism have emerged from the nine-teenth century egg-crate structures of teacher isolation that we described in earlier chapters. Similarly, balkanized teacher cultures are often a product of subject departmental structures.

We have shown how struggles to build collaborative cultures or to make other important changes can easily be defeated by unchanged and unbending structures, developed for other purposes in previous times. Rigid schedules can wear teachers down by not allowing them to meet together other than outside the regular school day. They become captives of their schedule, 'prisoners of time' (National Commission on Time and Learning, 1994). Teaching and learning also takes place in time warps. Existing time structures warp the possibilities for teaching and learning instead of time being redesigned around the learning needs of early adolescents.

Restructuring is about changing time and space, rules and relationships, roles and responsibilities in schools, to meet the pressing challenges of pre-sent times. Murphy (1991) argues that 'restructuring . . . involves fundamental alterations in the relationships among the players involved in the educational process' (p. 15) — teachers, students, parents, administrators and communities.

Chapter 4 explored a number of alternative structures that seemed to support early adolescent learning. These included block scheduling, mini schools and sub-schools where small teams of teachers worked together and no teacher met more than eighty students or so a week. Yet we have also shown how mini-school structures created to build student community needs can be perceived by students as leading only to monotony. Teachers will also resent new structures if they are imposed without consent and will find little difficulty in subverting them — for example, by teaching in their classes side-by-side, even though they are nominally a team; or slowly recreating their own depart-mental work spaces, after the administration has tried to merge or abolish them (Siskin, 1994).

Restructuring can be administratively attractive. But it is also dangerous and seductive — a threat to the commitment of teachers and indeed students, if it is imposed on them without their understanding and consent. Cultural changes in attitudes and relationships are repeatedly frustrated by existing structures. Structural changes can destroy cultural qualities of collaboration, com-mitment and support on which their success depends. Both are important, but each seems to negate the other. Change only the culture and you will regret it. Change only the structure and you will regret it. Make sweeping changes to the culture and structure together then teachers will be overwhelmed and you will regret both. We will return to this paradox in our final section.

Organizational Learning

Working together is not just a way of building relationships and collective resolve. It is also a source of learning. Learning is probably the most important

resource for organizational renewal in the post-modern age. It helps people to
see problems as things to be solved, not as occasions for blame; to value the
different and even dissident voices of more marginal members of the organization and to sort out the wheat from the chaff of policy demands.

Collaborative cultures turn individual learning into shared learning. Attending to structures so that they help people connect, and designing tasks so they
increase our capacity and opportunities for learning, spreads such learning across
the entire organization. This is what Senge (1990) means by organizational learning. Learning organizations, he says, are

> organizations where people continually expand their capacity to cre-
> ate the results they truly desire, where new and expansive patterns of
> thinking are nurtured, where collective aspiration is set free, and where
> people are continually learning how to learn together. (p. 3)

Professional learning is important to create awareness and build capacity among teachers in ways that will help them become more effective with
their students. Such learning includes the customary workshops, lectures and
'in-service training sessions', but extends far beyond these to embrace dozens
of other practices, including peer coaching, collaborative action research,
intervisitation between classrooms, school quality review, use of critical friends,
personal professional learning portfolios, joint planning, computerized professional learning networks, teacher support groups, school-university partnerships
and teachers' centers. School change is often accompanied by specific shots of
inservice training, the effects of which are debatable at best. Meaningful professional learning is more subtle and sophisticated than this. It engages teachers
in thinking about, renewing and improving how they teach on an ongoing basis.
Professional learning sponsors teacher-initiated change. In-service training
implements other people's changes.

But organizational learning in schools does not only build teacher capacity.
It also improves the school's capacity for improvement and problem solving
in a world of paradox and uncertainty — by getting people to own problems
together instead of seeing them as someone else's responsibility; by valuing
the diverse perspectives and expertise that everyone has to bring to the problem;
and by including those who appear to be part of the problem (including parents, students, or marginalized teachers) in devising its solution.

Organizational learning is quickly becoming one of the strongest intellectual
inspirations for educational change (for example, Louis, 1994; Fullan, 1993).
But the theory of organizational learning is not without limitations. For example,
the admirable commitment to *continuous improvement* can easily degenerate
into *interminable improvement* or endless change where no value is given to
heritage, continuity, consolidation and tradition (which are vital ingredients of
schooling); where only incurable change addicts prosper and survive. Some
teachers are habitual explorers, voracious readers, enthusiastic conference-goers,
willing volunteers for committees, task-forces and writing-teams (but sometimes

173

away from school too much as a result!). Others, especially classroom teachers in mid- to late career, prefer to cultivate their own gardens, making small changes with their own classes where they know their efforts will make a difference (Richardson, 1991; Huberman, 1993). No one should be closed to change and continuous learning. But in institutions that value cultural transmission and stable socialization among their many goals, there are moments and places for consolidation and routine as well. Organizational learning is a fundamental principle of positive change. But our commitment to it, as to all other change principles, should always be somewhat skeptical, and never euphoric and blind.

Positive Politics

Politics is as much part of schooling as is learning. Power is everywhere in education. Teachers exercise power over their students, administrators exercise power over their teachers, and the smarter teachers know how to manipulate or maneuver around administrators. In complex, post-modern times, these political realities are more inescapable and transparent. Schools are becoming more and more subject to the pressures of diverse groups with single-issue interests, in a chaotic competition for the minds of the young. Business organizations, computer companies, chambers of commerce, environmental lobbies, fundamentalist religions, parents wanting traditional standards, and pressure groups opposing sexism, racism and violence against women are all competing for space and influence in the schools of today (Emberley and Newell, 1994). The moves toward site-based management are also making schools more competitive and what they do more overtly political. And when change efforts threaten those with power-advantage, such people will always try to undermine the changes or protect their children against them. Politics is now everyone's responsibility. It cannot be avoided.

Many teachers feel that getting involved in politics is self-seeking and distasteful. Yet, not all politics is bad. Blase (1988) describes what he calls positive politics where power is used *with* other people rather than *over* them. How can teachers apply positive politics to benefit their students? Some key strategies are to:

- *Understand the micropolitical configurations of your school*: Who has formal and informal power? How do they exercise it? How are resources allocated? This will help you steer clear of moral martyrdom — pursuing noble but futile causes without considering whose interests they threaten, and whose support you need etc.
- *Act politically to secure support and resources of your own students and indeed all students.* Use influence, persuasion, assertiveness, diplomacy, charm, self-mockery (to get you off your pedestal) and flattery (not idle). Trade favors, influence power brokers, build coalitions, involve

others, lobby for support, plant seeds of a proposal before presenting them in detail, and find how what you want meets the interests of others. Altruism and opportunism are not necessary opposites! Brilliant arguments achieve little by themselves: The emotional and political work of change is what ultimately gives them their persuasiveness.

- *Empower and assisting others to be more competent and committed.* Empower students through cooperative learning strategies, active involvement in innovation, and by making them partners in their assessment through self-assessment and peer assessment. Empower parents by building partnerships with them (even when they are a problem!), communicating with them in plain language, and involving them in the uncertainties of change (rather than making change a secret professional activity). Empower colleagues by collaborating with them, involving them in decision-making, sharing leadership, and sharing with them your vulnerabilities and uncertainties as a leader as well as your successes. This also works with marginalized teachers if they are placed on school improvement teams (rather than these teams being made up of rather than just the usual innovative elite) and if they are involved in change efforts early rather than being the last to be told, in ways that confirm their marginalization.
- *Embrace conflict as a necessary part of change.* If there isn't any conflict, the change is probably superficial. Productive conflict brings differences into the open, allows many otherwise silenced voices to be heard, shows sensitivity to opposing interests and positions, avoids false or premature consensus and promotes movement beyond early (and perhaps unfounded) anxieties about one's own threatened interests.
- *Reclaim the discourse of education.* Explain yourself to parents and the public as well as you do to your students. Avoid defensive professional euphemisms. Instead, convey your principles through memorable phrases, vivid examples and simple stories. Teachers are highly skilled at explaining the world to their students, but are often much less skilled at explaining to the world what they do with their students. Language is power. Taking control of your language will help you keep hold of your purposes too.

These are some of the key change principles that can help teachers and others improve education for early adolescents within the paradoxes of the post-modern age. Teachers can take charge of change rather than being its conduits or its victims. They can develop the collective learning, moral strength and common language to expose and resist the most unreasonable and unworkable aspects of the paradoxes. They can unleash creativity and virtuosity that are needed to work with complexity and rapid change. They can renew their purposes as teachers of young teenagers; become agents rather than tools of policy; work more collaboratively with children, colleagues and the community;

design and experiment with better structures to support what they do; be as interested in and committed to their own learning as they are to the learning of their students; and pursue positive politics with others for those who matter most — the young people that they teach.

The Paradox of Hope

If we now have some sense of what the desirable destinations might be for the education of early adolescents, we are still often baffled about how to get there. Getting there might eventually be half the fun, but only if you know the viable modes of transportation. Daunted by the difficulties, some people panic and try to make changes on too many fronts — changing the curriculum *and* the assessment, classroom practices *and* school structures, setting up elementary-secondary liaison meetings *and* making all teachers into mentors for individual students. Our experience of schools attempting to make changes in the transition years on too many fronts before they were ready, is that they quickly experienced exhaustion and disillusionment, because of dissipated efforts and little visible success.

Other people often develop tunnel vision and try to simplify things by concentrating on one change strategy at once. They might try building grand missions or developing strategic plans, only to find that the talk goes on forever, and none of it makes a difference in the classroom (university faculties of education, with their addiction to debate and argument, are even more prone to this error!). Or they might engineer changes in structure to force teachers to work in other ways, only to find for example that teachers assigned to team-based structures haven't developed sufficient trust to work together as a team.

We have seen that successful school change is necessarily multi-dimensional and requires attention to structure and culture, politics and purpose, continuous learning and administrative discretion. Yet changing everything at once seems to bring only chaos and exhaustion. Conversely, making modest changes or adopting a narrow focus, may mean there is no real change at all, or that the change is undermined by all the other unaltered aspects of school that haven't been attended to.

This is a profound paradox and one that leads many educational leaders into utter despair. But there are ways to resolve it: to be *both* modest *and* ambitious, focused *and* broad. When starting out, it is important to have all the change principles we have reviewed in one's sight but not to make each one into an innovation or an action-plan. These principles should help inform thinking about and management of change efforts, as well as being a constant reminder of how everything affects everything else. But they should not become separate, disembodied change efforts of their own.

These multidimensional understandings can be helpful guides to change efforts if they are then applied together to specific areas of the school's work, such as a grade level, integration between two or three subject departments, links between elementary schools and high schools, and so on. Volunteers can usually be found for such programs, and sometimes, the most unlikely staff members will respond positively to active invitations to join them. Reviewing the literature in this area, Fullan (1994) has found that:

> isolated pockets of change reflecting new behaviors led to new thinking that eventually pushed structures and procedures to change. People learn new behaviors primarily through their interactions with others, not through front-end training designs. Training builds on and extends new momentum . . . Reform is much more powerful when teachers and administrators begin working in new ways, only to discover that school structures must be altered, than the reverse situation. (p. 194)

'Getting there' is most likely to be achieved by grounding multi-dimensional thinking in one or more localized initiatives. Learning and further change arising from these initiatives then requires inquiry and dialogue about their effectiveness through open lines of communication with the rest of the staff, as well as students and parents. Enough organizational frameworks of dialogue and decision-making need to be in place to enable this communication to occur. This creates the kind of generative politics we described earlier.

Throughout all this, persistence is essential, and patience is a virtue. For example, administrators may want teachers to *teach* in teams, but should not be despondent if initially they are only *planning* in teams. As we have found in a current project with grades 7 and 8 teachers, they may want teachers who are developing an integrated curriculum to agree on teaching a common content, but should not despair if initially the teachers can agree only on common principles and outcomes. If dialogue begins and can be sustained, action will usually deepen later.

So the paradox of educational change needing to be both fast and slow, narrow and broad, need not be a paradox of despair. It can be a paradox of hope where 'getting there' through the accumulation of small but significant initiatives informed by multidimensional thinking will lead teachers and students not to ultimate nirvanas of perfect education for early adolescents, but to significant ongoing improvements in an excitingly imperfectible world where even greater successes always lie just around the corner.

The final words of this book are being written by one of us in an airplane coming in to land. The flight attendant knows I'm trying to complete the manuscript on this flight. A moment ago, she leaned across and inquired encouragingly — 'Getting there?' Now I and my other authors have 'got there'. But it does not mean we will never want to go anywhere else, geographically or educationally. Getting to lots of 'theres' is both hard work and great fun, and so it should be for adolescent students and those who teach them, as much as it has been for us. Have the courage to strike out for exciting new destinations where schooling might look very different for you and your students. Overcome the obstacles, or go around them. Enjoy the journey. Getting there will be more than half the fun: it will be worth it for all of you.

References

Acker, S. (1995) 'Gender and teachers' work' in Apple, M. (Ed.) *Review and Research in Education*, 21, Washington, DC, AERA.

Adler, M. (1982) *The Paedia Proposal: An Educational Manifesto*, New York, MacMillan Publishing Co.

Ahola-Sidaway, J.A. (1988) 'From Gemeinschaft to Gesellschaft: A case study of student transition from elementary school to high school', paper presented at the annual meeting of the American Educational Research Association, New Orleans, ERIC Document ED 297450.

Ainley, J. (1991) 'High school factors that influence students to remain in school', *Journal of Educational Research*, **85**, 2.

Ainley, J. (1993) 'Parents in the transition years' in Hargreaves, A., Leithwood, K. and Gerin-Lajoie, D. (Eds) *Years of Transition: Times for Change*, Toronto, Ontario Ministry of Education and Training.

Alexander, K.A., Cook, M. and McDill, E.L. (1978) 'Curriculum tracking and educational stratification: Some further evidence', *American Sociological Review*, **43**, pp. 47–66.

Alexander, W. (1968) *The Emerging Middle School*, New York, Holt, Rinehart & Wilson.

Allen, R.R. and Kellner, R.W. (1983) 'Putting humpty dumpty together again: integrating the language arts', in *The Talking and Writing Series, K-12: Successful Classroom Practices*, Washington, DC, Dingle Associates.

Anderson, J.O. (1989) 'Evaluation of student achievement: Teacher practices and educational measurement', *The Alberta Journal of Educational Research*, XXXV, pp. 123–33.

Appleton, N. (1983) *Cultural Pluralism in Education*, New York, Longman.

Archibald, D. and Newman, F. (1988) *Beyond Generalized Testing: Assessing Achievement in the Secondary School*, Reston, VA, NASSP.

Armstrong, T. (1994) *Multiple Intelligences in the Classroom*, Alexandria, VA, ASCD.

Ascher, C. (1987) *The Ninth Grade — A Precarious Time for the Potential Dropout*, New York, Eric Clearinghouse on Urban Education, ERIC Document ED 284922.

Ashton, P. and Webb, R. (1986) *Making a Difference: Teacher's Sense of Efficacy and Student Achievement*, New York, Longman.

Association of Universities and Colleges of Canada (1982) 'Money may itself have become a philosophy of life for students', *University Affairs*, October, p. 27.

ATKINSON, P. and DELAMONT, S. (1977) 'Mock ups and cock ups: The stage management of guided discovery' in HAMMERSLEY, M. and WOODS, P. (Eds) *School Experience*, London, Croom Helm.

ATWOOD, V.A. *et al* (1989) 'In the soup: An integrative unit, Part 1', *Social Studies and the Young Learner*, **2**, 1, pp. 17–19.

AUBREY, R. (1985 November) 'A counseling perspective on the recent educational reform reports', *The School Counsellor*, **33**, pp. 91–9.

BABCOCK, E.H., DANIELS, D.B., ISLIP, J., RAZZELL, A.G. and ROSS, A.M. (1972) *Education in The Middle Years*, London, Evans/Methuen Educational.

BAILEY, W., DEERY, N., GEHRKE, M., PERRY, N. and WHITLEDGE, J. (1989) 'Issues in elementary school counseling: Discussion with American school counselor association leaders', *Elementary School Guidance and Counseling*, **24** October, pp. 4–13.

BALDWIN, J. and WELLS, H. (1981) *Active Tutorial Work: Books 1–5*, Oxford, Basil Blackwell.

BALL, S. (1980) *Beachside Comprehensive*, Cambridge, Cambridge University Press.

BALL, S. (1983) 'A subject of privilege: English and the school curriculum: 1906–35' in HAMMERSLEY, M. and HARGREAVES, A. (Eds) *Curriculum Practice: Some Sociological Case Studies*, Philadelphia, PA, Falmer Press.

BALL, S. and BOWE, R. (1992) 'Subject departments and the implementation of the national curriculum', *Journal of Curriculm Studies*, **24**, pp. 97–116.

BANTOCK, G. (1980) *Dilemmas of the Curriculum*, Oxford, Martin Robertson.

BARELL, J. (1991) *Teaching for Thoughtfulness: Classroom Strategies to Enhance Intellectual Development*, New York, Longmans.

BARKER, B. (1985) 'Curricular offerings in small and large high schools: How broad is the disparity?', *Research in Rural Education*, **3**, 1.

BARKER-LUNN, J. (1970) *Streaming in the Primary School*, Slough, NFER.

BARLOW, M. and ROBERTSON, H.-J. (1994) *Class Warfare: The Assault on Canada's Schools*, Toronto, Key Porter Books.

BARNES, D. (1976) *From Communication to Curriculum*, Harmondsworth, Penguin.

BARNES, D. (1982) 'Integrating the curriculum' in BARNES, D. (Ed.) *Practical Curriculum Study*, London, Routledge & Kegan Paul, pp. 121–40.

BARNES, D. and SHEMILT, D. (1974) 'Transmission and interpretation', *Educational Review*, **26**, 3.

BARROW, R. (1979) *The Canadian Curriculum: A Personal View*, London Ontario, Faculty of Education, University of Western Ontario.

BASSEY, M. (1978) *Nine Hundred Primary School Teachers*, Slough, NFER.

BATES, R. (1987) 'Corporate culture, schooling and educational administration', *Education Administration Quarterly*, **23**, 4, November pp. 79–155.

BEANE, J. (1991) 'The middle school: The natural home of integrated curriculum', *Educational Leadership*, **49**, 2, pp. 9–13.

BEATON, J., BOTH, S., FINE, J. and HEMBER, D. (1988) *The Peel Board of Education Science Review*, Report PGSCIECE/4436, Peel Board of Education.

BELL, D. (1973) *The Coming of Postindustrial Society*, New York, Basic Books.

BENNETT, K. and LeCOMPTE, M. (1990) *The Way Schools Work: A Sociological Analysis of Education*, New York, Longman.

BENNETT, N. (1976) *Teaching Styles and Pupil Progress*, London, Open Books.

BERG, M. (1988) 'The integrated curriculum', *Social Studies Review*, **28**, 1, pp. 38–41.

BERLAK, A. and BERLAK, H. (1981) *Dilemmas of Schooling*, London, Methuen.

BERMAN, P. and McLAUGHLIN, M. (1977) *Federal Programs Supporting Educational Change, Vol. VII, Factors Affecting Implementation and Continuation*, Santa Monica, CA, Rand Corporation.

BERNSTEIN, B. (1971) 'On the classification and framing of educational knowledge' in YOUNG, M.F.D. (Ed.) *Knowledge and Control*, London, Collier-MacMillan.

BEST, R. (1994) 'Teachers' supportive roles in a secondary school: A Case study and discussion', *Support for Learning*, **9**, 4, November.

BEST, R., RIBBINS, P., JARVIS, C. and ODDY, D. (1980) 'Interpretations of teachers' views of 'pastoral care' in BEST, C., JARVIS, C. and RIBBINS, P. (Eds) *Perspectives in Pastoral Care*, London, Heinemann.

BETTS, F.M. (1983) 'A qualitative model of the integrative learning process', *Issues in Integrative Studies*, **2**, pp. 93–122.

BIBBY, R. and POSTERSKI, D. (1992) *Teen Trends: A Nation in Motion*, Toronto, Stoddart Publishing.

BLACKBURN, K. (1975) *The Tutor*, London, Heinemann.

BLACKMORE, J. (forthcoming) *Feminism, Leadership and Educational Change*, Milton Keynes, Open University Press.

BLASE, J. (1988) 'The teachers' political orientation vis-a-vis the principal: The micropolitics of the school', *Politics of Education Association Yearbook*, London, Falmer Press, pp. 113–26.

BLOOM, B. (1970) 'Toward a theory of testing which includes measurement-evaluation-assessment' in WITTROCK, M.C. and WILEY, D.W. (Eds) *The Evaluation of Instruction*, New York, Holt, Rinehart and Winston.

BLOOM, B.S. (1971) 'Learning for mastery' in BLOOM, B.S., HASTING, J.T. and MADAUS, G.F. (Eds) *Handbook on Formative and Summative Evaluation of Student Learning*, New York, McGraw Hill.

BLOOMER, J.M. (1986) 'Conquering the new frontier', *NASSP Bulletin*, **70**, 487, pp. 95–6.

BOARD OF EDUCATION (1911) *Report of the Consultative Committee on Examinations in Secondary Schools*, (Cd 6004). London, HMSO.

BOLAM, R. and MEDLOCK, P. (1985) *Active Tutorial Work: Training and Dissemination — An Evaluation*, Oxford, Basil Blackwell.

BOOK, C. and FREEMAN, D.J. (1986) 'Differences in entry characteristics of elementary and secondary teacher candidates', *Journal of Teacher Education*, **37**, 2, pp. 47–51.

Bowan, R. (1986) 'Peer facilitators for middle grades: Students helping each other grow up', *The School Counsellor*, January.

Boyd, W. and Crowson, R. (1982) 'The changing conception and practice of public school administration', *Review of Research in Education*, **9**, pp. 311–73.

Boyer, E. (1983) *High School: A Report On Secondary Education In America*, New York, Harper and Row.

Braddock, J.H. II, *et al* (1988) *School Organization in the Middle Grades: National Variations and Effects*, Baltimore, MD, Center for Research on Elementary and Middle Schools, ERIC Document ED 301320.

Breen, J.M. (1983) 'Transition — hit or miss? A case study of a secondary school in Westernport region', Masters thesis, Melbourne, Monash University.

Brent, D. *et al* (1985) 'Effective integration of computer technology into a secondary school: Writing across the curriculum', *Technological Horizons in Education*, **13**, 3, pp. 103–6.

Bresler, L. (1993) 'The social organization of achievement: A case study of a music theory class', *Curriculum Journal*, **4**, 1, pp. 37–58.

Broadfoot, P. (1979) *Assessment, Schools and Society*, London, Methuen.

Broadfoot, P. (1984) 'From public examinations to profile assessment — the French experience' in Broadfoot, P. (Ed.) *Selection, Certification and Control*, London, Falmer Press.

Broadfoot, P. (1986) 'Alternatives to public examinations' in Nuttall, D. (Ed.) *Assessing Educational Achievement*, London, Falmer Press.

Broadfoot, P., James, M., McMeeking, S., Nuttall, D. and Stierer, B. (1988) *Records of Achievement: Report Of The National Evaluation Of Pilot Schemes*, London, HMSO.

Brophy, J. (1987) 'Syntheses of research on strategies for motivating children to learn,' *Educational Leadership*, **45**, 2, pp. 40–8.

Brophy, J. (1992) 'Probing the subtleties of subject-matter teaching', *Educational Leadership*, **49**, 7, ASCD.

Brophy, J. and Alleman, J. (1991) 'A caveat: Curriculum integration isn't always a good idea', *Educational Leadership*, **49**, 2, p. 66.

Brophy, J. and Good, T. (1974) *Teacher-Student Relationships: Causes and Consequences*, New York, Holt Rinehart and Winston, Inc.

Brown, B. (1984) *Crisis In Secondary Education: Rebuilding America's High Schools*, Princeton, NJ, Prentice Hall.

Bruner, J. (1994) 'How children learn', *The Executive Educator*, **16**, 8, pp. 31–6.

Bulson, T. (1984) *Bridging the Gap*, Aurora, Ontario, York Region Board of Education.

Burgess, R. (1983) *Experiencing Comprehensive Education*, London, Methuen.

Burgess, R. (1987) 'The politics of pastoral care', paper presented at the International Sociology of Education Conference, January, Westhill College, Birmingham.

Burgess, T. and Adams, E. (1985) *Records of Achievement*, Windsor, NFER-Nelson.

BURKE, A.M. (1987) *Making a Big School Smaller: The School-Within-a-School Arrangement for Middle Level Schools*, Orting, WA, Orting Middle Schools, ERIC Document ED 303890.

BUTTON, L. (1981) *Group Tutoring for the Form Teacher. 1. Lower Secondary School; (1982) 2. Upper Secondary School*, London, Hodder and Stoughton.

CALABRESE, R.L. (1987) 'Adolescence: A growth period conducive to alienation', *Adolescence*, **22**, 88, pp. 929–38.

CAMPBELL, R.J. (1985) *Developing the Primary Curriculum*, London, Holt, Rinehart and Winston.

CANADIAN TEACHERS FEDERATION (1990) *A CAPPELLA: Report on the Realities, Concerns, Expectations and Barriers Experienced by Adolescent Women in Canada*, Ottawa, CTF.

CAPUZZI, D. (1988) 'Personal and social competency: Developing skills for the future' in WALZ, G. (Ed.) *Building Strong School Counseling Programs*, Alexandria, VA, American Association for Counseling and Development, pp. 49–90.

CARDINALE, G. (1988) 'The four A's of history/social science education: A question of priorities', *Social Studies Review*, **28**, 1, pp. 14–18.

CARROLL, J. (1990) 'The Copernican plan: Restructuring the American high school', *Phi Delta Kappan*, **71**, 3.

CARTER, L. (1984) 'The sustaining effects of study of compensatory and elementary education', *Education Research*, **13**, pp. 4–13.

CASE, R. (1991) *The Anatomy of Curricular Integration. Forum on Curriculum Integration. Tri University Integration Project*, Occasional Paper #2, Burnaby, British Columbia, Simon Fraser University.

CASE, R. (1994) 'Our crude handling of educational reforms: The case of curricular integration', *Canadian Journal of Education*, **19**, 1, pp. 80–93.

CAZDEN, C.B. and LEGGETT, E.L. (1973) 'Cultural responsive education: recommendations for achieving lau remedies II' in TRUEBA, H., GUTHERIE, G. and AU, K. (Eds) *The Cultural and Bilingual Classroom*, London, Newbury.

CENTRAL ADVISORY COUNCIL FOR EDUCATION (England) (1967) *Children and Their Primary Schools (The Plowden Report)*, London, HMSO.

CHASKIN, R. and RAUNER, D. (1995) 'Youth and caring: An introduction', *Phi Delta Kappan*, **76**, 9, pp. 667–74.

CHENG, M.L. and ZIEGLER, S. (1986) *Moving from Elementary to Secondary School: Procedures which May Facilitate the Transition Process*, Toronto, Toronto Board of Education.

CICOUREL, A.V. and KITSUSE, J.F. (1963) *The Educational Decision Makers*, New York, Bobbs-Merrill.

CLARK, C. (1996) *Thoughtful Teaching*, New York, Teachers' College Press.

CLIFTON, R. (1975) 'Self-conception and attitudes: A comparison of Canadian Indian and non-Indian students', *Canadian Review of Sociology and Anthropology*, 12.

COHEN, D. and BARNES, C. (1992) 'Conclusion: A new pedagogy for policy' in

Cohen, D., McLaughlin, M. and Talbert, J. (Eds) *Teaching for Understanding: Challenges for Policy and Practice*, San Francisco, CA, Jossey-Bass.

Cohen, M. and Shapiro, R. (1979) *Report of the High School Articulation Project*, Brooklyn, NY, New York City Board of Education, Office of Educational Evaluation, ERIC Document ED 182377.

Cole, C. (1988) 'The school counselor: Image and impact, counselor role and function, 1960s to 1980s and beyond' in Walz, G. (Ed.) *Building Strong School Counseling Programs*, Alexandria, VA, American Association for Counseling and Development, pp. 127–50.

Cole, M. and Scribner, S. (1973) 'Cognitive consequences of formal and informal education', *Science*, **182**, pp. 553–9.

Cole, N. (1990) 'Conceptions of educational achievement', *Educational Researcher*, **19**, 3, pp. 2–7.

Conference Board of Canada (1991) *Employability Skills Profile*, Ottawa, National Bureau and Education Centre.

Conklin, K.R. (1966) 'The integration of the disciplines', *Educational Theory*, **16**, pp. 225–38.

Connell, R., Ashenden, D.J., Dessler, S. and Dowsett, G.W. (1982) *Making the Difference*, Boston, MA, Allen and Unwin.

Connelly, C.H. (1954) 'Integration in the organization of curriculum', *School and Society*, **80**.

Cooper, B. (1985) *Renegotiating Secondary School Mathematics*, Philadelphia, PA, Falmer Press.

Cooper, M. (1987) 'Whose culture is it anyway?' in Lieberman, A. (Ed.) *Building a Professional Culture in Schools*, New York, Teachers' College Press.

Corbett, H., Dickson, R., Firestone, W. and Rossman, G. (1987) 'Resistance To planned change and the sacred in school cultures', Educational *Administration Quarterly*, **23**, 4, pp. 36–59.

Corcoran, B.T. (1985) *Competency Testing and At-Risk Youth*, Philadelphia, PA, Research for Better Schools.

Corson, D. (1988) *Oral Language Across the Curriculum*, Clevedon, Multilingual Matters.

Corson, D. (1990) *Language Policy Across the Curriculum*, Clevedon, Multilingual Matters.

Corson, D. (1992) 'Minority cultural values and discourse norms in majority cultural classrooms', *The Canadian Modern Language Review*, **48**, 3, pp. 472–96.

Corson, D. (1993) *Language, Minority Education and Gender: Linking Social Justice and Power*, Clevedon, Multilingual Matters Ltd.

Costa, A. (1991) 'The School as a Home for the Mind', paper presented at the Annual International Conference on Critical Thinking and Educational Reform, Rohhert Park, CA, August 5–8.

Coulter, R. and McNay, M. (1993) 'Exploring one's experiences as an elementary school teacher', *Canadian Journal of Education*, **18**, 4, pp. 398–413.

Cox, C. and Scruton, R. (1984) *Peace Studies: A Critical Survey*, Occasional

Paper No. 7, Institute for European Defence and Strategic Studies, London, Alliance Publishers.

CRAIG, C. (1987) 'Addressing subject integration', *History and Social Science Teacher*, **23**, 1, pp. 31–4.

CREMIN, L. (1961) *The Tranformation Of The School*, New York, Teachers College Press.

CROOKS, T. (1988) 'The impact of classroom evaluation practices on students', *Review of Educational Research*, **58**.

CSIKZENTMIHALYI, M. (1990) *Flow: The Problem of Optimal Experience*, New York, Harper Collins.

CUBAN, L.J. (1984) *How Teachers Taught: Constancy and Change in American Classrooms 1890–1980*, New York, Longman.

CUMMINS, J. and SAYERS, D. (1995) *Brave New Schools: Challenging Cultural Illiteracy through Global Learning Networks*, Toronto, OISE Press.

CUNNINGHAM, D. (1986) 'Transition in languages other than English from primary to postprimary schools', *Babel*, **21**, 3, pp. 13–19.

CURTIS, B. (1988) *Building the Educational State: Canada West*, Philadelphia, PA, Falmer Press.

CUSICK, P.A. (1983) *The Egalitarian Ideal and the American High School: Students of These Schools*, London, Longman.

DARLING-HAMMOND, L. (1990) 'Instructional policy into practice: "The power of the bottom over the top"', *Educational Evaluation and Policy Analysis*, **12**, 3, pp. 233–41.

DARLING-HAMMOND, L. (1995) 'Policy for restructuring' in LIEBERMAN, A. (Ed.) *The Work of Restructuring Schools*, New York, Teachers' College Press.

DAS, J., KIRBY, J. and JARMAN, R. (1979) *Simultaneous and Successive Cognitive Processes*, New York, Academic Press.

DAVID, K. (1983) 'Personal and social education in secondary schools', *Schools Council, Programme 3*, London, Longman.

DAVIS, J. (1988) *The Small School*, Toronto, Department of Educational Administration, OISE.

DAVIS, J. (1989) 'Effective schools, organizational culture and local policy initiatives' in HOLMES, M. *et al* (Eds) *Educational Policy for Effective Schools*, Toronto, OISE Press.

DAVIS, J. and WANG, S. (1995) 'Organizational culture in Chinese and Canadian secondary school settings', paper presented at the CSSE Conference, Montreal.

DAVYDOV, V. (1995) 'The influence of L.S. VYGOTSKY on educational theory, practice and research', *Educational Researcher*, **24**, 3, pp. 12–21.

DE BONO, E. (1990) *Six Thinking Hats for Schools*, Perfection Learning. Boston, Little Brown and Co.

DEAL, T. and KENNEDY, A. (1982) *Corporate Cultures*, Reading MA, Addison-Wesley.

DEAL, T. and PETERSON, K. (1990) *The Principal's Role in Shaping School Culture*, Washington, DC, United States Government Printing Office.

DEAL, T. and PETERSON, K. (1994) *The Leadership Paradox: Balancing Logic and Artistry in Schools*, San Francisco, CA, Jossey-Bass.

DELHI, K. (1995) 'Travelling tales: Thinking comparatively about education reform and parental "choice" in post-modern times', paper presented at the annual meeting of the American Educational Research Association, San Francisco, April.

DELLER, D.K. (1980) 'A model for improving parent orientation to the middle schools', EdD Practicum Report, Florida, Nova University, ERIC Document ED 202083.

DELPIT, L. (1988) 'The Silenced dialogue: Power and pedagogy in educating other people's children', *Harvard Educational Review*, **58**, 3, pp. 280–98.

DEPARTMENT OF EDUCATION and SCIENCE (1983) *Teaching Quality*, London, HMSO.

DEPARTMENT OF EDUCATION and SCIENCE (1984) *Records of Achievement: A Statement of Policy*, London, HMSO.

DEPARTMENT OF EDUCATION and SCIENCE (1988) *Education Reform Act*, London, HMSO.

DEPARTMENT OF EDUCATION (1987) *What Works: Research About Teaching and Learning*, Washington, DC, Department of Education.

DERRICOTT, R. (1985) *Curriculum Continuity: Primary to Secondary*, Philadephia, PA, NFER-Nelson.

DERRICOTT, R. and RICHARDS, C. (1980) 'The middle school curriculum: Some uncharted territory' in HARGREAVES, A. and TICKLE, L. (Eds) *Middle Schools: Origins, Ideology and Practice*, London, Harper and Row.

DEUTSCH, M. (1979) 'Education and distributive justice: Some reflections on grading systems', *American Psychologist*, **34**, pp. 391–401.

DEYHLE, D. (1983) 'Between games and failure: a micro-ethnographic study of Navajo and testing', *Curriculum Inquiry*, **13**, 4, pp. 347–76.

DEYHLE, D. (1986) 'Success and failure: A micro-ethnographic comparison of Navajo and Anglo students' perceptions of testing', *Curriculum Inquiry*, **16**, 4, pp. 365–89.

DICKINSON, G. *et al* (1980) *Adult Basic Literacy Curriculum and Resource Guide*, Victoria, BC, British Columbia Department of Education.

DIVOKY, D. (1988) 'The model minority goes to school', *Phi Delta Kappan*, **70**, 3, pp. 219–22.

DORE, R. (1976) *The Diploma Disease*, London, Allen and Unwin.

DRAKE, S. (1991) 'How our team dissolved the boundaries', *Educational Leadership*, **49**, 2, pp. 20–22.

DRESSEL, P.L. (1958) 'The meaning and significance of integration' in HENRY, N.B. (Ed.) *The Integration of Educational Experiences: 57th Yearbook of the NSSE, Part III*, Chicago, IL, University of Chicago Press, pp. 3–25.

DUFFY, T. and JONASSEN, D. (1992) *Constructivism and the Technology of Instruction: A Conversation*, Princeton, NJ, Lawrence Erlbaum Associates.

DUNCAN, V.A. (1987) *English Language Arts Comprehensive Curriculum Goals: A Model for Local Curriculum Development*, Salem, OR, Oregon State Department of Education.

DUNN, R. and DUNN, K. (1982) 'Teaching students through their individual learning styles: a research report', *Student Learning Styles and Brain Behaviour*, Reston, VA, NASSP.

DURKHEIM, E. (1956) *Education and Sociology*, New York, Free Press.

EARL, L.M. (1987) *Organization of Schools for Intermediate Students: Literature Review*, Research Report 87–18, London, Ontario, Board of Education for the City of London.

EARL, L. and COUSINS, J.B. (1995) *Classroom Assessment: Changing the Face: Facing the Change*, Mississauga, Ontario, Canada: Ontario Public Service Teachers' Federation.

EBEL, R.L. (1980) 'Evaluation of students: implications for effective teaching', *Educational Evaluation and Policy Analysis*, **2**, 1, pp. 47–51.

ECCLES, J., LORD, S. and MIDGLEY, C. (1991) 'What are we doing to early adolescents? The impact of educational contexts on early adolescents', *American Journal of Education*, April, pp. 521–42.

EGAN, K. (1988) *Teaching as Storytelling*, London, Routledge.

ELKIND, D. (1993) 'School and family in the post-modern world', *Phi Delta Kappan*, **77**, 1, pp. 8–14.

EMBERLEY, P. and NEWELL, W. (1994) *Bankrupt Education: The Decline of Liberal Education in Canada*, Toronto, University of Toronto Press.

ENTWISTLE, N. (1981) *Styles of Learning and Teaching*, Chichester, John Wiley.

EPSTEIN, J.L. (1988) *Schools In the Center: Schools, Family, Peer and Community. Connections for More Effective Middle Grade Schools and Students*. Baltimore, MD, John Hopkins University Center for Research on Elementary and Middle Schools.

EPSTEIN, J.L. (1990) 'What matters in the middle grades — grade span or practices?', *Phi Delta Kappan*, **71**, 3.

EPSTEIN, J. (1995) 'School/family/community partnerships', *Phi Delta Kappan*, **76**, pp. 701–12.

EPSTEIN, J. and PETERSON, A. (1991) 'Discussion and outlook: Research on education and development across the years of adolescence', *American Journal of Education*, **99**, 4, pp. 643–57.

ERICKSON, F. (1993) 'Transformation and school success: The politics and culture of educational achievement' in JACOB, E. and JORDAN, C. (Eds) *Minority Education: Anthropological Perspectives*, Norwood, NJ, Ablex Publishing Corporation.

ERICKSON, F. and MOHATT, G. (1982) 'Cultural organization of participant structures in two classrooms of Indian students' in SPINDLER, G. (Ed.) *Doing the Ethnography of Schooling*, Toronto, Holt, Rinehart and Winston.

Esposito, D. (1973) 'Homogeneous and heterogeneous ability grouping: principal findings and implications for evaluating and designing more effective educational environments', *Review of Educational Research*, **43**, pp. 163–79.

ETZIONI, A. (1982) *An Immodest Agenda: Rebuilding America*, New York, McGraw Hill.

ETZIONI, A. (1993) *The Spirit of Community: Rights, Responsibilities and the Communitarian Agenda*, New York, Croan Publishers.

EVANS, M.J. (1983) 'From school to school: The integration into the secondary school of pupils in the transition from primary to secondary schooling', paper presented at the National Conference of the Australian Association for Research in Education, Canberra, November.

EYERS, V. (1992) *The Report of the Junior-Secondary Review: The Education of Young Adolescents in South Australian Government Schools*, Adelaide, Department of Education of South Australia.

FINDLEY, W. and BRYAN, M. (1975) 'The pros and cons of ability grouping', *PDK Fastback Series*, **66**.

FINE, M. (1986) 'Why urban adolescents drop into and out of public high schools', *Teachers College Record*, **87**, 3.

FINE, M. (1993) 'Sexuality, schooling and adolescent females: the missing discourse of desire' in WEISS, L. and FINE, M. (Eds) *Beyond Silenced Voices: Class, Race and Gender in United States Schools*, Albany, NY, State University of New York Press.

FIRESTONE, W. and ROSENBLUM, S. (1987) 'First year project: A study of alienation and commitment in five urban districts', paper presented at the annual meeting of the American Educational Research Association, Washington, DC.

FOGARTY, R. (1991) 'Ten ways to integrate curriculum', *Educational Leadership*, **49**, 2, pp. 61–5.

FOGARTY, R. (1994) *How to Teach for Metacognition*, Palatine, IL, IRI/Skylight.

FORD, F. (1985) 'Beginning again: A study of post-secondary student transition in a Victorian catholic schools network during 1982 and 1983', MEd studies thesis, Monash University.

FOWLER, J. (1992) 'What do we know about school size? What should we know?', paper presented at the annual meeting of the American Educational Research Association, San Francisco.

FRAM, I., GODWIN, R. and CASSIDY, P. (1976) *The Junior High School and the Social and Educational Needs of the Early Adolescent*, North York, Ontario, Board of Education for the Borough of North York.

FREUND, P. (1985) 'The transition from primary to secondary school: An investigation of the procedures of transfer and induction at eleven years', unpublished diploma dissertation, University of Oxford, Department of Educational Studies.

FRIEND, H. (1984) *The Effect of Science and Mathematics Integration on Selected Seventh Grade Students' Attitudes Toward and Achievement in Science*, New York, New York City Board of Education.

FULLAN, M. (1982) *The Meaning of Educational Change*, Toronto, OISE Press.

FULLAN, M. (1991) *The New Meaning of Educational Change* (with S. Stiegelbauer) New York, Teachers College Press.

FULLAN, M. (1993) *Change Forces: Probing the Depths of Educational Reform*, Philadelphia, PA, Falmer Press.

FULLAN, M. (1994) 'Coordinating top-down and bottom-up strategies for educational reform' in ELMORE, R. and FUHRMAN, S. (Eds) *The Governance of Curriculum. The 1994 ASCD Yearbook*, Alexandria, VA, Association for Supervision and Curriculum Development.

FULLAN, M. (1996) 'Leadership for change' in LEITHWOOD, K. (Ed.) *International Handbook of Educational Leadership*, The Netherlands, Kluwer Press.

FULLAN, M. and HARGREAVES, A. (1991) *What's Worth Fighting For In Your School*, Toronto, Ontario Public School Teacher's Federation.

FULLER, F. (1969) 'Concerns of teachers: A developmental characterisation', *American Educational Research Journal*, **6**, pp. 207–26.

FURTHER EDUCATION CURRICULUM (1982) *Profiles: A Review of Issues and Practice in the Use and Development of Student Profiles*, London, HMSO.

GALLOWAY, D. (1985) 'Pastoral care and school effectiveness' in REYNOLDS, D. (Ed.) *Studying School Effectiveness*, London, Falmer Press.

GALTON, M. and DELAMONT, S. (1980) 'Pupil anxiety and transfer to middle school' in HARGREAVES, A. and TICKLE, L. (Eds) *Middle Schools: Origins, Ideology and Practice*, London, Harper and Row.

GALTON, M., SIMON, B. and CROLL, P. (1980) *Inside the Primary Classroom*, London, Routledge and Kegan Paul.

GALTON, M. and WILLCOCKS, J. (1983) *Moving from the Primary Classroom*, London, Routledge and Kegan Paul.

GARCIA, E. (1990) 'An Analysis of literacy enhancement for middle school Hispanic students through curriculum integration', paper presented at the annual meeting of the National Reading Conference, Miami.

GARDNER, H. (1983) *Frames of Mind: The Theory of Multiple Intelligences*, New York, Basic Books.

GARDNER, H. (1985) *The Mind's New Science*, New York, Basic Books.

GARDNER, H. (1991) *The Unschooled Mind: How Children Think and How Schools Should Teach*, New York, Basic Books.

GARDNER, H. (1993) *Multiple Intelligences: The Theory in Practice*, New York, Basic Books.

GARDNER, H. (1994) 'Howard Gardner on learning for understanding', *The School Administrator*, January, pp. 26–31.

GARTON, A.F. (1987) 'Specific aspects of the transition from primary school to high school', *Australian Educational and Developmental Psychologist*, **4**, 1, pp. 11–16.

GEDGE, J. (1991) 'The hegemonic curriculum and school dropout: The Newfoundland case', *Journal of Education Policy*, **6**, 2, pp. 215–24.

GEORGE, P.S. and OLDAKER, L.L. (1985) *Evidence for the Middle School*, Columbus, OH, National Middle School Association.

GIBSON, M. (1987) 'The school performance of immigrant minorities: a comparative view', *Anthropology and Education Quarterly*, **18**, 1, pp. 262–75.

GIDDENS, A. (1995) *Beyond Left and Right*, Stanford, CA, Stanford University Press.

GILLIGAN, C. (1982) *In a Different Voice: Psychological Theory and Women's Development*, Cambridge, MA, Harvard University Press.

GILLIGAN, C. (1989) 'Making connections: the relational worlds of adolescent girls at Emma Willard School', Reviewed in *Toronto Star*, (1990, January 16), pp. B1, B4.

GINSBURG, M.B., MEYENN, R.J., MILLER, H.D.R. and RANCEFORD-HADLEY, C. (1977) *The Role of the Middle School Teacher*, Aston Educational Monograph No. 7, Birmingham, University of Aston.

GIRE, J. and POE, B. (1988) 'Implementing a transition-to-work model at the junior high school level', *Pointer*, **32**, 2, pp. 15–17.

GLATTER, R. (1994) 'Managing dilemmas in education: The tightrope walk of strategic choice in more autonomous institutions', paper presented at the 8th International Intervisitation Program in Educational Administration, Toronto, May.

GOLDMAN, S. and McDERMOTT, R. (1987) 'The culture of competition in American schools' in SPINDLER, G. (Ed.) *Education and Cultural Process: Anthropological Approaches* (2nd edn) Prospect Heights, Waveland Press.

GOODLAD, J.I. (1984) *A Place Called School: Prospects For The Future*, New York, McGraw-Hill.

GOODLAD, J. and OAKES, J. (1988) 'We must offer equal access to knowledge', *Educational Leadership*, February.

GOODMAN, K.S., SMITH, E.B., MEREDITH, R. and GOODMAN, Y.M. (1987) *Language and Thinking in School — A Whole Language Curriculum*, New York, Richard C. Owen.

GOODSON, I.F. (1983) *School Subjects and Curriculum Change*, London, Croom Helm.

GOODSON, I.F. (1988) *The Making of Curriculum*, Philadelphia, PA, Falmer Press.

GOODSON, I.F. (1992) 'Sponsoring the teacher's voice' in HARGREAVES, A. and FULLAN, M. (Eds) *Understanding Teacher Development*, New York, Teachers' College Press.

GOODSON, I.F. (1994) *Studying Curriculum: Cases and Methods*, Buckingham, Open University Press.

GOODSON, I.F. and BALL, S. (Eds) (1985) *Defining the Curriculum*, Philadelphia, PA, Falmer Press.

GOODSON, I.F. and MANGAN, J.M. (1992) 'Computers in schools as symbolic and ideological action: The genealogy of the ICON', *The Curriculum Journal*, **3**, 3, pp. 261–276.

GORWOOD, B. (1986) *School Transfer and Curriculum Continuity*, New Hampshire, Croom Helm.

GOULD, C. (1981) *Career Education Management Activity Guide*, Augusta, ME, Maine State Department of Educational and Cultural Services. Office of Career Education, ERIC Document ED 215099.

GOVERNMENT OF NEWFOUNDLAND and LABRADOR (1989) *Towards an Achieving Society*, Task Force on Mathematics and Science Education.

GRAY, J., McPHERSON, A.F. and RAFFE, D. (1983) *Reconstructions of Secondary Education*, London, Routledge and Kegan Paul.

GREENAN, J.P. and TUCKER, P. (1990) 'Integrating science knowledge and skills in vocational education programs: Strategies and approaches', *Journal for Vocational Special Needs Education*, **13**, 1, pp. 19–22.

GREENBERG, A. and HUNTER, A. (1982) 'Striving for excellence: Middle schoolers study "Work",' *Ideas for Action in Education and Work*, Issue 5.

GREENE, M. (1985) 'Jeremiad and the curriculum: The haunting of the secondary school', *Curriculum Inquiry*, **15**, 3.

GREGORC, A.F. (1979) *ORGANON: Theory Manual*, Working Paper, University of Connecticut, School of Education.

GRIFFITHS, D.E. (1980) 'Beyond the basics', *New York University Education Quarterly*, **12**, 1, pp. 2–6.

GRONN, P. (1995) 'Greatness revisited: The current obsession with transformational leadership', *Leading and Managing*, **1**, 1, autumn, pp. 14–27.

GUE, L. (1975) 'Patterns in native education', *CSSE Yearbook*, **1**, pp. 7–20.

GUE, L. (1977) *Links, Sponsored International Development Projects. An Introduction to Educational Administration in Two Canadian Universities*, Ottawa, Canadian Bureau for International Education.

GULLICKSON, A.R. (1982) 'The Practice of Testing in Elementary and Secondary Schools', unpublished report, ED229391.

GULLICKSON, A.R. (1984) 'Teacher perspectives of their instructional use of tests', *Journal of Educational Research*, **77**, pp. 244–8.

GUSKEY, T. (Ed.) (1994) *High Stakes Performance Assessments: Perspectives on Kentucky's Educational Reform*, Thousand Oakes, CA, Corwin Press.

GUTTMAN, M.A. (1985) 'A peer counselling model: Social outreach', *Canadian Counsellors*, **19**, pp. 135–43.

HAASE, S.E. (1981) 'Thoughts on an integrated approach to curriculum', *Journal of American Indian Education*, **20**, 3, pp. 32–3.

HAIRSTON, L. (1983) *Getting to the Core of Education in the Omaha Public School System*, Omaha, NE, Omaha Public Schools.

HALE, M. (1990) *Chronicling the Implementation of Selected Key Concepts at R.H. King Academy*, Scarborough Board of Education Report No. 90/91–06.

HAMBLIN, D. (1978) *The Teacher and Pastoral Care*, Oxford, Basil Blackwell.

HAMILTON, D. (1973) 'The integration of knowledge: Practice and problems', *Journal of Curriculum Studies*, **2**, pp. 146–55.

HAMILTON, D. (1975) 'Handling innovation in the classroom: Two Scottish examples' in REID, W.A. and WALKER, D.F. (Eds) *Case Studies in Curriculum Change*, London, Routledge and Kegan Paul.

HAMILTON, D. (1989) *Towards a Theory of Schooling*, Philadelphia, PA, Falmer Press.

HAMMERSLEY, M. (1985) 'From ethnography to theory: A program and paradigm for case study research in the sociology of education', *Sociology*, **19**, 2, pp. 244–59.

HAMMERSLEY, M. and SCARTH, J. (1986) *The Impact of Examinations on Secondary School Teaching*, Final Research Report, School of Education. Milton Keynes: Open University Press.

HAMRE-NIETUPSKI, S. *et al* (1989) 'Enhancing integration of students with severe disabilities through curricular infusion: A general/special educator partnership', *Education and Training in Mental Retardation*, **24**, 1, pp. 78–88.

HANDY, C. (1994) *The Age of Paradox*, Cambridge, MA, Harvard Business Press.

HANEY, W. (1991) 'We must take care: Fitting assessments to function' in PERRONE, V.C. (Ed.) *Expanding Student Assessment*, Alexandria, VA, Association for Curriculum Development and Supervision.

HANEY, W. and MADAUS, G. (1989) 'Searching for alternatives to standardized tests: Whys, whats and whithers', *Phi Delta Kappan*, **70**, 9, pp. 683–87.

HARGREAVES, A. (1977) 'Progressivism and pupil autonomy', *Sociological Review*, **25**, 3.

HARGREAVES, A. (1986) *Two Cultures of Schooling: The Case of Middle Schools*, London, Falmer Press.

HARGREAVES, A. (1989) *Curriculum and Assessment Reform*, Milton Keynes, Open University Press.

HARGREAVES, A. (1991) 'Restructuring restructuring: postmodernity and the prospects for educational change', paper presented to the Second International Conference on Teacher Development, Vancouver, February, later published in the *Journal of Education Policy*, **9**, 1, pp. 47–65.

HARGREAVES, A. (1992) 'Cultures of teaching' in HARGREAVES, A. and FULLAN, M. (Eds) *Understanding Teacher Development*, London, Cassell.

HARGREAVES, A. (1994) *Changing Teachers, Changing Times: Teachers' Work and Culture in the Postmodern Age*, Toronto, Ontario Institute for Studies in Education.

HARGREAVES, A. (forthcoming) 'Rethinking educational change' in HARGREAVES, A. (Ed.) *Positive Change for School Success. The 1997 ASCD Yearbook*, Alexandria, VA, Association for Supervision and Curriculum Development.

HARGREAVES, A., BAGLIN, E., HENDERSON, P., LEESON, P. and TOSSELL, T. (1988) *Personal and Social Education: Choices and Challenges*, Oxford, Blackwell.

HARGREAVES, A., DAVIS, J., FULLAN, M. *et al* (1992) *Secondary School Work Cultures and Educational Change*, Toronto, Ontario Institute for Studies in Education.

HARGREAVES, A. and DAWE, R. (1990) 'Paths of professional development: contrived collegiality, collaborative culture and the case of peer coaching', *Teaching and Teacher Education*, **4**, 3.

HARGREAVES, A. and EARL, L. (1990) *Rights of Passage: A Review of Selected Research About Schooling in the Transition Years*, Toronto, Queen's Printer for Ontario.

HARGREAVES, A. and GOODSON, I. (1996) 'Teachers' professional lives: Aspirations and actualities' in GOODSON, I. and HARGREAVES, A. (Eds) *Teachers' Professional Lives*, London, Falmer Press.

HARGREAVES, A., LEITHWOOD, K., GERIN-LAJOIE, D., THIESSEN, D. and COUSINS, B. (1993) *Years of Transition: Times for Change*, Toronto, Ontario Institute for Studies in Education.

HARGREAVES, A. and MACMILLAN, R. (1995) 'The balkanization of secondary school teaching' in Siskin, L.S. and Little, J.W. (Eds) *The Subject in Question*, New York, Teachers' College Press.

Hargreaves, A. and Tickle, L. (1980) *Middle Schools: Origins, Ideology and Practice*, London, Harper and Row.

Hargreaves, A. and Wignall, R. (1989) *Time for the Teacher: A Study of Collegial Relations and Preparation Time Use Among Elementary School Teachers*, Final report of Transfer Grant Project 51/1070, Toronto, Ontario Institute for Studies in Education.

Hargreaves, D. (1967) *Social Relations in a Secondary School*, London, Routledge and Kegan Paul.

Hargreaves, D. (1980) 'The occupational culture of teaching' in Woods, P. (Ed.) *Teacher Strategies*, London, Croom Helm.

Hargreaves, D. (1982) *The Challenge for the Comprehensive School: Culture, Curriculum and Community*, London, Routledge and Kegan Paul.

Hargreaves, D. (1994) 'The new professionalism: The synthesis of professional and institutional development', *Teaching and Teacher Education*, **10**, 4, pp. 423–38.

Hargreaves, D. (1995) 'School culture, school effectiveness and school improvement', *School Effectiveness and School Improvement*, **6**, 1, pp. 23–46.

Hawking, S. (1988) *A Brief History of Time*, New York, Bantam Books.

Hawkins, J.A. *et al* (1983) *Grade Organization Patterns in Schools: A Review of the Research*, Rockville, MD, Montgomery County Public Schools.

Heath, B.E. (1988) 'Motivating teachers to utilize the integrated and correlated approach to teaching history-social science', *Social Studies Review*, **28**, 1, pp. 42–7.

Helsby, G. and McCulloch, G. (1996) 'Teacher professionalism and curriculum control' in Goodson, I. and Hargreaves, A. (Eds) *Teachers' Professional Lives*, London, Falmer Press.

Henrikson, G. (1973) *Hunters in the Barrens: The Naskapi on the Edge of the White Man's World*, St. John's Memorial University Institute of Social and Economic Research.

Henry, M.E. (1994) 'Parent-school partnerships: Public school reform from a feminist perspective', paper presented at the annual meeting of the American Educational Research Association, New Orleans, April.

Her Majesty's Inspectorate (1978) *Primary Education in England: A Survey by HM Inspectorate of Schools*, London, HMSO.

Her Majesty's Inspectorate (1979) *Aspects of Secondary Education in England: A Survey by HM Inspectors*, London, HMSO.

Her Majesty's Inspectorate (1983) *Curriculum 11–16: Towards a Statement of Entitlement*, London, HMSO.

Herman, J. and Dorr-Bremme, D.W. (1984) *Testing and Assessment in American Public Schools: Current Practices and Directions for Improvement*, Los Angeles, Center for the Study of Evaluation, University of California at Los Angeles.

Hewitt, J. (1994) *Teaching Teenagers: Making Connections in the Transition Years*, Thorndale, Ontario, Willsdowne Press.

HIRST, P. (1975) *Knowledge and the Curriculum*, London, Routledge and Kegan Paul.

HIRST, P.H. (1974) 'Curriculum integration' in HIRST, P.H. (Ed.) *Knowledge and the Curriculum*, London, Routledge and Kegan Paul, pp. 15–132.

HO, C. (1992) 'Grade 8 to 9 orientation program in Scarborough schools: Student survey', *Guidance and Counseling*, **7**, 4, pp. 41–7.

HOUT, M. and GARNIER, M. (1979) 'Curriculum placement and educational stratification in France', *Sociology of Education*, **52**, 3, pp. 146–56.

HUBERMAN, M. (1992) 'Teacher development and instructional mastery' in HARGREAVES, A. and FULLAN, M. (Eds) *Understanding Teacher Development*, New York, Teachers' College Press.

HUBERMAN, M. (1993) *The Lives of Teachers*, London, Cassell.

HUBERMAN, M. and MILES, M. (1984) *Innovation Up Close*, New York, Plenum.

HUNT, DAVID, E. (1987) *Beginning with Ourselves: In Practice, Theory and Human Affairs*, Cambridge, MA, Brookline Books.

HUNTER, B. (1980) *An Approach to Integrating Computer Literacy into the K-8 Curriculum*, Alexandria, VA, Human Resources Research Organization.

IANNI, F. (1989) 'Providing a structure for adolescent development', *Phi Delta Kappan*, **70**, 69.

INGVARSSON, L., CHADBOURNE, R. and CULTON, W. (1994) 'Implementing new career structures for teachers: A study of the advanced skills teacher in Australia', paper presented at the annual meeting of the American Educational Research Association, New Orleans, April.

INNER-LONDON EDUCATION AUTHORITY (1984) *Improving Secondary Schools*, London, Inner London Education Authority.

INNER LONDON EDUCATION AUTHORITY (1988) *Improving Secondary School Transfer*, London, Inner London Education Authority.

JACKSON, P. (1988) *The Practice of Teaching*, New York, Teachers' College Press.

JEFFCUTT, P. (1993) 'From interpretation to representation' in HASSARD, J. and PARKER, M. (Eds) *Postmodernism and Organizations*, London, Sage.

JEWETT, A.E. and ENNIS, C.D. (1990) 'Ecological integration as a value orientation for curricular decision making', *Journal of Curriculum and Supervision*, **5**, 2, pp. 120–131.

JOHNSON, D.W. and JOHNSON, P.T. (1990) 'Social skills for successful group work', *Educational Leadership*, **47**, 4, pp. 29–33.

JOHNSON, S.M. (1990) *Teachers at Work*, New York, Basic Books.

KALTSOUNIS, T. (1990) 'Interrelation between social studies and other curriculum areas: A review', *Social Studies*, **81**, 6, pp. 283–6.

KARP, E. (1988) *The Dropout Phenomenon in Ontario Secondary Schools: A Report to the Ontario Study of the Relevance of Education and the Issue of Dropouts*, Toronto, Queen's Printer for Ontario.

KASTEN, K.L. *et al* (1989) 'Self-managing groups and the professional lives of teachers: A case study', *Urban Review*, **21**, 2, pp. 63–80.

KEARNS, JOHN, R. (1990) 'Self-esteem: A place to begin', in *The Middle: Journal of the Saskatchewan Middle Years Association*, **8**, 2, pp. 4–5.

KEFFORD, R. (1981) 'From narratives to note taking: differential demands in writing tasks, year six to year seven', *English in Australia*, **58**, pp. 36–41.

KENNEY, A.M. (1987) 'Teen pregnancy: An issue for schools', *Phi Delta Kappan*, **68**, 10.

KENWAY, J., BIGUM, C. and FITZCLARENCE, L. (1993) 'Marketing education in the post-modern age', *Journal of Education Policy*, **8**, 2, pp. 105–22.

KERSH, M.E. *et al* (1987) 'Techniques and sources for developing integrative curriculum for the gifted', *Journal for the Education of the Gifted*, **7**, 1, pp. 56–68.

KING, A. (1986) *The Adolescent Experience*, Toronto, Research Committee of the Ontario Secondary School Teachers' Federation.

KING, A., WARREN, W., MICHALSKI, C. and PEART, M. (1988) *Improving Student Retention in Ontario Secondary Schools*, Toronto, Ontario Ministry of Education.

KING, J. and EVANS, K. (1991) 'Can we achieve outcomes-based education?', *Educational Leadership*, October, pp. 73–5.

KNIGHT, T. (Ed.) (1984) *Inservice Education with Primary Schools*, La Trobe University School of Education (Series in Primary School Innovation), ISBN 0858165406.

KOMSKI, K. (1990) 'Integrated learning systems take integrated effort', *School Administrator Special Issue: Computer Technology Report*, pp. 25–7.

KORETZ, D. (1994) *The Reliability of Vermont Portfolio Scores in the 1992–93 School Year*, Interim Report, Rand Reprint Series.

KULIK, C. and KULIK, J. (1982) 'Effects of ability grouping on secondary school students: A meta-analysis of evaluation findings', *American Educational Research Journal*, **19**.

KULIK, J. and KULIK, C. (1987) 'Effects of ability grouping on student achievement', *Equity and Excellence*, **23**.

KUTNICK, P. and MARSHALL, D. (1993) 'Development of social skills and the use of the microcomputer in the primary school classroom', *British Education Research Journal*, **11**, 5, pp. 517–33.

LACEY, C. (1970) *Hightown Grammar*, Manchester, Manchester University Press.

LACEY, C. (1977) *The Socialization of Teachers*, London, Methuen.

LAKE, S. (1988a) *Equal Access to Education: Alternatives to Tracking and Ability Grouping. Practitioner's Monograph, #2*, Sacramento, CA, California League of Middle Schools, ERIC Document ED 303553.

LAKE, S. (1988b) *Scheduling the Middle Level School: Philosophy into Practice*. Sacramento, CA, California League of Middle Schools, ERIC Document ED 300920.

LANG, P. (1983) 'Review of perspectives in pastoral care', *Pastoral Care in Education*, **1**, 1.

LANG, P. (Ed.) (1985) *New Directions in Pastoral Care*, Oxford, Basil Blackwell.

LASCH, C. (1979) *The Culture of Narciscism*, New York, W.W. Norton.

LASH, S. and URRY, J. (1994) *Economies of Signs and Space*, London, Sage.

LAWTON, D. (1975) *Class, Culture and Curriculum*, London, Routledge and Kegan Paul.

LAWTON, S., LEITHWOOD, K., BATCHER, E., DONALDSON, E. and STEWART R. (1988) *Student Retention and Transition in Ontario High Schools*, Toronto, Ministry of Education.

LAZEAR, R. (1991) *Seven Ways of Knowing: Teaching for Multiple Intelligences*, Palatine, IL, IRI/Skylight.

LECOMPTE, M. (1987) 'The culture context of dropping out: why remedial programs fail to solve the problem', *Education and Urban Society*, **19**, 3.

LECOMPTE, M. and DWORKIN, A. (1991) *Giving Up on School: Teacher Burnout and Student Dropout*, Newbury Park, CA, Corwin Press.

LEINHARDT, G. (1992) 'What research on learning tells us about teaching', *Educational Leadership*, **49**, 7, pp. 20–5.

LEITHWOOD, K., LAWTON, S. and HARGREAVES, A. (1988) 'Recommendations Concerning Ontario Education Policy and Policy Making Process'. A presentation to the Select Committee on Education of the Legislative Assembly of Ontario, Toronto, Ontario Institute for Studies in Education, September.

LEVI, M. and ZIEGLER, S. (1991) *Making Connections: Guidance and Career Education in the Middle Years*, Toronto, Queen's Printer for Ontario.

LEVIN, B. (1994) 'Improving educational productivity: putting students at the centre', *Phi Delta Kappan*, **75**, 10, pp. 758–60.

LEVY, T. (1988) 'Making a difference in the middle school', *Social Education*, **52**, 2, pp. 104–6.

LOUIS, K.S. and MILES, M. (1990) *Improving the Urban High School: What Works and Why*, New York, Teachers' College Press.

LICATA, V.F. (1987) 'Creating a positive school climate at the junior high school level', paper presented at the annual meeting of the Michigan Association of Middle School Educators, ERIC Document ED 280143.

LIEBERMAN, A. (1986) 'Collaborative work', *Educational Leadership*, February, pp. 4–8.

LIEBERMAN, A. (Ed.) (1995) *The Work of Restructuring Schools*, New York, Teachers' College Press.

LIEBERMAN, A. and MILLER, L. (1990) 'Restructuring schools: What matters and what works', *Phi Delta Kappan*, June.

LIGON, G.D. (1983) 'Preparing students for standardized testing', *New Directions for Testing and Measurement*, 19, pp. 19–27.

LINN, M. and SANGER, N. (1991) 'How do students' views of science influence knowledge integration?', *Journal of Research in Science and Teaching*, **28**, 9, pp. 761–84.

LIPSITZ, J. (1995) 'Prologue: Why we should care about caring', *Phi Delta Kappan*, **76**, 9, pp. 665–6.

LITTLE, J.W. (1984) 'Seductive images and organizational realities in professional development', *Teachers' College Record*, **86**, 1, pp. 84–102.

LITTLE, J.W. (1989) 'The persistence of privacy: Autonomy and initiative in teachers' professional relations', paper presented at the annual meeting of the American Educational Research Association, San Francisco.

LITTLE, J.W. (1990a) 'The mentoring phenomenon and the social organization of teaching', *Review of Research in Education*, **15**.

LITTLE, J.W. (1990b) 'The persistence of privacy: Autonomy and initiative in teachers' professional relations', *Teachers' College Record*, **91**, 4, pp. 509–36.

LITTLE, J.W. (1993) 'Professional community in comprehensive high schools: the two worlds of academic and vocational teachers' in LITTLE, J.W. and McLAUGHLIN, M.W. (Eds) *Teachers' Work: Individuals, Colleagues and Contexts*, New York, Teachers' College Press.

LITTLE, J.W. and BIRD, T. (1984) *Report on a Pilot Study of School-Level Collegial Teaming*, San Francisco, CA, Far West Laboratory for Educational Research and Development, ERIC Document ED 266540.

LIVINGSTONE, D. (1993) 'Lifelong education and chronic underemployment: Exploring the contradiction' in ARISEF, P. and AXELROD, P. (Eds) *Transitions: Schooling and Employment in Canada*, Toronto, Thomas Educational Publishing Co.

LLOYD, J. (1987) 'The opportunity of private sector training', *Vocational Education Journal*, **62**, 3, pp. 20–4.

LOGAN, L., SACKS, J. and DEMPSTER, N. (1994) 'Who said planning was good for us?: School development planning in Australian primary schools', *Report of the Primary School Planning Project*, Brisbane, Griffith University.

LORTIE, D. (1975) *Schoolteacher: A Sociological Study*, Chicago, IL, University of Chicago Press.

LOUIS, K.S. (1994) 'Beyond managing change: Rethinking how schools improve', *School Effectiveness and Improvement*, **5**, 1, pp. 2–24.

LOUNSBURY J. (Ed.) (1982) *This We Believe*, Columbus, OH, National Middle School Association, ERIC Document ED 226513.

LOUNSBURY, J. and CLARK, D. (1991) *Inside Grade Eight: From Apathy to Excitement*, Reston, VA, National Association of Secondary School Principals.

LYMAN, N. and FOYLE, H.C. (1989) 'Cooperative learning in the middle school', paper presented at the annual Kansas Symposium for Middle Level Education, February, ERIC Document ED 302866.

McCARTHY, B. (1980) *The 4MAT System: Teaching to Learning Styles with Right/ Left Mode Techniques*, Barrington, IL, Excel, Inc.

McCARTHY, C. (1993) 'After the canon: Knowledge and ideological representation in the multicultural discourse on curriculum reform' in McCARTHY, C. and CRICHLOW, W. (Eds) *Race, Identity and Representation in Education*, London, Routledge, pp. 289–305.

McCLELLAND, D. (1987) *Human Motivation*, New York, Cambridge University Press.

McGANNEY, M.L. *et al* (1989) 'Ninth grade houses: The program and its impact in New York city public high schools', paper presented at the annual meeting of the American Educational Research Association, San Francisco, ERIC Document ED 306284.

MacIVER, D. and EPSTEIN, J. (1991) 'Response practices in the middle grades: Teacher teams, advisory groups, remedial instruction and school transition programs', *American Journal of Education*, August, pp. 587–622.

McLaughlin, M. (1990) 'The rand change agent study revisited: macro perspectives and micro realities', *Educational Researcher*, December, pp. 11–16.

McLaughlin, M. and Talbert, J. (1993) *Contexts that Matter for Teaching and Learning*, Stanford University, CA, Centre for Research on the Context of Secondary School Teachers.

McLean, L.D. (1985) *The Craft of Student Evaluation in Canada*, Toronto, Canadian Education Association.

McPartland, J. *et al* (1987) *Balancing High Quality Subject-Matter Instruction with Positive Teacher-Student Relations in the Middle Grades: Effects of Departmentalization. Tracking and Block Scheduling on Learning Environments*, Report No. 15, Centre for Research on Elementary and Middle Schools, Johns Hopkins University, Baltimore, MD, Johns Hopkins University, ERIC Document ED 291704.

McPartland, J., Coldiron, J. and Braddock, J. (1987) *A Description of School Structures and Classroom Practices in Elementary, Middle, and Secondary Schools*, Baltimore, MD, John Hopkins University.

Maguire, J. (1976) *An Outline of Assessment Methods in Secondary Education in Selected Countries*, Edinburgh, Scottish Council for Research in Education.

Makins, V. (1977) 'Why cream of sixth go sour', *The Times Educational Supplement*, 29 July, p. 3.

Manning, M.L. and Allen, M.G. (1987) 'Social development of early adolescence: Implications for middle school educators', *Childhood Education*, **63**, 3.

Manning, S. (1992) *The Campbell-Kelsey Transition Years Survey*, Scarborough Board of Education Report No. 92/93–05.

Manning, S., Freeman, S. and Earl, L. (1991) *Charting the Voyage of Planned Educational Change: Year One — The Scarborough Pilot Projects*, Scarborough Board of Education Research Report 91/92–11.

Mansfield, B. (1989) 'Students' perceptions of an integrated unit: A case study', *Social Studies*, **80**, 4, pp. 135–40.

Marland, M. (Ed.) (1974) *Pastoral Care*, London, Heinemann.

Marx, R. and Grieve, T. (1988) 'The learners of British Columbia', *British Columbia Royal Commission on Education*, Vol. 2, Victoria, Queen's Printer for British Columbia.

Marzano, R. (1992) *A Different Kind of Classroom: Teaching with the Dimensions of Learning*, Alexandria, Virginia, ASCD.

Mattingly, R. and VanSickle, R. (1991) *Cooperative Learning and Achievement in Social Studies: Jigsaw II*, Germany, US Dept. of Defense Research/Technical Report PT 143.

May, S. (1994) *Making Multicultural Education Work*, Clevedon, Multilingual Matters.

Measor, L. and Woods, P. (1984) *Changing Schools*, Milton Keynes, Open University Press.

Mertin, P., Haebich, E. and Lokan, J. (1989) 'Everyone will be bigger than me: Childrens' perceptions of the transition to high school', *Australian Educational and Developmental Psychologist*, **6**, 2, pp. 1–4.

MESSICK, S. (1969) *The Criterion Problem in the Evaluation of Instruction*, Princeton, NJ, Educational Testing Service.

METZ, M. (1991) 'Real school: A universal drama amid disparate experience' in MITCHELL, D. and GNESTA, M. *Education Politics for the New Century, The Twentieth Anniversary Yearbook of the Politics of Education Association*, London, Falmer Press.

METZ, M. (1988) 'The American high school: A universal drama amid disparate experience', paper presented at the annual meeting of the American Educational Research Association, New Orleans.

MEYENN, R.J. and TICKLE, L. (1980) 'The transition model of middle schools: two case studies' in HARGREAVES, A. and TICKLE, L. (Eds) *Middle Schools: Origins, Ideology and Practice*, London, Harper and Row.

MILES, M.B. and HUBERMAN, A.M. (1984) *Innovation Up Close: How School Improvement Works*, New York, Plenum Press.

MILLS, C.W. (1959) *The Power Elite*, New York, Oxford University Press.

MOON, B. (1983) *Comprehensive Schools: Challenge and Change*, Windsor, NFER-Nelson.

MORTIMORE, J. and MORTIMORE, P. (1984) *Secondary School Examinations*, Bedford Way Papers, London, Institute of Education.

MORTIMORE, J., SAMMONS, P., STOLL, L., LEWIS, D. and ECOB, R. (1988) *School Matters*, Berkeley, CA, University of California Press.

MUNBY, S. (1989) *Assessing and Recording Achievement*, Oxford, Blackwell.

MUNN, P. and MORRISON, A. (1984) 'Approaches to collaboration in Scottish secondary schools in multidisciplinary courses 14–16', *Stirling Educational Monographs*, No. 13, Department of Education, University of Stirling.

MURPHY, J. (1991) *Restructuring Schools: Capturing and Assessing the Phenomena*, New York, Teachers' College Press.

MURPHY, J. and HALLINGER, P. (1989) 'Equity as access to learning: curricular and instructional treatment differences', *Journal of Curriculum Studies*, **21**.

MURPHY, R. and TORRANCE, H. (1988) *The Changing Face of Educational Assessment*, Milton Keynes, Open University Press.

MUSGRAVE, F. (1973) 'Power and the integrated curriculum', *Journal of Curriculum Studies*, **5**, 1, pp. 3–12.

NAGY, P., TRAUB, R.E. and MacRURY, K. (1986) *Strategies for Evaluating the Impact of Province-Wide Testing*, Toronto, Queen's Printer for Ontario.

NATIONAL EDUCATION COMMISSION ON TIME and LEARNING (1994) *Prisoners of Time*, Washington, DC, US Government Printing Office.

NATIONAL INSTITUTE OF EDUCATION (1979) *Testing, Teaching and Learning. Report of a Conference on Research on Testing*, Washington, DC, National Institute of Education.

NATIONAL MIDDLE SCHOOL ASSOCIATION (1982) *This We Believe*, Columbus, OH, National Middle School Association.

NATIONAL PANEL ON HIGH SCHOOL and ADOLESCENT EDUCATION (NPHSAE) (1976) *The Education of Adolescents*, Washington, DC, US Dept. of Health, Education and Welfare, ERIC Document ED 130379.

NATRIELLO, G. (1982) *Organizational Evaluation Systems and Student Disengagement in Secondary Schools*, St. Louis, MO, Washington University, Final Report to the National Institute of Education.

NATRIELLO, G. (1987) *Evaluation Processes in Schools and Classrooms*, Baltimore, MD, Social Organization of Schools, Johns Hopkins University, ERIC Document ED 294890.

NEAL, P.D. (Ed.) (1975) *Continuity in Education — EDC Project Five*, Birmingham, City of Birmingham Education Department.

NEW YORK STATE SCHOOL BOARDS ASSOCIATION (NYSBA) (1987) *Meeting in the Middle: Directions in Schooling for Young Adolescents*, Albany, NY, New York State School Boards Association, ERIC Document ED 290207.

NEUFELD, J. (1991) 'Curriculum reform and the time of care', *Curriculum Journal*, **2**, 3, pp. 285–300.

NIAS, J. (1989) *Primary Teachers Talking*, London, Routledge & Kegan Paul.

NIAS, J., SOUTHWORTH, G. and YEOMANS, R. (1989) *Staff Relationships in the Primary School*, London, Cassells.

NISBET, J.D. and ENTWISTLE, N.J. (1966) *Age of Transfer to Secondary Education*, London, University of London Press.

NISBET, J.D. and ENTWISTLE, N.J. (1969) *The Transition to Secondary Education*, London, University of London Press.

NODDINGS, N. (1992) *The Challenge to Care in Schools*, New York, Teachers' College Press.

NORFOLK MIDDLE SCHOOL HEADTEACHERS (1983) *Discussion Document: Patterns of Liaison — Middle to Secondary*, Norwich, Norfolk Association of Middle School Headteachers.

NORTHWESTERN EDUCATIONAL SERVICE DISTRICT (1989) *'Restructuring' Schools: Integrating the Curriculum*, Mount Vernon, WA, Northwestern Educational Service District.

NORTON, R. (1988) 'Similarities between history-social science framework and English-language arts framework: What it means for elementary teachers', *Social Studies Review*, **28**, 1, pp. 48–52.

NYSTRAND, M. *et al* (1992) *Using Small Groups for Responses to and Thinking About Literature*, Centre on the Organization and Restructuring of Schools, Madison, WI, Centre for Educational Research.

OAKES, J. (1985) *Keeping Track: How Schools Structure Inequality*, Yale University Press.

OAKES, J. (1992) 'Can tracking research inform practice?', *Educational Researcher*, May.

OAKES, J., GAMORAN, A. and PAGE, R. (1992) 'Curriculum differentiation: opportunities, consequences and meanings' in JACKSON, P. (Ed.) *Handbook of Research in Curriculum*, New York, Macmillan Publishing and Co.

OAKES, J., LIPTON, M. and JONES, M. (1992) *Changing minds: deconstructing intelligence in detracking schools,* Paper delivered to the annual meeting of the American Educational Research Association, San Francisco, April.

OGBU, J. (1992) 'Understanding cultural diversity and learning', *Educational Researcher,* **21**, 8, pp. 5–14.

OLSON, J. (1982) *Innovation in the Science Curriculum,* London, Croom Helm.

OLSON, L. (1988) 'Crossing the schoolhouse border: Immigrant children in California', *Phi Delta Kappan,* **70**, 3, pp. 211–18.

ONTARIO MINISTRY OF EDUCATION and TRAINING (1995) *The Common Curriculum: Policies and Outcomes, Grades 1–9,* Toronto, The Queen's Printer.

OPPENHEIMER, J. (1990) *Getting It Right: Meeting the Needs of the Early Adolescent Learner,* Ontario, Federation of Women Teachers in Ontario.

O'ROURKE, K. (Ed.) (1990) *The Challenge of Counselling in Middle Schools,* Michigan, Office of Educational Research and Improvement.

OSBORNE, K. (1984) *Middle Years Sourcebook: Some Suggestions for the Education of Early Adolescents,* Winnipeg, Manitoba Department of Education.

OUCHI, W.G. (1980) 'Markets, bureaucracies and clans', *Administrative Science Quarterly,* **25**, pp. 125–41.

OXFORD CERTIFICATE OF EDUCATIONAL ACHIEVEMENT (OCEA) (1984) *The Personal Record Component: A Draft Handbook for Schools,* Oxford, OCEA.

PAGE, R. (1987) 'Teachers' perceptions of students: A link between classrooms, school cultures and the social order', *Anthropology and Education Quarterly,* **18**, pp. 77–97.

PALOMARES, U. and BALL, G. (1980) *Grounds For Growth,* Spring Valley, CA, Palomares and Associates.

PAPPAS, C.C. *et al* (1990) *An Integrated Language Perspective in the Elementary School: Theory into Action,* Trading, MA, Addison, Wesley and Longman Publishing Co.

PARIS, S., LAWTON, T., TURNER, J. and ROTH, J. (1991) 'A development perspective on standardized achievement testing', *Educational Researcher,* **20**, 5, pp. 12–20.

PERKINS, D. (1995) *Outstanding IQ: The Emerging Science of Learnable Intelligence,* New York, Free Press.

PERKINS, D. and BLYTHE, T. (1994) 'Putting understanding up front', *Educational Leadership,* February, pp. 4–7.

PETERSON, P. and KNAPP, N. (1993) 'Inventing and reinventing ideas: Constructivist teaching and learning in mathematics' in *Challenges and Achievements of American Education,* ASCD Yearbook.

PHILIPS, S.U. (1983) *The Invisible Culture: Communication in the Classroom and Community on the Warm Springs Reservation,* New York, Longman.

PICKARD, S. (1990) 'Integrating math skills into vocational education curricula: Beyond providing specific occupational skills', *Journal for Vocational Special Needs Education,* **13**, 1, pp. 9–13.

PIKE, T. (1983) 'Science and years 7 to 8 interface', *SASTA Journal,* **832**, pp. 25–8.

PINK, W. (1988) 'Implementing an alternative program for at risk youth: A school within a school model for school reform', paper presented at the annual meeting of the American Educational Research Association, New Orleans.

PINKEY, H.B. (1981) 'Is it time to stop busing?', *American School Board Journal*, **168**, 10, pp. 21–3.

POLLARD, A. (1985) *The Social World of the Primary School*, London, Cassell.

POSTMAN, N. (1992) *Technopoly: The Surrender of Culture to Technology*, New York, Alfred A Knopf.

POWELL, B. (1982) 'Transition in mathematics: Year 7 to 8', paper presented to the fourth annual conference of the Mathematics Education Research Group of Australia.

POWER, C., and COTTERELL, J. (1981) *Changes in Students in the Transition Between Primary and Secondary School*, Education Research and Development Committee Report #27, Australian Government Publishing Service.

PRATT, D. (1987) 'Characteristics of Canadian curricula', *Canadian Journal of Education*, **14**, 3, pp. 295–310.

PRAWAT, R. (1989) 'Promoting access to knowledge, strategy and disposition in students: A research synthesis', *Review of Educational Research*, **59**, 1, pp. 9–13.

PRING, R. (1973) 'Curriculum integration: The need for clarification', *New Era*, **54**, 3, pp. 59–64.

PUGH, W.C. (1988) 'A study of school grade organization: Policy implications for middle schools', paper presented at the annual meeting of the Eastern Educational Research Association, Miami Beach, ERIC Document ED 296459.

PURKEY, S.C. and SMITH, M. (1983) 'Effective schools: A review', *Elementary School Journal*, **83**, 4.

PURKEY, W. and NOVAK, J. (1984) *Inviting School Success*, Belmont, CA, Wadsworth.

QUATTRONE, D.F. (1989) 'A case study in curriculum innovation: Developing an interdisciplinary curriculum', *Educational Horizons*, **68**, 1, pp. 28–35.

RADWANSKI, G. (1987) *Ontario Study of the Relevance of Education and the Issue of Dropouts*, Toronto, Ontario Ministry of Education.

RAMIREZ, M. (1983) 'A bicognitive-multicultural model for pluralistic education', *Early Childhood Development and Care*, **51**, pp. 129–36.

RATSOY, E.W. (1983) *Public Reactions to the Proposed Provincial Student: Evaluation Policy*, Edmonton, Alberta Education.

REDDINGTON, R. (1988) 'Knowledge and power in the subarctic', *American Anthropologist*, **90**, 1, pp. 98–110.

REID, M.I., CLUNIES-ROSS, L., GOACHER, B. and VILE, C. (1981) *Mixed Ability Teaching: Problems and Possibilities*, Windsor, NFER-Nelson Publishing Co.

RESNICK, D.P. and RESNICK, L.B. (1985) 'Standards, curriculum, and performance: A historical and comparative perspective', *Educational Researcher*, **14**, 4, pp. 5–20.

RESNICK, D.P. and RESNICK, L.B. (1992) 'Assessing and thinking curriculum: New tools for educational Reform' in CLIFFORD, B. and O'CONNOR, M. (Eds) *Changing Assessments: Alternative Views of Aptitude, Achievement and Instruction*, Boston, MA, Klewer Academic Publishers.

REYNOLDS, D. and SULLIVAN, M. (1987) *The Comprehensive Experiment*, London, Falmer Press.

RICHARDS, N.J. (1980) 'The relationship between background factors and parental interest in and expectation of schooling and the satisfaction and confidence in transition', ME thesis, School of Education, Monash University.

RICHARDSON, V. (1991) 'How and why teachers change?' in CONLEY, S.C. and COOPER, B.S. (Eds) *The School as a Work Environment*, Needham, MA, Allyn and Bacon.

RICHMOND, W.K. (1975) 'Integration or disintegration?', *The Scottish Educational Journal*, **58**, 4, p. 1089.

RIMMINGTON, G.T. (1977) 'Evaluation in history and the social sciences: The longitudinal aspect and its problems', *History and Social Science Teacher*, **12**, pp. 207–11.

ROBERTSON, H.J. (1992) 'Teacher development and gender equity' in HARGREAVES, A. and FULLAN, M. (Eds) *Understanding Teacher Development*, London, Cassell.

ROSENHOLTZ, S. (1989) *Teachers' Workplace*, New York, Longman.

ROSSMAN, G., CORBETT, H. and FIRESTONE, W. (1985) *Professional Cultures, Improvement Efforts and Effectiveness: Findings from a Study of Three High Schools*, Philadelphia, PA, Research for Better Schools.

ROWNTREE, D. (1980) 'The side effects of assessment' in FINCH, A. and SCRIMSHAW, P. (Eds) *Standards, Schooling and Education*, London, Hodder and Stoughton.

RUDDUCK, J. (1991) *Innovation and Change: Developing Involvement and Understanding*, Milton Keynes, Open University Press.

RUTGERS, THE STATE UNIVERSITY, NEW JERSEY DEPARTMENT OF VOCATIONAL-TECHNICAL EDUCATION (1981) *Introduction to Vocations: Building Occupational Exploration at the Middle School Level*, New Brunswick, NJ, New Jersey, State Department of Education and Cancer Preparation.

RUTTER, M., MAUGHAN, B., MORTIMORE, P., OUSTEN, J. and SMITH, A. (1979) *Fifteen Thousand Hours*, London: Open Books.

RYAN, D.W. (1976) *The Education of Adolescents in Remote Areas of Ontario*, Toronto, Ontario Ministry of Education, Ontario Government Publications Services.

RYAN, J. (1991) 'Finding time: The impact of space and time demands on post-secondary native students', paper presented at the annual conference of the Canadian Society for the Study of Education. Kingston.

RYAN, J. (1992a) 'Formal schooling and deculturation: nursing practice and the erosion of native communication styles', *The Alberta Journal of Educational Research*, **38**, 2, pp. 91–103.

RYAN, J. (1992b) 'Aboriginal learning styles: A critical review', *Language, Culture and Curriculum*, **5**, 3, pp. 161–83.

RYAN, J. (1992c) 'Eroding innu cultural tradition: individuality and communality', *Journal of Canadian Studies*, **26**, 4, pp. 94–111.

RYAN, J. (1994) 'Organizing the facts: Aboriginal education and cultural differences in discourse and knowledge', *Language and Education*, **8**, 4, pp. 251–71.

RYAN, J. (1995a) *Student Communities in a Culturally Diverse School Setting: Identity, Representation and Association*, Toronto, Ontario Institute for Studies in Education.

RYAN, J. (1995b) 'Organizing for teaching and learning in a culturally diverse school setting', paper prepared for the annual conference of the Canadian Society for the Study of Education. Montreal.

RYAN, J. (in press) 'Experiencing urban education: the adjustment of native students to the out-of-school demands of a post-secondary education program', *Canadian Journal of Native Studies*.

RYAN, J. with WIGNALL, R., MOORE, S., ANTHONY, S. and HARRIS, M. (1994) *Teaching and Learning in a Multiethnic School*, Toronto, Ontario Ministry of Education and Training.

SAMMONS, P. (1993) 'Differential school effectiveness: Results from a reanalysis of the inner London Education Authorities Junior School's project data', *British Educational Research Journal*, **19**, 4, pp. 381–405.

SARASON, I.G. (1983) 'Understanding and modifying test anxiety' in ANDERSON, E.B. and HELMING, J.S. (Eds) *On Educational Testing*, San Francisco, CA, Jossey-Bass, pp. 133–49.

SARASON, S. (1971) *The Culture of the School and the Problem of Change*, Boston, MA, Allyn and Bacon.

SARASON, S. (1972) *The Creation of Settings and the Future Societies*, San Francisco, CA, Jossey-Bass.

SARASON, S. (1990) *The Predictable Failure of Educational Reform*, San Francisco, CA, Jossey-Bass.

SATTERLY, D. (1981) *Assessment in Schools*, Oxford, Blackwell.

SCARTH, J. (1987) 'Teaching to the exam? — The case of the School Council History Project' in HORTON, T. (Ed.) *GCSE: Examining the New System*, London, Harper and Row.

SCHEIN, E.H. (1984) 'Coming to a new awareness of organizational culture', *Sloan Management Review*, winter, pp. 13–16.

SCHLECHTY, P. (1990) *Schools for the Twenty-First Century: Leadership Imperatives for Educational Reform*, San Francisco, CA, Jossey-Bass.

SCOTTISH COUNCIL FOR RESEARCH IN EDUCATION (SCRE) (1977) *Pupils in Profile*. Edinburgh, Hodder and Stoughton.

SCRIVEN, M. (1978) 'How to anchor standards', *Journal of Educational Measurement*, **15**, pp. 273–5.

SCRUTON, R. (1985) *World Studies: Education or Indoctrination?*, Occasional Paper, No. 15, Institute for European Defence and Strategic Studies, London, Alliance Publishers.

SCRUTON, R., ELLIS-JONES, A. and O'KEEFE, D. (1985) *Education or Indoctrination?*, London, Sherwood Press.

SELTZER, V. (1982) *Adolescent Social Development: Dynamic Functional Interaction*, Lexington, MA, Lexington Books.

SENGE, P. (1990) *The Fifth Discipline: The Art and Practice of the Learning Organization*, New York, Doubleday.

SERGIOVANNI, T. (1994) *Building Community in Schools*, San Francisco, CA, Jossey-Bass.

SHAINLINE, M. (1987) *Program to Integrate Math and Science*, Evaluation report, Alburquerque, NM, Alburquerque Public Schools: Planning, Research and Accountability.

SHEPARD, L. (1989) 'Why we need better assessments', *Educational Leadership*, **47**, 7, pp. 4–9.

SHEPARD, L. (1991) 'Psychometricians' Beliefs about learning', *Educational Researcher*, **20**, 6, pp. 2–16.

SHIPMAN, M. (1983) *Assessment in Primary and Middle Schools*, London, Croom Helm.

SHOEMAKER, B. (1989) 'Integrative education: A curriculum for the twenty-first century', Oregon School Study Council, Eugene, *OCCS Bulletin*, **33**, 2.

SHULTZ, H. (1981) 'The middle years study — Future of division three', *Saskatchewan Educational Administrator*, **13**, 4, pp. 32–50.

SIKES, P., MEASOR, L. and WOODS, P. (1985) *Teacher Careers: Crises and Continuities*, London, Falmer Press.

SILBERMAN, C.E. (1970) *Crisis in the Classroom: The Revaluing of American Education*, New York, Random House.

SILBERMAN, C.E. (Ed.) (1973) *The Open Classroom Reader*, New York, Vintage Books.

SIMMONS, R.G. and BLYTH, D.A. (1987) *Moving into Adolescence: The Impact of Pubertal Change and School Context*, New York, Aldine de Gruyter.

SIMON, B. (1981) 'The primary school revolution: Myth or reality?' in SIMON, B. and WILLCOCKS, J. (Eds) *Research and Practice in the Primary Classroom*, London, Routledge and Kegan Paul.

SIMON, S.B. (1972) 'Grades must go', *Pennsylvania Education*, **3**, 5, pp. 19–21.

SISKIN, L. (1994) *Realms of Knowledge*, London, Falmer Press.

SISKIN, L. and LITTLE, J. (Eds) (1995) *The Subjects in Question*, New York, Teachers' College Press, Columbia University.

SIZER, T. (1992) *Horace's School: Redesigning the American High School*, Boston, MA, Houghlin Mifflin Co.

SKELTON, A. (1990) 'Towards confusion and retreat: The changing face of curriculum integration in Sheffield, 1986–90', *School Organization*, **10**, 2 and 3, pp. 229–38.

SKILBECK, M. (1984) *School-Based Curriculum Development*, London, Harper and Row.

SLAVIN, R.E. (1987a) 'Developmental and motivational perspectives on cooperative learning: a reconciliation', *Child Development*, **58**, 5, pp. 1161–7.

SLAVIN, R.E. (1987b) *Student Teams: What Research Says to the Teacher*, (2nd edn) Washington, DC, National Education Association.

SLAVIN, R.E. (1987c) 'Ability grouping and student achievement in elementary schools: A best-evidence synthesis', *Review of Educational Research*, **57**.

SMEDLEY, S. and WILLOWER, D. (1981) 'Principal's pupil control behavior and school robustness', *Education Administration Quarterly*, **17**, pp. 40–56.

SMITH, B. (1987) 'On teaching thinking skills: A conversation with B. Othanel Smith' in BRANT, R. (Ed.) *Educational Leadership*, **5**, pp. 16–19.

SNYDER, D. and EDWARDS, G. (in press) 'America in the 1990s: An economy in transition, a society under stress', *Future Forces*.

SOLOMON, P. (1992) *Black Resistance in High School: Forging a Separatist Culture*, Albany, NY, State University of New York Press.

SPADY, W. (1994) *Outcomes Based Education: Critical Issues and Answers*, Virginia, American Association of School Administrators.

SPADY, W. and MARSHALL, K. (1991) 'Beyond traditional outcomes-based education', *Educational Leadership*, **49**, 2, pp. 67–72.

SPELMAN, B.J. (1979) *Pupil Adaptation to Secondary School*, Belfast, Northern Ireland Council for Educational Research.

STAHL, S.A. and MILLER, P.D. (1989) 'Whole language and language experience approaches for beginning reading: A quantitative research synthesis', *Review of Educational Research*, **59**, pp. 87–116.

STANSBURY, D. (1980) 'The record of personal experience' in BURGESS, T. and ADAMS, E. (Eds) *Outcomes of Education*, London: MacMillan.

STEER, D.R. (Ed.) (1980) *The Emerging Adolescent: Characteristics and Educational Implications*, Fairborn, OH, National Middle School Association, ERIC Document ED 198626.

STENHOUSE, L. (1980) *Curriculum Research and Development in Action*, London, Heinemann.

STENNETT, R.G. (1987) *Student Evaluation Policy and Philosophy: A Survey of Principals*, London, Board of Education for the City of London.

STENNETT, R.G. and ISAACS, L. (1979) *The Elementary to Secondary Transition: A Follow-up of 'High Risk' Students*, London, London Board of Education.

STEVENS, P. and LICHTENSTEIN, S. (1990) 'Integrating communication skills into vocational programs: Critical role of vocational educators', *Journal for Vocational Special Needs Education*, **13**, 1, pp. 15–18.

STEVENSON, H. and STIGLER, J. (1991) 'How Asian teachers polish each lesson to perfection', *American Educator: The Professional Journal of the American Federation of Teachers*, **15**, 1, pp. 12–20 and pp. 43–47.

STIGGINS, R. (1988) 'Revitalizing classroom assessment: The highest instructional priority', *Phi Delta Kappan*, **69**, 5, pp. 363–8.

STIGGINS, R. and BRIDGEFORD, N. (1985) 'The ecology of classroom assessment', *Journal of Educational Measurement*, **22**.

STIGGINS, R.J., GRISWORD, P. and FRISBIE, D. (1989) 'Inside high school grading practices: Building a research agenda', *Educational Measurement, Issues and Practices*, summer.

STILLMAN, A. and MAYCHELL, K. (1984) *School to School*, New Jersey, NFER-Nelson.

STODOLSKY, S.S. (1988) *The Subject Matters: Classroom Activity in Math and Social Studies*, Chicago, IL, University of Chicago Press.

STOLL, C. (1995) *Silicon Snakeoil: Second Thoughts on the Information Highway*, New York, Doubleday.

STOLL, L. and FINK, D. (1996) *Changing Our Schools*, Milton Keynes, Open University Press.

STRADLING, R., PROCTOR, M. and BAINES, B. (1984) *Teaching Controversial Issues*, London, Edward Arnold.

STRONG, R., SILVER, H. and ROBINSON, A. (1995) 'What do students want (and what really motivates them?)', *Educational Leadership*, **53**, 1.

SUGRUE, C. (1996) 'Student teachers' lay theories: Implications for professional development' in GOODSON, I. and HARGREAVES, A. (Eds) *Teachers' Professional Lives*, London, Falmer Press.

SULLIVAN, B.M. (1988) *A Legacy for Learners: The Report of the Royal Commission on Education*, Victoria, British Columbia, British Colombia Provincial Government.

SWALES, T. (1980) *Records of Personal Achievement: An Independent Evaluation of the Swindon RPA Scheme*, London, Schools Council.

TASK FORCE ON EDUCATION OF YOUNG ADOLESCENTS (TFEYA) (1989) *Turning Points: Preparing American Youth for the 21st Century*, New York, Carnegie Council on Adolescent Development.

TAYLOR, D. and TEDDLIE, C. (1992) 'Restructuring and the classroom: A view from a reform district', paper presented at the annual meeting of the American Educational Research Association, San Francisco.

TAYLOR, M. and GARSON, Y. (1982) *Schooling in the Middle Years*, Trentham, Trentham Books.

TAYLOR, J. and HOLSINGER, D. (1975) 'Locus of control differences between rural American Indian and white children', *Journal of Social Psychology*, **95**, pp. 149–55.

TENNYSON, W., WELSEY, G., SKOVHOLT, T. and WILLIAMS, R. (1989) 'How they view their role: A survey of counselors in different secondary schools', *Journal of Counseling and Development*, **67**, pp. 399–403.

THARP, R. and GALLIMORE, R. (1988) *Rousing Minds to Life: Teaching, Learning and Schooling in Social Context*, New York, Cambridge University Press.

THOMAS, C. (1984) 'An Ethnographic Study of Sixth Form Life', M.Phil. Thesis, Department of Educational Studies, University of Oxford.

THOMAS, N. (1984) *Improving Primary Schools*, London, ILEA.

THORNBURG, D. (1994) 'On the birth of the communication age: a conversation with David Thornburg' in BETTS, F. (Ed.) *Educational Leadership*, **51**, 7, pp. 20–3.

THORNBURG, H.D. (1982) 'The total early adolescent in contemporary society', *High School Journal*, **65**, 8, pp. 272–8.

TICHY, N.M. and DEVANNA, M.A. (1990) *The Transformational Leader*, New York, Wiley Press.

TIZARD, B. (1984) 'Problematic aspects of nuclear education' in BISHOP OF SALISBURY, WHITE, P., ANDREWS, R., JACOBSEN, B. and TIZARD, B. (Eds) *Lessons Before Midnight: Education for Reason in Nuclear Matters*, Bedford Way, Paper No. 19, Institute of Education, University of London.

TOMKINS, G.S. (1986) *A Common Countenance: Stability and Change in the Canadian Curriculum*, Scarborough, Prentice-Hall.

TONNIES, F. (1887) *Gemeinschaft and Gesellschaft.* (C.P. Loomis Ed. and Translator), New York, Harper Collins (1957).

TORRANCE, H. (1986) 'Expanding school-based assessment: Issues, problems and future possibilities', *Research paper in Education*, **1**, 1, pp. 48–59.

TRAUB, R. and NAGY, P. (1988) *Teacher Assessment Practices in a Senior High School Mathematics Course*, Toronto, Ontario Institute for Studies in Education.

TRAUB, R., NAGY, P., MacRURY, K. and KLEIMAN, R. (1988) *Teacher Assessment Practices in a Senior High School Math Course*, Final Report of OISE Transfer Grant Project #52–1028. Toronto, Ontario Institute for Studies in Education.

TRAUB, R.E., WOLFE, R., WOLFE, C., EVANS, P. and RUSSELL, H.H. (1977) *Secondary-Postsecondary Interface Project II: Nature of Students, Volumes I and II*, Toronto, Ministry of Education and Ministry of Colleges and Universities.

TREBILCO, G.R., ATKINSON, E.P., and ATKINSON, J.M. (1977) 'The transition of students from primary to secondary school', paper presented at the annual conference of the Australian Association for Research in Education, Canberra.

TRIMBLE, K. and SINCLAIR, R. (1987) 'On the wrong track: Ability grouping and the threat to equity', *Equity and Excellence*, **23**.

TROMAN, G. (1989) 'Testing tensions: The politics of educational assessment', *British Educational Research Journal*, **15**, 3, pp. 279–95.

TROYNA, B. (1993) *Racism and Education: Research Perspectives*, Buckingham, Open University Press.

TURNER, G. (1983) *The Social World of the Comprehensive School*, London, Croom Helm.

TYACK, D. and TOBIN, W. (1994) 'The grammar of schooling: Why has it been so hard to change?', *American Educational Research Journal*, **31**, 3, Fall, pp. 453–80.

TYE, B. (1985) *Multiple Realities: A Study of 13 American High Schools*, Lanham, University Press of America.

TYE, K. (1985) *The Junior High: Schools in Search of a Mission*, Lanham, University Press of America.

TYLER, J. and HOLSINGER, D. (1975) 'Locus of control differences between rural American Indian and white children', *Journal of Social Psychology*, **95**, pp. 149–55.

UNITED STATES NATIONAL COMMISSION ON EXCELLENCE IN EDUCATION (1983) *A Nation at Risk: The Imperative for Educational Reform*, Washington, DC, United States Department of Education.

References

WAGNER, H. (1983) 'Discipline in schools is inseparable from teaching', *Education*, **103**, 4, pp. 390–4.

WAHLSTROM, M. and DALEY, R. (1976) *Assessment of Student Achievement*, Toronto, Ontario Ministry of Education.

WAKE, R., MARBEAU, V. and PETERSON, A. (1979) *Innovation in Secondary Education in Europe*, Council for Cultural Cooperation.

WALKER, R. and ADELMAN, C. (1972) *A Guide to Classroom Observation*, London, Routledge and Kegan Paul.

WALSH, M.E. (1995) 'Rural students' transitions to secondary school: culture, curriculum and context', *The Curriculum Journal*, **6**, 1, pp. 115–127.

WATKINS, C. (1994) 'Personal-social education and the whole curriculum' in BEST, R., LANG, P., LODGE, C. and WATKINS, C. (Eds) *Pastoral Care and Personal-Social Education: Entitlement and Provisions*, London, Cassells.

WATTS, J. (1980) 'English in an integrated curriculum — Practice at Countesthorpe College, Leicestershire', paper presented at the third annual meeting of the International Conference on the Teaching of English, Sydney.

WEHLAGE, G. and RUTTER, R. (1986) 'Dropping out: how much do schools contribute to the problem?', *Teachers College Record*, **87**, 3.

WEIS, L. (1993) 'White male working class youth: An exploration of relative privilege and loss' in WEIS, L. and FINE, M. (Eds) *Beyond Silenced Voices: Class, race and gender in United States Schools*, Buffalo, NY, State University of New York Press.

WEISS, C. (1993) 'Shared decision-making about what? A comparison of schools with and without teacher participation', *Teachers' College Record*, **95**, 1, pp. 69–92.

WELLS, A. (1993) 'Public funds for private schools: Politics and first amendment considerations', *American Journal of Education*, **101**, 3, pp. 209–33.

WERNER, W. (1991a) 'Curriculum integration and school cultures', *Forum on Curriculum Integration*, Tri-University Integration Project, Occasional Paper #6. Burnaby, Simon Fraser University.

WERNER, W. (1991b) 'Defining curriculum policy through slogans', *Journal of Education Policy*, **6**, 2, pp. 225–38.

WERTSCH, J. (1991) 'A sociological approach to mental action' in CARRETERO, M., POPE, M., SIMONS, R. and POZO, J. (Eds) *Learning and Instruction: European Research in an International Context*, Vol. 3, Oxford, Pergamon Press.

WESTBURY, I. (1973) 'Conventional classrooms, open classrooms, and the technology of teaching', *Journal of Curriculum Studies*, **5**, 2.

WESTON, P. (1979) *Negotiating the Curriculum*, Windsor, NFER-Nelson.

WEXLER, P. (1992) *Becoming Somebody: Toward a Social Psychology of School*, London, Falmer.

WHEELOCK, A. (1986) *The Way Out: Student Exclusion Practices in Boston Middle Schools*, Boston, MA, Massachusetts Advocacy Centre, ERIC Document ED 303529.

WHEELOCK, A. (1992) *Crossing the Tracks: How 'Untracking' Can Save America's Schools*, New York, The New Press.

WHITE, R. (1992) 'Implications of recent research on learning for curriculum and assessment', *Journal of Curriculum Studies*, **24**, 2, pp. 153–64.

WHITFORD, B. and GAU, S. (1995) 'With a little help from their friends: Teachers making changes at Wheeler School' in LIEBERMAN, A. (Ed.) *The Work of Restructuring Schools*, New York, Teachers' College Press.

WHITTY, G. (1985) *Sociology and School Knowledge*, London, Methuen Books.

WIDEEN, M., MAYER-SMITH, J. and MOON, B. (1996) 'Knowledge, teacher development and change' in GOODSON, I. and HARGREAVES, A. (Eds) *Teachers' Professional Lives*, London, Falmer Press.

WIDEEN, M. and PYE, I. (1989) *The Struggle for Change in a Complex Setting: A Literature Review of the High School*, Research study of high schools for School District No. 36. Surrey, Simon Fraser University.

WIGGINS, G. (1989) 'A true test: Toward more authentic and equitable assessment', *Phi Delta Kappan*, **70**, 9, pp. 703–13.

WIGGINS, G. (1992) 'Creating tests worth taking', *Educational Leadership*, **49**, 8, pp. 26–33.

WILES, J. *et al* (1982) 'Miracle on Main Street: The St. Louis story', *Educational Leadership*, **40**, 2, pp. 52–3.

WILKINS, A. and OUCHI, W. (1983) 'Effective cultures: Exploring the relationship between culture and organizational performance', *Administrative Science Quarterly*, **28**, 3, pp. 468–81.

WILLIAMS, R. (1961) *The Long Revolution*, London, Chatto and Windus.

WILLIAMS, S. (1980) 'Continuity and diversity in the classroom', *Outlook*, **37**, pp. 9–19.

WILLIAMSON, D. (1980) '"Pastoral care" or "Pastoralization"?' in BEST, C., JARVIS, C. and RIBBINS, P. (Eds) *Perspectives in Pastoral Care*, London, Heinemann.

WILLIS, P. (1977) *Learning to Labour*, London, Saxon House.

WILSON, A. (1983) *A Consumer's Guide to Bill 82: Special Education in Ontario*, Toronto, Ontario Institute for Studies in Education.

WILSON, E. (1971) *Sociology: Rules, Roles, and Relationships*, Homewood, IL, Dorsey Press.

WILSON, R. (1989) 'Evaluating student achievement in an Ontario high school', *The Alberta Journal of Educational Research*, xxxv.

WILSON, R., REES, R. and CONNOCK, M. (1989) 'Classroom practices in evaluation: A progress report from the ecology of evaluation project', *Research Forum*, 4, School District #36, Surrey.

WOLF, A. (1988) 'The new history-social science framework: Will it become a reality or remain a dream?', *Social Studies Review*, **28**, 1, pp. 5–13.

WOLF, D., BIXBY, J., GLENN, J. and GARDNER, H. (1991) 'To use their minds well: Investigating new forms of student assessment' in GRANT, G. (Ed.) *Review of Research in Education*, **17**.

WOOD, R. and POWER, C. (1984) 'Have national assessments made us wiser about standards?', *Comparative Education*, **20**, pp. 307–21.

WOODS, P. (1993) *Critical Events in Teaching and Learning*, London, Falmer Press.

References

WOODS, P. (1996) 'Critical students: Breakthroughs in learning', *International Studies in Sociology of Education*, **4**, 2, pp. 123–46.

YOUNG, M.F.D. (Ed.) (1971) *Knowledge and Control*, London, Collier-MacMillan.

YOUNGMAN, M.B. and LUNZER, E.A. (1977) *Adjustment to Secondary Schooling*, Nottingham, Nottinghamshire County Council and University of Nottingham School of Education.

ZLATOS, B. (1993) 'Outcomes-based outrage', *Educational Leadership*, **15**, 9, pp. 12–16.

Index

Index